W9-DDS-973

Thinking Theory Thoroughly

Thinking Theory Thoroughly

Coherent Approaches to an Incoherent World

James N. Rosenau
The George Washington University

Mary Durfee
Michigan Technological University

Westview Press
Boulder • San Francisco • Oxford

All rights reserved. No part of this publication may be reproduced or transmitted in any form or by any means, electronic or mechanical, including photocopy, recording, or any information storage and retrieval system, without permission in writing from the publisher.

Copyright © 1995 by Westview Press, Inc.

Published in 1995 in the United States of America by Westview Press, Inc., 5500 Central Avenue, Boulder, Colorado 80301-2877, and in the United Kingdom by Westview Press, 12 Hid's Copse Road, Cumnor Hill, Oxford OX2 9JJ

Library of Congress Cataloging-in-Publication Data
Rosenau, James N.
  Thinking theory thoroughly : coherent approaches to an incoherent
world / James N. Rosenau, Mary Durfee.
     p.   cm.
  ISBN 0-8133-2594-3 — ISBN 0-8133-2595-1 (pbk.)
  1. International relations.   I. Durfee, Mary.   II. Title.
JX1391.R5848   1995
327.1'01—dc20   95-1095
                                                                                   CIP

Printed and bound in the United States of America

The paper used in this publication meets the requirements
of the American National Standard for Permanence of Paper
for Printed Library Materials Z39.48-1984.

10   9   8   7   6   5   4   3   2   1

For all those who are willing to
acknowledge and probe the
complexities of world affairs

Contents

Tables and Figures

Preface

We are as proud of the origins of this book as we are of the final product. The ideas presented here were inspired by undergraduates who were taking an introductory international relations (IR) course taught by Mary Durfee at the University of Dayton in fall 1991. Their insights in coping with the challenges of abstract theorizing about world politics motivated us to refine our thinking about IR theory.

The story is a simple one. Durfee offered the students an option of no term paper in exchange for separate weekly meetings and short papers devoted to a systematic, chapter-by-chapter reading of Rosenau's *Turbulence in World Politics: A Theory of Change and Continuity.* Seven students chose the option and then, week after week, sustained a surprising level of remarkably insightful and broad discussions of world affairs. Put off at first by the abstract formulations early in the book, they soon began to interpret the diverse dimensions of the subject in complex ways and became unusually adept at being playful with the ideas underlying the turbulence model, often advancing their own theories even as they found flaws in Rosenau's formulations. At the last meeting of the group, on December 1, 1991, Rosenau was present and had the exhilarating experience of participating in a sophisticated discussion of the book's complex propositions with seven sophomores who were just completing their first IR course.

Over dinner that evening the two of us firmed up our plans to coauthor this book. The day's invigorating discussion reinforced our respective experiences in teaching the turbulence model. It seemed clear to us that, despite its length and new ways of probing the basic parameters of international affairs, *Turbulence in World Politics* made a difference for undergraduates, even for those starting from scratch in the field. At the same time, we agreed that the encounter with the turbulence model would be enriched by an alternative framework against which to compare its premises, that comparing coherent approaches to an incoherent world was the quickest way to deepen one's understanding of the course of events. Accordingly, we decided to develop a volume organized around comparisons of the turbulence model and the theory, realism, that has long dominated the field. What follows offers overviews of both theories and a chapter that compares them along key dimensions.

In addition, our respective teaching experiences had taught us that theories are more fully grasped when applied to specific issues. Thus we have included three "case" chapters, each more complex and ambiguous than the previous one, to bring out the differences between the theories and thereby demonstrate how the raw materials of IR take on different meanings when interpreted from different theoretical perspectives. Through it all we have sought to highlight the joys and rewards of theorizing. That, in the end, is the central purpose of the book.

The project seemed straightforward enough at the start: Lay out the main dimensions of the two theories, then use them to interpret some standard IR phenomena, and conclude with a few suggestions as to how one might undertake theorizing on one's own. Wanting to be fair to both approaches, we pressed each other in the case chapters to revise any wording that appeared to favor one theory over the other. In fact, we sought to develop the theories with enough detachment that the reader would find it difficult to discern our own theoretical preferences. We hope the debates we had over the phone, through letters, in face-to-face meetings, and via E-mail between Houghton and Hong Kong have had that result.

The collaboration, however, proved more invigorating and certainly less straightforward than we had anticipated. In a test of the manuscript with a class of beginning IR students at Michigan Technological University, students challenged us to show how the two theories explained international crises. In effect, they argued that we had failed to put the two theories to a fair trial because not a word on crises appeared in the original draft even though the world seems beset today by an endless series of tense and critical situations. So we undertook to add a chapter on the subject and found ourselves continuously challenged by the task of applying such all-encompassing schemes as the realism and turbulence models to the specifics of those abbreviated moments in history when events are overtaken by climactic conflicts. Since most inquiries into crises focus on foreign policy decisional processes, the literature of the field provided little guidance, compelling us to forge the links between crises and systemic theories on our own. Two of Durfee's students, Matthew Hoffmann and Peter Ouillette, were particularly helpful in this regard, and we are indebted to them for their incisive observations. Throughout this effort to extend the scope of the book in Chapter 7, we tried to live by our advice on how to think theoretically. Whether we did so thoroughly is for the reader to judge.

*   *   *

Parts of Chapter 3 originally appeared in James N. Rosenau, *Turbulence in World Politics: A Theory of Change and Continuity* (Princeton: Princeton University Press, 1990), and James N. Rosenau, *The United Nations in a Turbulent World* (Boulder: Lynne Rienner, 1992), and we are grateful to the Princeton University Press and the International Peace Academy for permission to reprint revised versions of these materials. Chapter 8 is a revision of James N. Rosenau, "Thinking Theory Thoroughly," originally published in K. P. Misra and Richard Smith Beal, eds., *International Relations Theory: Western and Non-Western Perspectives* (New Delhi: Vikas Publishing House, 1980), pp. 14–28, and again we are grateful to the Vikas Publishing House for permission to reprint this revision.

Many students and colleagues contributed to the evolution of the manuscript. We extend special thanks to the "Rosenau Group" of students at the University of Dayton who provided the impetus for the book: Tory Callaghan, Michelle D. Crone, Rico Falsone, Lizanne Martin, Amy McGough, Dan Okenfuss, and Suzanne Schlak. In the summer of 1994, students at Michigan Tech read the entire first draft of the manuscript and did exercises based on it, thus helping us to identify problems that required further thoughts and revision. We are happy to acknowledge our gratitude to these students: Natalie Dimitruck, Scot Eichorst, Peter Ouillette, Chris Porter, Diana Richardson, Kashif Siddiqui, Ognjen Similjanic, Mike Stachnik, Douglas Stark, and Karie Toronjo. We also appreciate the comments on early drafts of the Antarctica chapter by students in an introductory IR course at Wittenberg University and by those at Michigan Tech who took Durfee's course in environmental problems, especially Misi Boge.

We are also grateful to several colleagues for their criticisms and suggestions, especially Christopher Joyner, who commented on the Antarctica chapter; Martha Finnemore, Richard Friman, and Hongying

Wang, who read early versions of the realism chapter; Joseph Lepgold, who made suggestions on the first four chapters; and Margaret P. Karns, who read much of the manuscript. Indeed, it was Margaret who brought us together for the end-of-the-semester meeting with the students and who was a supportive colleague to both of us throughout the subsequent writing of the book. A good friend makes a huge difference and Peg is all of that! Likewise, we feel especially fortunate to have had the assistance of Jennifer Knerr, Brenda Hadenfeldt, Jane Raese, and Eric Wright at Westview Press. A good editor makes a huge difference and Jennifer is all of that!

Hilary Levin's help in preparing the index is also gratefully acknowledged.

Needless to say, we owe much to the support of our spouses—to Don, who managed the turbulence a book produces in family life so very well, and to Hongying, who did the same in her own inimitable way.

Valuable as was the help of all those we have named, however, they are not responsible for the final product. For that we alone are answerable.

James N. Rosenau
Mary Durfee

Thinking Theory Thoroughly

1
The Need for Theory

It is sheer craziness to dare to understand world affairs. There are so many collective actors—states, international organizations, transnational associations, social movements, and subnational groups—and billions of individuals, each with different histories, capabilities, and goals, interacting to create historical patterns that are at all times susceptible to change. Put more simply, world affairs are pervaded with endless details—far more than one can hope to comprehend in their entirety.

And if these myriad details seem overwhelming during relatively stable periods, they seem that much more confounding at those times when dynamism and change become predominant. Such is the case as the twentieth century draws to a close. In all parts of the world, long-established traditions, institutions, and relationships are undergoing profound and bewildering transformations. Indeed, the pace of change has been so rapid, with the collapse of the Soviet Union following so soon after the end of the Cold War—to mention only the most dramatic of the changes that have cascaded across the global landscape—that it becomes reasonable to assert that change is the only constant in world affairs.

And we dare to think we can make sense of this complex, swift-moving world, with its welter of details, intricate relationships, mushrooming conflicts, and moments of cooperation! How nervy! How utterly absurd! What sheer craziness!

But the alternatives to seeking comprehension are too noxious to contemplate, ranging as they do from resorting to simplistic and ideological interpretations to being propelled by forces we can neither discern nor influence. So dare we must! However far-fetched and arrogant it may seem, we have no choice as concerned persons but to seek to fathom the meaning and implications of the events and stunning changes that bombard us from every corner of the world.

Happily, there are at least two handy mechanisms available for easing the task. One involves a sense of humility. If we can remain in awe of the complexities and changes at work in the world, ever ready to concede confusion and always reminding ourselves that our conclusions must perforce be tentative, then it should be possible to avoid excessive simplicity and intellectual paralysis. Second, and much more important, we can self-consciously rely on the core practices of theory to assist us in bringing a measure of order out of the seeming chaos that confronts us. For it is through theorizing that we can hope to tease meaningful patterns out of the endless details and inordinate complexities that sustain world politics.

Moving Up the Ladder of Abstraction

Being self-consciously theoretical is not nearly as difficult as it may seem at first glance. For inevitably we engage in a form of theorizing whenever we observe world affairs. It is impossible to perceive and describe all that has occurred (or is occurring), and there is just too much detail to depict every aspect of any situation, much less numerous overlapping situations. Put more forcefully, asking a student of world affairs to account for all the dimensions of an event is like asking geographers to draw a life-sized map of the world. Clearly, such a map could not be drawn (where would they store it?); thus, one is compelled to make choices among all the possible details that could be described, to select some as important and dismiss others as trivial for the purposes at hand (much as geographers might select mountains and rivers as salient and treat hills and streams as irrelevant). And it is at the very point when one starts selecting the relevant details that one begins to theorize. For we do not make the selections at random, for no reason, capriciously. Rather, crude and imprecise as they may be, our observations derive from some notion of what is significant and what is not— distinctions that amount to a form of theory, a sorting mechanism that enables us to move on to the next observation.

To acknowledge that the selection process always accompanies effort to develop understanding is not, however, to insure a self-consciousness about theory. It is all too tempting to lapse into thinking that the aspects of a situation selected form an objective reality that any observer would perceive. From the perspective of our unrecognized theories, everything can seem so self-evident that we may be inclined to equate our understanding of events with the "truth" about them, a practice that can lead to all kinds of problems once we try to share our understandings with others.

To avoid or overcome these difficulties, and thereby heighten our theoretical sensitivities, it is useful to conceive of raw observations—the endless details noted above—as located at the lowest rung on a huge ladder of abstraction. One then ascends the ladder each time one clusters details at a given level into a more encompassing pattern. The broader the generalizations one makes, of course, the higher one goes on the ladder, stopping the ascent at that rung where one is satisfied that the kind of understanding one seeks has been achieved. In a like manner, one descends the ladder when one perceives that more detail is needed to clarify the understanding developed at higher rungs.

The notion of understanding arrayed at different levels of abstraction promotes theoretical self-consciousness because it constantly reminds us that we are inescapably involved in a process of selecting some details as important and dismissing others as trivial. Aware that, perforce, we must teeter precariously on a rung of delicately balanced interpretations whenever we move beyond raw facts, we are continuously impelled to treat any observation we make as partly a product of our premises about the way things work in world politics.

Another way of developing a keen sensitivity to the imperatives of theorizing is to evolve a habit of always asking about any phenomenon we observe, "Of what is this an instance?" Though brief, the question is powerful because it forces us to move up the ladder of abstraction in order to identify a more encompassing class of phenomena of which the observed event is an instance. Suppose, for example, one is investigating the Soviet Union and observes that in 1991 it underwent a coup d'état that failed, and further suppose that one then asks of what is this failure an instance. Immediately one comes upon a number of possible answers at different rungs on the ladder. At the next highest rung the coup attempt may loom as a botched power grab by a small clique of politicians frustrated by their progressive loss of influence. At a higher rung it can be seen as an instance of factional and ideological tension among an elite accustomed to unquestioned leadership. At a still higher rung it might be interpreted as an instance of the kind of political tensions that follow when an economy enters a period of steep decline. Near the top rung the failed coup can readily be viewed as an instance of profound change in a long-stagnant society. At the very top it might be seen as the final stage in a long process of systemic collapse.

In the sense that they are broadly explanatory, each of these interpretations is profoundly theoretical. None of them is more correct than any other—since they offer explanations at different levels of aggregation—but all of them select certain aspects of the failed coup as relevant and impute meaning to them. And, in so doing, they nicely demonstrate how the of-what-is-this-an-instance question impels us to use theory as a means of enlarging our understanding. More than that, the several interpretations of the coup highlight the satisfactions inherent in the theoretical enterprise. For there is little to get excited about at the lowest rungs on the ladder of abstraction. To be sure, the raw facts and historical details are important—one could hardly theorize without them—but it is only as one moves up the ladder that the interesting questions begin to arise and allow one's mind to come alive, to probe and ponder, to delve and discard, to roam and revise. Taken by itself, the failed coup in August 1991 was no more than nine men imprisoning a president and issuing orders; but as an instance of more encompassing processes, it was one of the most dynamic moments of recent history.

The Refinements of Theory

It follows that at least crude forms of theorizing are at work whenever we undertake observation. The facts of history or current events do not speak to us. They do not cry out for attention and impose themselves upon us. Rather, it is we who make the facts speak, accord them salience, give them meaning, and in so doing endlessly engage in the theoretical enterprise. Since this is the case irrespective of whether we are aware of ourselves as theoreticians, it is obviously preferable to move consciously up and down the ladder of abstraction. Indeed, since theorizing is the surest and most expeditious route to understanding, there is much to be said for making a habit out of the of-what-is-this-an-instance question, of training oneself to ask it constantly in order to insure that one proceeds explicitly from observation to inference to explanation. By being habitual about the question, that is, one assures always seeing larger meanings even as one focuses on particular events. And by being explicit, one can identify where one may have erred if it turns out that an interpretation proves unwarranted in the light of subsequent developments.

Explicitness, in other words, is a crucial refinement of the theoretical enterprise. It is what allows us to test and revise our theories. By being explicit we can not only check our reasoning against further observations but also submit our theories to the scrutiny of those who doubt the soundness of our theorizing. In this way knowledge cumulates and both specific events and broad trends come into focus and pave the way for ever more enriched understanding. Thus is a task that may seem like sheer craziness transformed by the theorist into a challenging and rewarding endeavor.

There are, of course, many other rules and procedures that underlie the theoretical enterprise. Theory is not a means of giving vent to one's intuitions, of randomly asserting whatever pops to mind as a response to the of-what-is-this-an-instance question. A hunch or impression may serve as an initial stimulus to theory building, but no observation acquires a theoretical context until such time as it is integrated into a coherent and more encompassing framework and then subjected to the rigors of systematic analysis. Like any other intellectual enterprise, in other words, theorizing is founded on rules—in this case, rules for transforming raw observations into refined hypotheses and meaningful understandings. In themselves, the rules are neutral; they allow for weak theory as well as powerful theory, for narrow theory that explains a limited set of observations as well as broad theory that purports to account for a wide array of phenomena. Whatever the strength and scope of any theory, however, it is unlikely to advance understanding if it strays far from the core rules that underlie the enterprise.

Toward the Higher Rungs

Although this is not the place to elaborate the rules to which theoreticians adhere, it is useful to note that the higher one moves up the ladder of abstraction, the less one worries about anomalous situations and the more one focuses on patterns that reflect central tendencies. At the top of the ladder sit comprehensive perspectives that organize our overall understanding of cause and effect. We all have such theories, even if we are not consciously aware of them. Pluralists, for example, understand social life to be moved by a variety of groups with differing agendas that may nevertheless intersect. Any such broad perspective is consistent with several more specific theories; pluralism implies interest-group liberalism or "world society" approaches. Even though such theories require somewhat different testable hypotheses, they are fundamentally related in that they share basic axioms about social and political life.

Consequently, as one approaches the rungs at the top of the ladder, one's theories subsume diverse details and become all-encompassing, ranging across the full gamut of human affairs. At the highest rung, a theory may also be called a paradigm or a model, terms that refer to an integrated set of propositions that account for any development within the purview of the theory.[1] Virtually by definition, therefore, paradigmatic formulations rest on simple propositions that subsume many diverse forms of activity and thus cannot be readily overturned or embarrassed by exceptions to the central tendencies they depict. Put differently, paradigms tend to be closed systems of thought that cannot be broken by the recitation of specific examples that run counter to their premises. A thoroughgoing paradigm closes off the anomalies by resort to deeper explanations that bring the exceptions within the scope of its central tendencies. Marxists, for example, were long able to preserve their paradigm by treating any challenge to their theoretical perspective as conditioned by class consciousness and thus as explicable within the context of their core premises. It follows that the only way one can break free of an entrapping paradigm is by rejecting its core premises and framing new ones that account in a different way for both the central tendencies and the anomalies. Once one develops a new formulation out of the new premises, of course, one acquires a new paradigm that, in turn, is both all-encompassing and all-entrapping.

In short, we inevitably bring to world politics a broad paradigmatic perspective that enables us to infuse meaning into the latest development. And inescapably, too, we are bound to feel quarrelsome with respect to those who rely on different paradigms to explain the same events.

Notwithstanding the combative impulses induced by paradigmatic commitments and the occasional moments of insecurity over being entrapped in a conceptual jail of one's own making, the higher rungs of the ladder serve the valuable purpose of infusing coherence into all that we observe in global politics. The paradigm of our choice may be excessively simple and it may be closed to all challenges, but it does guide us through the complexities of an ever more interdependent world. Our perch high on the ladder of abstraction enables us to identify key questions and develop a perspective on how to answer them. Without a self-conscious paradigmatic commitment, one is destined for endless confusion, for seeing everything as relevant and thus being unable to tease meaning out of the welter of events, situations, trends, and circumstances that make up international affairs at any and every moment in time. Without a readiness to rely on the interlocking premises of a particular paradigm, our efforts at understanding would be, at best, transitory, and at worst they would be arbitrary, filled with gaping holes and glaring contradictions.

In order to demonstrate the virtues of climbing to the highest rungs on the ladder of abstraction, as well as to show how thoroughly the substance of the field is a product of the broad theories we employ, in the following chapters we present two very different paradigms and then contrast them through a series of case studies. There are, of course, more than two well-developed theories available for use by students of the subject. Rather than attempting to be exhaustive, however, we have chosen to be intensive, to show how a theory founded on continuity and stability (the realism paradigm) yields a very different picture of global politics than one organized around change and fluidity (the turbulence or postinternational paradigm). In the next two chapters we present, respectively, these two paradigmatic perspectives in broad outline, and in Chapter 4 we compare the points at which they overlap and diverge. Chapters 5, 6, and 7 carry the comparisons into the empirical realm with several very different case studies—one on the Antarctic Treaty, a second on the United Nations, and others on major crises that mark recent history. The final chapter offers some suggestions for readers who would like to improve their capacities as theorists.

It must be emphasized that in both the presentations and the comparisons we have sought to be fair and to avoid loading the analysis in the direction of our own preferences. Paradigms are not superior or inferior to each other, and we do not wish to imply that they are. Their purpose is to clarify and explain phenomena in the context of underlying premises. Hence they are not either right or wrong; rather, they are either useful or not useful depending on what one wishes to emphasize and accomplish through systematic inquiry. We hope that the ensuing pages will help readers to develop paradigmatic commitments appropriate to their substantive interests and philosophic orientations.

2
The Realist Paradigm

In 1948 Hans Morgenthau published a remarkable book, *Power Among Nations*. His aim was nothing less than to expound a theory of international relations designed to explain past and current events and suggest the likely direction and shape of future relations. He explicitly attached a label—"political realism"—to his theory. Some of the ideas he offered bore a resemblance to earlier writings on world politics; others have been radically changed by newer members of the realism school. The older writers did not, however, share Morgenthau's belief in the value of theory. In contrast, the new writers on realism most certainly do. In this chapter we offer an overview of the major claims that modern realists make about the nature of world politics.

Realism hopes to explain why states behave the way they do. Since states engage in a number of behaviors with considerable regularity, something must underlie that regularity. What, for instance, accounts for war and peace? Why do states survive or fail? These are the questions central to realist theory.

Realism, Neorealism, and Idealism

The realist approach to world politics can be traced back as far as Thucydides, the chronicler of the ancient Peloponnesian War, who wrote, "The strong do what they have the power to do, the weak accept what they have to accept."[1] During this great ancient war, which dragged on for more than a quarter century, Athens and Sparta fought each other on land and sea. They tried to make peace, but their agreements failed to hold. They sought, lost, coerced, and destroyed allies; allies and neutrals made their own calculations of power and chose sides.

Thucydides made it clear that a first-class navy and the wealth of empire gave an edge to Athens. Indeed, it was "the growth of Athenian power and the fear this caused in Sparta" that, in Thucydides's opinion, caused the war.[2] The fact of Athenian power and the fact, known to his readers, that Athens ultimately lost the war creates a terrible tension in his book.[3] Why, if Athens was so powerful, did it lose? The answer, according to Thucydides, was that the city-state overextended itself and fell victim to its own sense of grandeur. Its citizens forgot the necessity for moderation and denigrated the virtues of taking justice as well as advantage into its political calculations. Both raw power, as expressed in ships and money, and the moral character of the warring cities accounted for the final outcome of the war.

The concept of power also underlies the two strands of realism that have evolved in the modern era. The first, which we will call traditional realism, evolved in the 1930s and in the immediate post–World War II period as a reaction, among scholars as well as policymakers, to an excessive reliance on idealism during the interwar period. This form of realism is grounded in a view of human nature. It argues that humans are self-interested, rational, and seek power, qualities that lead to the consistent, regular behavior of states. Traditional realism holds that we live in "a world of opposing interests and of conflict among them, moral principles can never be fully realized, but must at best be approximated through the ever temporary balancing of interest and the very precarious settlement of disputes."[4] What matters in the realm of politics, in short, is interest defined in terms of power.

In contrast, the idealism that produced the realist reaction assumed that humans are reasonable, good, and moral. Idealism, wrote Hans Morgenthau, "assumes the essential goodness and infinite malleability of human nature, and blames the failure of the social order to measure up to the rational standards on lack of knowledge and understanding, obsolescent social institutions, or the depravity of certain isolated individuals or groups. It trusts in education, reform, and the sporadic use of force to remedy these defects."[5]

When idealists of the 1920s and 1930s sought to bring an end to war in the conduct of international relations, they relied on law and morality. This reliance, according to realist writers like E. H. Carr[6] and Morgenthau, led to an inadequate response to the aggressions of Germany, Italy, Japan, and the Soviet Union. Had the leaders of Britain, France, and the United States paid more attention to power and not imagined that good will and accommodation would be adopted by all, then actions to counter the aggressions of the 1930s might have prevented the outbreak of World War II.

The second strand of realism, neorealism (also called structural realism), shares much with traditional realism but emphasizes the structure of the international system rather than human nature to account for the behavior of states.[7] What individuals might prefer does not particularly matter, because individuals themselves do not matter a great deal in explaining the behavior of states. It is the lack of central authority in the international system that causes states to behave the way they do.[8] The structure of the international system forces states to attend not just to their own interests but to any changes in the power of other states. Thus, according to one theorist, "The fundamental goal of states in any relationship is to prevent others from achieving advances in their relative capabilities."[9]

The Main Assumptions of Realist Theory

Both schools of modern realist thought would agree that the use of war and diplomacy by states is as important to the international system today as they were to the Greek city-state world 2,500 years ago. For realists of any stripe, the nature of interstate politics has not changed significantly over the millennia, nor is it likely to do so any time soon. Then, as now, the search for power motivated state behavior. Compared to neorealism, however, traditional realism more readily admits the possibility of restraint, choice, and even some moral foundations, in the sense of prudence, as a source of state behavior. We can catch a glimpse of this difference by considering how traditional and neorealists would explain the Peloponnesian War. Neorealists would focus on "the rise of Athenian power" in a system where no authority was greater than that of the city-states themselves. Sparta had to respond to the growth in Athenian power because no matter how powerful Sparta was in absolute terms, Athens was gaining (or growing) in power relative to Sparta and the other cities. For neorealism, conflict is the natural condition for members of the international community (or for members of the Greek city-state system). In contrast, although traditional realists would not ignore the search for power in their evaluation of the causes of the war, they would also focus on the quality of diplomacy and the rational incentives for cooperation that prudential calculations of interest might suggest. (In all probability, Thucydides would have placed the greatest emphasis on the moral failure.)

Neither school of modern realism concerns itself with the internal structures, histories, and cultures of states. It does not matter whether a state is organized along authoritarian, nonmarket or democratic, capitalist lines. Given the same external stimuli, all states will behave in a similar manner. Faced with attack, they will defend themselves. If one state seems to be growing in power, the other states will either match that growth or find allies. If some states agree to regulate a problem by law, then other states may seize the opportunity of—temporarily—solving the problem by also signing the agreement.

Realism assumes that states are unitary actors, that is, that a state does not speak to the rest of the world through multiple voices. If a conflict arises between a state's foreign and defense departments, realists say it will be resolved authoritatively: Only one policy will be directed toward the world.[10] Since realists assume that states are able to rely on a single position in their foreign policy, they need not take domestic politics into account when explaining a state's international behavior.

Both realist schools conceive of states as rational. For traditional realism, a wide range of behaviors are available to states that are rationally consistent with their perceived interests. For neorealists, however, choices are strongly constrained by the international system, which has no centralized authority presiding over states.[11] Rational decision derives from calculations in which states link means and ends in a logical fashion. Presumably, states do not act in any way that might injure their own self-interests. Rationality also means that state preferences are consistent, not just purposeful.[12] Given a number of ends and means, the rational-actor state will order them from the least to the most optimal. "Rationality," says George Tsebelis, "is nothing more than an optimal correspondence between ends and means."[13] In sum, the premises of modern realism posit that states "behave in ways that are, by and large, rational, and therefore comprehensible to outsiders in rational terms."[14]

States must meet a number of requirements to make their claim to rationality. "To say that governments act rationally ... means that they have consistent, ordered preferences, and that they calculate the costs and benefits of all alternative policies in order to maximize their utility in light both of those preferences and of their perceptions of the nature of reality."[15] This observation suggests that states do not hold contradictory beliefs at a particular point in time because then any option might be viewed as logically acceptable. If a state believed that peace and war were equally important goals, it could choose either course and be consistent with its preferences. That approach would not be rational, and other states would have considerable difficulty coping with a state that behaved in this way. The reader may wonder whether states *are* rational in the way described. Although it would not be correct to say that, in actual practice, states always act in perfectly rational ways, it would be generally correct to say that states presume that other states act to maximize their preferences.

Similarly, states tend to assume that the preferences of other states are always transitive. Realist theory claims that security is more important than economics and economics is more important than, say, human rights. According to realist theory, then, states faced with a choice between their security interests and their human rights concerns will choose security. Likewise, they will choose economics over human rights, but security over economic goals.[16] In trying to maximize their preferences, states will take the value of what they expect to get from some action and multiply it by the likelihood they can actually get it (producing what is known as an "expected utility"). A state might highly value getting industrialized tomorrow, but this value will be sharply reduced for the state because there is little reason to expect that it can get rich so quickly. Of course, sometimes states misjudge the probability of a desired outcome and take actions that seem "crazy." Nevertheless, both realists and policymakers presume that states behave rationally most of the time.

For scholars who adhere to this perspective, the assumption of rationality makes theoretical analysis possible. When realist scholars want to understand some action, they engage in what is called "rational reconstruction."[17] This process entails imagining that one is a rational decisionmaker for a state and then explaining international behavior from that perspective.

The Modern International System

Most theorists regard 1648 as the date when the modern international system was founded. That year, the states of Europe signed the Treaty of Westphalia, which ended the Thirty Years War over the religion to be practiced in different territories. Until this treaty it was not clear whether leaders "owned" their territories and the people in them or whether other authorities, like the Catholic Church, claimed some rights over citizens. The Thirty Years War ended the dispute: The religion of the ruler would be the religion of the region. Westphalia, in effect, clarified questions of property and authority.

Thus it is that the modern international system is based on the building blocks of sovereign states. There are many theories about the nature of sovereignty.[18] For realists, though, only a few main ideas need be stressed. First, states occupy a given bit of territory and control what happens inside that territory. Second, no "superstate" or "world government" can tell that state what to do. Sovereignty entails "the lack of any links which place the state concerned in a subordinate constitutional position in relation to another state. ... Sovereignty may be seen as a moat, cutting the state off from constitutional subordination to other states and thus expressing the fact of its own constitutional independence."[19] Sovereignty does not mean that states have some kind of impenetrable barrier. States open their borders in more ways than one, often leaving the "drawbridge" down to others; thus, the moat metaphor is apt.

The Westphalian system put states at the center of the world stage, unconstrained by any higher political authority. If all states are masters of their own fates, if no government exists above them, then the system lacks hierarchy. The absence of a higher authority is termed *anarchy*. Anarchy in this sense, it should be emphasized, does not mean chaos.[20] Rather, anarchy means that states have to protect and look out for themselves—that they must rely on themselves to insure order and obtain needed resources. *Self-help* is the basis for enforcing rules and protecting interests. Thus, according to neorealists, all states tend to perform the same functions for their people and in the international system (which is why there is no need to inquire into their domestic politics). Most notably, they seek to enhance their security from military threat. Without security they cannot maintain sovereignty.

Since security is the highest goal of states and since the anarchic nature of the international system prevents enforcement of contracts, self-help may lead to unfortunate—but quite comprehensible—behaviors on the part of states. Conspicuous among these unfortunate, but understandable, behaviors is the constant preparation for war. As realists see it, all states face what is called the *security dilemma*: An effort by one state to increase its security decreases the security of other states.

The other states respond by building arms of their own. The initiating state may feel even more insecure and build more arms, and therein lies a major source of arms races and possibly wars. The dilemma is that increasing one's own security decreases everyone else's; yet not working to improve one's security may prove disastrous.[21] The only way it can be resolved is for states to find ways, through law and diplomacy, to keep an eye on each other. Arms control agreements are one approach. Each state, however, will want to be sure that all the parties to an arms agreement are actually doing what they agreed to do to. Failure to comply or outright efforts to cheat could decrease the security of others while, at least in the short term, increasing that of the noncomplying state. Thus, states seek to verify that obligations are being met.[22] If all parties carefully comply with the agreement, the dilemma itself (should I trust that I'm secure) can at least temporarily be eased. For neorealists, such situations of assurance are few and far between and do not last very long.

For traditional realists, sovereignty also encourages states to keep each other in business. That is, states much prefer keeping their international system in operation over contributing to its demise. Thus, although states resort to war if that is the only means through which they can maintain their sovereignty, ordinarily they opt for the less risky paths of diplomacy, negotiation, and such tactics as economic sanctions when dealing with other states.

For some analysts, the recognition of mutual as well as conflicting interests means that the system of states is actually a society: an anarchical society.[23] According to this line of reasoning, the anarchical society attempts to achieve four goals. The goals reflect the transitivity requirement of rationality. That is, the first goal is the most important, followed by the second, and so on.

According to Hedley Bull, "First there is the goal of the preservation of the system and society of states itself."[24] Any challengers to the healthy existence of states will be met decisively by the states. One power will not be allowed to dominate, and entities that are not states will be consigned roles secondary to those of states. When push comes to shove, when nonstate entities (such as multinational corporations or the U.N.) attempt to act independently, they will be stopped or regulated by states.

"Second," according to Bull, "there is the goal of maintaining the independence or external sovereignty of individual states."[25] Although the first goal takes precedence and may result in some small states being destroyed or occupied by great powers (e.g., Tibet), most of the rules of international law and the informal behaviors of states aim at preserving the independence of states. This rule explains why states accept and obey international law: To get one's own independence recognized, one must extend the same courtesy to everyone else. Neorealists would tend to downplay this point, but it has a prominent place in traditional realism.

"Third, there is the goal of peace."[26] Most nations are at peace with most other nations most of the time. War is not the day-to-day experience of states, although it lurks constantly in the background. If threats to the first two goals arise, states may indeed prefer war to peace. For the most part, however, states go about their daily business in a peaceful fashion and have developed a large array of methods for the peaceful settlement of disputes.

"Fourth are ... the common goals of all social life: limitations of violence resulting in death or bodily harm, the keeping of promises, and the stabilization of possession by rules of property."[27] Evidence that states value this goal can be found across a wide range of issues. For example, there are rules aimed at protecting the lives of some soldiers and civilians during war; the most recent Law of the Sea treaty, outlining how states can claim mining areas in an effort to stabilize property rights; and the international agreement to protect the ozone layer by banning chlorofluorocarbons, which has provisions aimed at ensuring the performance of promises made.

Interests and Power

Since realism posits all politics as deriving from interests defined in terms of power, it is important to take note of the power concept as it is understood by realists.[28] Although all sovereign states are legal equals, not all states are equal in terms of either absolute or relative capabilities. Thus, the United States and the former Soviet Union were called superpowers, just as in an earlier age Britain, France, Russia, and Prussia were called great powers.[29]

Neorealist Kenneth Waltz and traditional realist Hans Morgenthau agree that a great power must excel in virtually all elements of physical power. A state's power status depends on how it scores on *all* of the following items: size of population and territory, resource endowment, economic capability, military strength, political stability, and competence in diplomacy.[30] Table 2.1 suggests the kinds of analyses to which this conception of international status leads.

Large land territory provides protection from attack. The Soviets traded space for time in World War II as they built up power to defeat the Nazi invaders. Without modern roads and railways, however, even a state occupying a large territory will find it difficult to go to war or to trade with others and gain wealth. Coastlines make one vulnerable to other sea powers but also provide ready access to the rest of the world during both peace and war. Britain, the United States, and Japan are all sea powers (the United States is unusual in that it is also a land power). The Soviet Union could be a sea power, but its location makes good, year-round ports difficult to maintain.[31]

Population fills armies and industries. Canada has the virtue of large space but has few people. Japan has many people but not much land. Mexico is in between. Other factors, such as literacy, also play a role in determining the population's contribution to a nation's strength. Mexico, for example, is closer in literacy rates to Iraq than it is to the industrial societies.

Natural resources provide a certain independence from economic control by others. They provide raw materials for economic development and for the engines of war. Japan's overall economic performance takes on a remarkable appearance seen in the light of its virtual lack of mineral and gas resources.

Iraq at one point had a military manpower strength that would have put it in the top ten of the world. Even after the Gulf War, it spends more on defense than Canada or Mexico and its manpower levels are higher than Japan, Canada, or Mexico, despite its small population. At first glance this seems like an impressive achievement, but it was won only by putting nearly 25 percent of all military-aged men in service and required enormous expenditures of hard-earned money in an economy of modest size. In contrast, the United States has the third largest military in the world (after China and Russia), but only a small proportion of its population serves in the armed forces. Moreover, its economy is by far the largest in the world.

When the war between the U.S.-led coalition and Iraq broke out, even critics of the United States were amazed at how quickly the United States delivered a large number of fully equipped forces to the scene. Without drawing down the numbers of units and ships stationed elsewhere, the United States put 230,000 troops in Saudi Arabia

TABLE 2.1 Power Comparisons

	U.S.	Japan	Canada	Mexico	Iraq
GNP/GDP US$ 1991	5,945.7 bn.	3,346.5 bn.	588.63 bn.	286.63 bn.	24.5 bn.
Population	252.5 mil.	124 mil.	26.8 mil.	90 mil.	19.5 mil.
Territory	9,384,658 sq.km.	377,441 sq.km.	9,976,139 sq.km.	1,972,546 sq.km.	446,713 sq.km.
Defense budget US$ 1992	276.3 bn.	39.71 bn. (1993 est.)	10.31 bn.	1.52 bn.	8.61 bn. 1990
Active Military	1,729,700	237,700	78,100	175,000	382,000
Literacy 1985	99%	99%	99%	74%	70%

Sources: International Institute for Strategic Studies, *The Military Balance, 1993–94* (London: Brassey's, 1993), pp. 20, 39, 98–99, 117, 157–158, 188–189; George Kurian, ed., *World Education Encyclopedia, Vols. 1–111* (New York: Facts on File Publications, 1988), pp. 179, 610, 696, 861, 1294, 1344; and *SIPRI Yearbook: 1993 World Armaments* (Stockholm: Stockholm International Peace Research Institute, 1993), pp. 343, 350, 355, 391.

in a matter of three months; the number was ultimately increased to half a million. No other nation in the world could have done this. Thus, with respect to military power, the United States appears preeminent; certainly the challenger state of Iraq could not hope to match the overall capacity and ability of the United States to project force abroad.

In terms of sheer economic size, too, no other state rivals the United States. Consider GNP. Japan's is not quite half that of the United States. Mexico looks like a great economic power compared to Iraq; once again we find Mexico has more in common economically with medium powers like Canada than with weaker developing nations like Iraq.

In terms of absolute capability, the United States is by far the strongest nation. Indeed, with the collapse of the Soviet Union it may well be the only great power. Still, many assert that the United States is in decline. What accounts for this concern with U.S. power? The answer lies in the concept of relative power. Waltz, a neorealist, says states care about *relative* position.[32] This is where doubts about U.S. power arise. The United States is weaker relative to other states than it was in 1947. In 1947 the United States accounted for 50 percent of all world manufacturing and had 70 percent of all the gold in the world. It had atomic weapons (and the USSR did not). It was virtually unscathed by the recently fought (and won) World War II. Yes, compared to 1947 the relative position of the United States has declined. Even so, according to historian Paul Kennedy, the United States has the relative strength today that Britain had at the height of its power in the 1870s.[33]

Susan Strange also maintains that the United States remains very powerful. Not only is it extremely capable in military affairs, but it still has important clout in other areas. First, virtually all international prices are determined and denominated in U.S. dollars. Although it is certainly true that Japanese yen increasingly grease international financial wheels, the centrality of the dollar remains. Second, the United States alone accounts for 20 percent of all world trade—an amount that is less than in 1947 but still very impressive. Third, when European and Japanese firms have research and development (R&D) dollars to spend, they generally spend it in U.S. universities. That means the United States dominates in knowledge production.[34] It should be added, moreover, that the English language has become the world's lingua franca; indeed, most of the world's knowledge has been stored in English.

System Polarity

One might ask how the distribution of capabilities between the interacting units in a situation of anarchy affects the structure of the international system. "Behavior and outcomes," according to neorealists, "change as interactions among a system's units become sparser or denser, as alliances shift, as nations adapt their policies to one another. These are changes within the system and often systems dynamics are identified with and limited to such changes."[35] In other words, the anarchical international system can change as the number of powerful states increases or decreases, but in so doing it does not lose its essential characteristic of anarchy.

Over the 350 years of the modern system, the number of great powers has varied between two and five. When there are two dominant powers, the international system is said to be *bipolar.* When there are four or more, it is viewed as *multipolar.* A system with three powers could be called multipolar but is usually called *tripolar.* A structure with only one great power is called *unipolar.*

Some writers say the current international scene is multipolar, with the United States, the People's Republic of China (PRC), Russia, Japan, and the European Union (EU) operating as the poles. Others say neither Japan nor the EU count as poles. The EU is rejected because its individual members still retain considerable independence in security affairs, and Japan is not viewed as meeting great-power standards because it is too weak militarily. According to this interpretation, the world is tripolar (United States, Russia, PRC). Still others say the world remains bipolar (United States and Russia), but recent changes in the former Soviet Union undermine this perspective. One hardy soul claims that the collapse of the USSR has put the world in a "unipolar moment," with the United States first among equals.[36] Historian Paul Kennedy does not think the world has quite become unipolar, but he does regard the power of the United States as exceptional. "Because it has so much power for good or evil, because it is the linchpin of the western alliance system and the center of the existing global economy, what it does, *or does not do,* is so much more important than what any of the other Powers decides to do" (emphasis in original).[37] Perhaps the best term for today's world, drawn from realists primarily interested in economic relations, is *hegemonic.* The United States (the hegemon) has the capacity and sometimes the desire to lead the world in a variety of contexts, but other states can clearly shape its behavior.

Attributes of the Balance of Power

Deciding who is a great power may seem like an exercise in bragging rights, but for realists the number of major powers matters considerably. There is reason to think that states alter their behaviors depending on the polarity of the international system. This changed behavior is expressed through the operation of the *balance of power*. The balance may operate differently depending on the polarity of the system.[38] Moreover, overall systemic stability and the propensity for war or peace may be affected by polarity.

The balance of power, according to one observer, serves three purposes:

1. to ensure the continued existence of the state system by preventing universal empire through conquest. In other words, "let no one power predominate";
2. to assist, at the regional level, in maintaining the independence of states; and
3. to facilitate the growth of law and organization by providing a kind of enforcement by great powers.[39]

Viewed in this way, it follows that the balance of power is essential to maintaining order in international politics. The balance is one of the methods, along with law, war, and diplomacy, that states use to serve the goal of maintaining the state system. Sometimes the powers may be unable to balance; in other cases, they may see no reason to do so. For example, China maintained a suzerain over East Asia for centuries. That is, it dominated all other regions so thoroughly that no actor could gain power internally or make enough allies to balance the power of China. A somewhat similar picture emerges in the Western hemisphere, where the United States dominates most countries in the region. At the same time, none of the Latin American states has built enough power or successfully allied with others to counterbalance the United States.[40]

Traditional realists and neorealists differ in their views on how much choice states have in balancing. Traditionalists see considerable leeway for states. Neorealists assume balances arise naturally from the anarchy of the system.[41] In either case, failure to balance is rather rare. Traditional realists take some pains to explain these rare occasions; neorealists do not. Balances may fail to arise, according to traditional realists, when states have low perceptions of threat or have no other options.

Sentiments favoring the threat perception view can be found in the writings of early writers on international relations. For example, Emerich von Vattel, who wrote about the law of nations in the eighteenth century, observed, "Power alone does not constitute a threat of injury; the will to injure must accompany the power. ... As soon as a State has given evidence of injustice, greed, pride, ambition, or a desire of domineering over its neighbours, it becomes an object of suspicion which they must guard against."[42]

Stephen Walt says proximity, growth in arms, and obvious hostile activities contribute to making a state seem threatening.[43] A state next door that adds a hundred aircraft to its military inventory is more threatening than a state 2,000 miles away that adds a similar number to its ledger. If the nearby state also tries to coerce other states to do things they otherwise would prefer not to do, then it becomes even more menacing. Very powerful states can take their time to react to such threats, but smaller ones cannot.

Walt also offers an explanation for the failure to balance based on the availability of allies. If a state lacks good external options and has only a limited capacity to build power domestically, it bandwagons with the threat. That explanation accounts for the lack of balancing against U.S. aggressive behavior in Latin America; these states have few options. If the states of Latin America build up power (and the United States dominates many of their economies, so this scenario is unlikely), then they may achieve greater success in balancing against the United States.

Although the functions of the balance of power remain constant irrespective of the polarity of the international system, polarity does affect the actual implementation of the balance. A set of categories for analyzing the means by which states keep a balance in bipolar and multipolar systems is shown in Table 2.2. Here, "alliance" refers to mutual agreements to assist (or not to get involved with) another state in military situations; "coalition" involves four or more states working together against a threat; "moderation" means preservation of essential players and includes allowances for those vanquished in war to have a say in postwar decisions; "vigilance" denotes sensitivity to changes in power; "intervention" entails intrusion into the affairs of another state; "holding the balance" refers to a third party that sits

TABLE 2.2   Operation of the Balance of Power in Two Types of Polarity

	Bipolar	*Multipolar*
Alliance	Permanent	Flexible
Coalition	Alliances become permanent coalitions	Rare; only formed in times of military crisis
Moderation	No; only with respect to nuclear weapons	Only toward great powers
Vigilance	Globalized	Other great powers only
Intervention	Endemic	Only when there is sudden shift in power of another great power
Holding the Balance	No; requires third party	Yes; Britain said this was its policy toward Europe
Compensation	No; closest analog is that main power sometimes transfers resources to allies	Yes
War	Yes, but not against the other power; may be a function of nuclear weapons	Yes, as last resort against other powers

Source: Categories and multipolar characteristics derived from Edward Vose Gulick, *Europe's Classical Balance of Power* (Ithaca, N.Y.: Cornell University Press, 1955), Chap. 3.

"outside" a major conflict and shifts its weight depending on who has the upper hand; and "compensation" involves agreements giving a state that lost land or people in one area equivalent land or people elsewhere.[44] The last row, war, is self-explanatory.

The operation of the balance of power was quite evident in 1990 in the Persian Gulf. President Saddam Hussein built up the military power of Iraq to the point where it became a regional power. This course of action was a response to both Iranian and Israeli power. He also evidently hoped to gain more economic resources via force of arms. Earlier he had warred with Iran; the world mostly ignored that war. But his grab for Kuwait was different: It sought the outright conquest of an independent state. As we have seen, one of the most important goals of the international society, and one of the major reasons for any balance of power, is to protect the independence of states. Beyond that, Kuwait had oil, a factor critical to the industrial lifeblood of many states. If Iraq had gained access to Kuwaiti oil, it would have controlled a large share of world petroleum resources. That would be too much power, in the view of many states who import large quantities of oil and gas from the gulf. Consequently, a thirty-two-nation coalition fought a quick and successful war to redress the balance by ousting Iraq from Kuwait.

Based on Table 2.2, this response to Iraq's aggression fits a multipolar operation of the balance better than a bipolar one. The coalition formed to solve the problem was temporary (many of the states were not under formal alliance). Iraq had perhaps gotten away with the invasion in the first place because it was not important enough to watch vigilantly. Once the war ended, considerable moderation was employed by the other states with respect to Iraq's independence. Iraq was not destroyed, and it still participates in decisions over its future. War was certainly the last resort; months of negotiations occurred before the U.S.-led coalition took military action. Only the entries for the holding-the-balance and the compensation rows in Table 2.2 do not conform to the facts of the Iraq conflict.

Cooperation and Realism

Given the large number of incentives to protect one's state against the possible military actions of other states, there would seem to be few reasons to cooperate. Is cooperation ever rational? For neorealists, the answer is a qualified no. For more traditional realists, the answer is yes. There are two related ways of approaching the problem. One approach uses the balance-of-power idea and the other takes us back to rationality. Traditional realists will argue that prudence should lead to cooperation at times; neorealists say that, in view of the attention to relative power that the anarchical system tends to force on states, it is possible but very difficult for them to engage in cooperation.

To grasp this distinction, let us return to the war between Athens and Sparta. Early in the war, Athens threatened Sicily. Thucydides recounts the speech Hermocrates of Syracuse gave to convince all the peoples of Sicily to unite against the impending Athenian aggression. Hermocrates begins with a line of reasoning that realists would find familiar: "If it is natural to want to dominate, it is also natural to want to resist domination."[45] Indeed, actors ought to take active preparation to resist domination.

Although this observation explains why states maintain the balance, it does not explain why states cooperate. Hermocrates' reasoning, however, takes a surprising turn as he makes an allowance for the fact that actions occur under conditions of uncertainty about the future.

Realism's assumption of rationality, strictly speaking, means that states act with perfect information; in the absence of such perfection, caution may be warranted. Uncertainty is likely to be quite high about the distant future[46] because it becomes difficult to calculate how one's moves will interact with countermoves by other states. The more variables that must be factored into the calculation, the harder the choice. This uncertainty ought to constrain any thought of aggrandizement. Wrote classicist Robert Connor, "The surest means of security is not ingenuity and speed in plotting nor a rational means of prediction, but a recognition of the limits of knowledge in a world that cannot totally be predicted or controlled. ... [Hermocrates] urges settlement, accommodation, and common action based on restraint."[47] In other words, because it is natural both to dominate and to resist domination, and also because uncertainty is a feature of political life, the best course for the powerful is to accommodate the weaker so that they will be less inclined to balance with others against the powerful.

The very prospect of retaliation is one reason why, as Bull has claimed, the balance of power may produce cooperation.[48] But since one cannot be sure whether retaliation will occur or what the effects of retaliation might be if executed, caution and preference for nonmilitary solutions may be the best course of action. It is easy to see why small states might be cautious—they have less power and hence fewer choices. Less clear are the reasons why the powerful should be cautious and attempt cooperative approaches to gain their desired ends. Just because one is powerful does not mean one should dominate in such a way as to injure others and thereby goad them into defensive action. Hans Morgenthau explained the enormous success of Great Britain, which was a great power well into this century, as follows:

> The only nation that in modern times could maintain a continuous position of preponderance owed that position to a rare combination of potential superior power, a reputation for superior power, and the infrequent use of that superior power. Thus Great Britain was able, on the one hand, to overcome all serious challenges to its superiority because its self-restraint gained powerful allies and, hence, made it actually superior. On the other hand, it could minimize the incentive to challenge it because its superiority did not threaten the existence of other nations.[49]

Similarly, U.S. restraint in the war with Iraq more readily generated cooperation on the part of other states. President Bush's use of the

United Nations to "restrain" and legitimate U.S. power in the gulf is yet another instance of this sort of leadership. Did he demand more than the U.N. asked? No. Did he demand the removal of Hussein—an action that would probably have been in contravention of international law? Not officially. Thus moderation and restraint by the dominant power probably increased international collaboration. Despite the United States's astonishing power, its actions did not directly threaten other states.

Neorealists and traditional realists diverge in their thinking about this kind of hegemonic leadership. Neorealists argue that if cooperation emerges at all it is because a powerful state sets the rules and helps implement them. Once that leadership declines, so will the cooperation. Traditional realists, as suggested by Morgenthau, can imagine leadership where other states believe the powerful state is acting legitimately.[50] In contrast, a power that forces other states to do things is exercising coercive leadership; other states do not believe the powerful state is acting legitimately. Legitimate leadership by a hegemon produces cooperative outcomes at a lower cost than does sheer coercion even as it is also less likely to engender counterbalances. Coercive leadership is expensive and may motivate those states being coerced to withdraw support for the powerful state and coalesce against it.

Thus, hegemonic leadership can be viewed as the powerful's use of "accommodation and common action based on restraint." Coercive leadership fails to accommodate others and lacks restraint. Any common action in a setting of coercive leadership comes, essentially, at the point of a gun. Walt's research into alliances touches on this point in describing the ever-increasing difficulties the former Soviet Union had in maintaining its leadership in its bloc compared to the United States.[51] David Forsythe puts the idea of hegemonic leadership like this: "Because the hegemon's policy position is seen as good and because the hegemon is seen as having the power to compel implementation of policy if necessary, or at least the power to induce compliance through payments, there is 'voluntary' deference from others."[52]

Hegemonic leadership may be critical to the creation of international regimes. Regimes are collections of rules, obligations, and decisionmaking procedures in specific issue areas.[53] There are, for instance, regimes for money, trade, human rights, and the Antarctic. In economic matters the United States was not just important, it was dominant in the decades following World War II. Its policies also made sense to others. Through negotiation the United States and its allies agreed to treaties and international organizations to facilitate international policy coordination. When the United States would not lead, however, inaction occurred: An International Trade Organization failed to form after World War II because the United States changed its mind about the value of the proposed organization.

Smaller powers can maneuver widely in the space created by the hegemon, especially if they can organize themselves—for example, as the Organization of Petroleum Exporting Countries (OPEC) did during its early years—or if they can make a bargain that advances their economic interests and the hegemon's security interests. By threatening not to cooperate—which would increase the costs of leadership to the hegemon—smaller states can gain more resources than they might otherwise be permitted. The hegemonic leader, moreover, understands the utility of cooperation and the danger that would be posed by states "resisting domination"; thus, hegemons may give way when—in sheer power terms—they need not.

For instance, the General Agreement on Tariffs and Trade (GATT) seeks to reduce tariffs and promote free trade. During the Cold War, however, the developing countries objected to free trade because their economies were so weak that they needed preferential arrangements. Preferential treatment meant that Third World goods could go more readily to the North than the other way around. This the United States in concert with other important powers agreed to do. The wealthier states made a short-term concession for long-term gain. Power considerations were not absent: Former colonial powers like Britain and France did it as a means of assisting—and retaining some control over—former colonies, whereas the United States accepted the idea as a means of keeping the countries out of Soviet hands. In short, U.S. power kept things in bounds and also moderated disputes between the rich countries.

Change in International Politics

One of the most difficult questions for an adherent of realism is accounting for change. More correctly, except for increases or decreases in the capabilities of states, the question of change is not an important one to realists. To be sure, states come and go, but the behavior of the system and the remaining states in the system stays quite constant. Be-

cause realism assumes all states perform similar functions and therefore does not inquire into their internal characteristics, it is not especially interested in the question of why any particular state drops out
of the picture.

Realism is concerned, however, about the impact of system polarity
on the behavior of states. Thus some realists speculate on what causes
the polarity of the system to undergo change. Two approaches, the effects of war and the role of hegemons, offer potential avenues for realists who want to explain polarity changes.

Major wars seem to ratify underlying power changes. The Napoleonic Wars marked the beginnings of Britain's dominance in world affairs; World War II marked the rise of the United States and the USSR to
preeminence. Jack S. Levy observes, "In spite of the traditional importance of 'balance of power' and related ... hypotheses in the study of
international conflict, there is no explicitly 'realist' theory of general
war and no compilation of wars based on realist assumptions."[54] Since
realism does not explain war very well, it is hard to say how war as a
cause of change would work within realist theory.

Possibly it is hegemonic leadership that causes change. Britain, after
the Napoleonic Wars, launched a virtual peace offensive toward the
United States and let it become dominant in the Western Hemisphere.
Britain attempted a similar operation in the early twentieth century
with respect to Japan. More recently, the United States rebuilt former
enemies, Japan and Germany, in order to counter Soviet power. But the
evidence on hegemonic leadership as a source of rule change and facil-
itator of power transitions remains unclear. After all, if all states still act
approximately the same way due to the anarchical nature of the system, a hegemon's efforts to order the world along its preferred lines is
hardly surprising or indicative of change.

A key question about change was raised by a critic of realism, John
Ruggie, who believes that major systemic changes have occurred and
thinks realists ought to account for them: How can we account for
changes in the system as a whole?[55] Waltz considers one component of
a system to be the differentiation of its units, in this case sovereign
states; at the same time he allows this component to drop out when he
explains the operation of the international system. For Waltz, the medieval and the modern state systems are essentially similar. But, notes
Ruggie, during the medieval period anarchy existed, but sovereignty
did not. Accordingly, one problem with Waltz's neorealism is that "it

provides no means by which to account for, or even to describe, the most important contextual change in international politics in this millennium: the shift from the medieval to the modern international system."[56] One could respond to this point by observing that realism is a theory that explains behaviors when there is anarchy in the system and sovereignty for its units.

How realism handles the dynamics of change is nicely summarized by the following observation: "If history is 'just one damn thing after another,' then for realists international politics is the same damn things over and over again: war, great power security and economic competitions, the rise and fall of great powers, and the formation and dissolution of alliances. International political behavior is characterized by continuity, regularity, and repetition because states are constrained by the international system's unchanging (and probably unchangeable) structure."[57]

Conclusion

By assuming states matter more than any other global entity, the realist paradigm simplifies the world. This factor, some may say, greatly impoverishes realism's capacity for explanation and for rich description. And yet, the main components of the theory do seem to account for much of world politics, so perhaps the loss is unimportant.

In addition, in assuming that states are rational and unitary, realism offers a simplification that assists one in imagining how any nation—in general or in particular—is likely to act. Vast amounts of subnational politicking can be collapsed into the utility-maximizing entity known as a state.

Realism helps us see how the lack of hierarchy in authority at the systemic level creates rules that confine the choices available to states. At the same time, the emphasis on power helps to explain why some states are more successful in achieving their goals than are others.

In summary, the theoretical approach to world politics called realism has a long, distinguished history and offers a coherent, parsimonious explanation for much of what goes on across the globe. It does not purport to explain every global phenomenon, but its simplicity and utility commends it to policymakers and theorists alike.

3
Postinternationalism in a Turbulent World

Although the realism and postinternational politics paradigms have some common elements, in most important respects they rest on very different, even contradictory, premises. Both the similarities and the differences are discussed in Chapter 4. Here the task is to set out the underlying rationale for viewing world politics as having undergone turbulent transformations that are so profound as to warrant the framing of a new, postinternational paradigm.[1]

As the label implies, the structures and processes depicted by the new paradigm are still in the process of taking shape. Its outlines are not so clear-cut as to be easily summarized by a distinctive phrase. Yet, "postinternational politics" is an appropriate label because it highlights the decline of long-standing patterns without at the same time indicating where the changes may be leading. It suggests flux and transition even as it implies the presence and functioning of some stable structures. It reminds us that "international" matters may no longer be the dominant dimension of global life, or at least that other dimensions have emerged to challenge or offset the interactions of nation-states. And, not least, it permits us to avoid premature judgment as to whether present-day turbulence is an enduring or a transitional condition.

Toward a New Paradigm

There is no dearth of indicators—such as the launching of wars by states and their efforts to negotiate postwar arrangements—to highlight the many ways in which world politics are marked by continuity. Nevertheless, it is also clear that huge changes have been at work in the global system, changes that are of sufficient magnitude to suggest the emergence of new global structures, processes, and patterns. Daily occurrences of complex and uncertain developments in every region, if not every country, of the world are so pervasive as to cast doubt on the viability of the long-established ways in which international affairs have been conducted and analyzed. It almost seems as if anomalous events—those developments that are unique and surprising because they deviate from history's normal paths—have replaced recurrent patterns as the central tendencies in world politics.

This is not the place to enumerate the many anomalous developments that point to profound and rapid change, but it is useful to recall the utter surprise that greeted the abrupt end of the Cold War. Pundits, professors, politicians, and others conversant with world politics were literally stunned, with not one claiming to have anticipated it and with all admitting to ad hoc explanations. Since the sudden collapse of the Communist world was the culmination of dynamics that had been subtly at work for a long time, the intensity and breadth of the surprise it evoked can only be viewed as a measure of the extent to which our understandings of world politics have lagged behind the deep transformations that are altering the global landscape. Anomalies indicative of profound change began to flow well before the end of the Cold War,[2] but the series of events that transformed Eastern Europe late in 1989 surely arrested attention on the presence of powerful change agents.

Equally important, in the years since 1989 the world has not settled back into the familiar patterns of international politics. The interactions of states have not again become the exclusive, or at least the predominant, form of transaction across national boundaries. States have not recovered strict control over the flow of people, goods, and money in and out of their countries. Publics have not subsided into quiescent acceptance of governmental policies. The United Nations and other international organizations are no longer mere loci for the power plays of states. The boundaries between domestic and international politics have continued to erode as the principles of sovereignty are no longer barriers to external interventions into situations where famine, civil war, and violations of human rights are out of control. In short, there is no lack of incentives to frame a new paradigm with which to comprehend the course of events.

Most notably perhaps, the removal of the Cold War from the equations of world affairs did not result in a return to earlier patterns.

Rather than simply being an extreme variant of great-power competition, the rivalry between the United States and the Soviet Union that lasted some forty years proved to be a lid that contained underlying transformations in the way people sustained their daily lives and societies conducted their public affairs. The Cold War, in other words, did not stimulate change so much as it masked it, thereby adding to the impulse to treat the swelling flow of anomalies as requiring a new paradigmatic formulation. As one analyst put it:

> Not only the configuration of great powers and their alliances but the very structure of political history has changed. ... The very sovereignty and cohesion of states, the authority and efficacy of the governments are not what they were.
>
> Are we going to see ever larger and larger political units? ... Or are we more likely going to see the break-up of several states into smaller ones? Are we going to see a large-scale migration of millions of peoples, something that has not happened since the last century of the Roman Empire? This is at least possible. The very texture of history is changing before our very eyes.[3]

Assuming that the quickening flow of anomalies preceded the end of the Cold War, what gave rise to them? What underlying dynamics were eroding the long-standing patterns of world politics and fostering the evolution of new, postinternational structures and processes? How can we begin to understand the emergence of a new global order at a level of deep and turbulent change that is more fundamental than the advent of a Gorbachev in the Soviet Union, the fashioning of a thirty-two-nation coalition against Iraq, and the reunification of Germany? How do we account, in short, for an acceleration of the pace of change in international affairs that has altered "the very texture of history"?

The Turbulence Paradigm

Postinternational politics are perhaps most conspicuously marked by turbulence, by dynamics that foster intense conflicts, unexpected developments, pervasive uncertainties, and swift changes. Indeed, the turbulence is so global in scope that we shall use the term "turbulence model" interchangeably with "postinternational politics" as a label for the new paradigm. Lest there be any terminological confusion, however, it must be stressed at the outset that the notion of turbulence is

used here as more than a metaphor for great commotion and uncertainty. The purpose is not to wax eloquent about change, but rather to
probe its underlying dynamics in a systematic way.

Put most succinctly, the precise meaning ascribed to the turbulence
concept focuses on changes in three prime parameters of world politics. When these fundamental patterns that normally bind and sustain
the continuities of international life are overcome by high degrees of
complexity and dynamism—that is, when the number, density,
interdependencies, and volatility of the actors occupying the global
stage undergo substantial expansion—world politics are viewed as
having entered into a period of turbulence.

The three parameters conceived to be primary include the overall
structure of global politics (a macro parameter), the authority structures that link macro collectivities to citizens (a macro-micro parameter), and the skills of citizens (a micro parameter). According to this
perspective, all three parameters are presently undergoing extensive
complexity and dynamism and the world is experiencing its first
period of turbulence since the era that culminated with the Treaty of
Westphalia some 350 years ago.[4] Perhaps more to the point, the relative simultaneity that marks the impact of much greater complexity
and dynamism on all three parameters has given rise to what might
well be the central characteristic of world politics today, namely, the
presence of persistent tensions between tendencies toward centralization and those that foster decentralization. Viewed in this way, for example, it is hardly anomalous that even as the former components of
Yugoslavia aspire to admission to the European Community, so are
they engaged in violent conflict with each other. As will be seen, these
interactive centralizing-decentralizing tensions are especially evident
in the transformation of each of the three prime parameters.

Table 3.1 summarizes the changes in the three parameters, but the
order of their listing should not be interpreted as implying causal sequences in which the actions of individuals are conceived to precede
the behavior of collectivities. On the contrary, incisive insights into
the turbulence of world politics are crucially dependent on an appreciation of the profoundly interactive nature of the three parameters—on
recognizing that even as individuals shape the actions and orientations of the collectivities to which they belong, so do the goals, policies, and laws of the latter shape the actions and orientations of individuals. Indeed, much of the rapidity of the transformations at work in

TABLE 3.1 Transformation of Three Global Parameters

	From	*To*
Micro parameter	Individuals less analytically skillful and emotionally competent	Individuals more analytically skillful and emotionally competent
Macro-micro parameter	Authority structures in place as people rely on traditional and/or constitutional sources of legitimacy to comply with directives emanating from appropriate macro institutions	Authority structures in crisis as people evolve performance criteria for legitimacy and compliance with the directives issued by macro officials
Macro parameter	Anarchic system of nation-states	Bifurcation of anarchic system into state- and multi-centric subsystems

world politics can be traced to the ways in which the changes in each parameter stimulate and reinforce the changes in the other two.

The Micro Parameter: A Skill Revolution

The transformation of the micro parameter is to be found in the shifting capabilities of citizens everywhere. Individuals have undergone what can properly be termed a skill revolution. For a variety of reasons ranging from the advance of communications technology to the greater intricacies of life in an ever more interdependent world, people have become increasingly more competent in assessing where they fit in international affairs and how their behavior can be aggregated into significant collective outcomes. Included among these newly refined skills, moreover, is an expanded capacity to focus emotion as well as to analyze the causal sequences that sustain the course of events.

Put differently, it is a grievous error to assume that citizenries are a constant in politics. Indeed, it is hard to imagine that such rapid changes and increasing complexity could not have consequences for the individuals who make up the collectivities that interact on the global stage. As long as people were uninvolved in and apathetic about world affairs, it made sense to treat them as a constant parameter and to look to variabilities at the macro level for explanations of what happens in world politics. Today, however, the skill revolution has expanded the learning capacity of individuals, extended the detail and concepts of the cognitive maps through which they perceive the

world, and elaborated their scenarios of how states, leaders, and publics will interact in the future. Among the many skills that populations
have refined, perhaps the most important is an enlarged capacity to
know when and how to participate in collective action.[5] It is no accident that the squares of the world's cities have lately been filled with
large crowds demanding change.

It is tempting to view the impact of the skill revolution as leading to
positive outcomes. Certainly the many restless publics that have protested authoritarian rule suggest a worldwide thrust toward an expansion of political liberties and a diminution in the central control of
economies. But there is nothing inherent in the skill revolution that
leads people in more democratic directions. The change in the micro
parameter is not so much one of new orientations as it is an evolution
of new capacities for cogent analysis. The world's peoples are not so
much converging around the same values as they are sharing a greater
ability to recognize and articulate their values. Thus, this parametric
change is global in scope because it has enabled Islamic fundamental-
ists, Asian peasants, and Western sophisticates alike to better serve
their respective orientations. And thus, too, the commotion in public
squares has not been confined to cities in any particular region of the
world. From Seoul to Prague, from Soweto to Beijing, from Paris to the
West Bank, from Belgrade to Rangoon—to mention only a few of the
places where collective demands have recently been voiced—the
transformation of the micro parameter has been unmistakably evident.

Equally important, evidence of the skill revolution can be readily
discerned in trend data for education, television viewing, computer us-
age, travel, and a host of other situations in which people are called
upon to employ their analytic and emotional skills. And hardly less relevant, in a number of local circumstances—from traffic jams to water
shortages, from budget crises to racial conflicts, from flows of refugees
to threats of terrorism—people are relentlessly confronted with social,
economic, and political complexities that impel them to forego their
rudimentary premises and replace them with more elaborate conceptions of how to respond to the challenges of daily life.

This is not say that people everywhere are now equal in the skills
they bring to bear upon world politics. Obviously, the analytically rich
continue to be more skillful than the analytically poor. But although
the gap between the two ends of the skill continuum may be no

narrower than in the past, the advance in the competencies of those at every point on the continuum is sufficient to contribute to a major transformation in the conduct of world affairs.

The Macro-Micro Parameter: A Relocation of Authority

This parameter consists of the recurrent orientations, practices, and patterns of aggregation through which citizens at the micro level are linked to their collectivities at the macro level. In effect, it encompasses the authority structures whereby large aggregations, including private organizations as well as public agencies, achieve and sustain the cooperation and compliance of their memberships. Historically, these authority structures have been founded on traditional criteria of legitimacy derived from constitutional and legal sources. Under these circumstances individuals were habituated to compliance with the directives issued by higher authorities. They did what they were told to do because, well, because that is what one did. As a consequence, authority structures remained in place for decades, even centuries, as people unquestioningly yielded to the dictates of governments or the leadership of any other organizations with which they were affiliated. For a variety of reasons, including the expanded analytic skills of citizens as well as a number of other factors noted below, the foundations of this parameter have undergone erosion. Throughout the world today, in both public and private settings, the sources of authority have shifted from traditional to performance criteria of legitimacy. Where the structures of authority were once in place, in other words, now they are in crisis, with the readiness of individuals to comply with governing directives being very much a function of their assessment of the performances of the authorities. The more the performance record is considered appropriate—in terms of satisfying needs, moving toward goals, and providing stability—the more are they likely to cooperate and comply. The less they approve the performance record, the more are they likely to withhold their compliance or otherwise complicate the efforts of macro authorities.

As a consequence of the pervasive authority crises, states and governments have become less effective in confronting challenges and implementing policies than they were in the past. They can still maintain public order through their police powers, but their ability to address substantive issues and solve substantive problems is declining as people find fault with their performances and thus question their authority, redefine the bases of their legitimacy, and withhold their cooperation. Such a transformation is being played out dramatically today in the former Soviet Union, as it did earlier within all the countries of Eastern Europe. But authority crises in the former Communist world are only the more obvious instances of this newly emergent pattern. It is equally evident in every other part of the world, although the crises take different forms in different countries and in different types of private organizations. In Canada the authority crisis is rooted in linguistic, cultural, and constitutional issues as Quebec seeks to secede or otherwise redefine its relationship to the central government, an effort that in turn has fostered the emergence of demands for rights by women, new ethnic groups, and indigenous peoples (and subsequent legislation on these issues). In France the devolution of authority was legally sanctioned through legislation that privatized several governmental activities and relocated authority away from Paris and toward greater jurisdiction for the provinces. In China the provinces enjoy a wider jurisdiction by, in effect, ignoring or defying Beijing. In the former Yugoslavia the crisis led to violence and civil war. In the crisis-ridden countries of Latin America the challenge to traditional authority originates with insurgent movements, human rights, and the drug trade. In Japan and Mexico the decades-long predominance of a single party has come to an end. And in those parts of the world where the shift to performance criteria of legitimacy has not resulted in the relocation of authority—such as the United States, Israel, Argentina, the Philippines, and South Korea—uneasy stalemates prevail in the policy-making process as governments have proven incapable of bridging societal divisions sufficiently to undertake the decisive actions necessary to address and resolve intractable problems.

Nor is the global authority crisis confined to states and governments. It is also manifest in subnational jurisdictions, international organizations, and nongovernmental transnational entities. Indeed, in some cases the crises unfold simultaneously at different levels: Just as the issue of Quebec's place in Canada became paramount, for example, so did the Mohawks in Quebec press for their own autonomy. Similarly, just as Moldavia rejected Moscow's authority, so did several ethnic groups within Moldavia seek to establish their own autonomy by rejecting Moldavia's authority. And, to cite but a few conspicuous examples of crises in international and transnational organizations, the

United Nations Educational, Scientific, and Cultural Organization (UNESCO), the Palestine Liberation Organization (PLO), and the Catholic Church have all experienced decentralizing dynamics that are at least partly rooted in the replacement of traditional with performance criteria of legitimacy.

The relocating of authority precipitated by challenges to states and governments at the national level occurs in several directions, depending in good part on the scope of the enterprises people perceive as more receptive to their concerns and thus more capable of meeting their increased preoccupation with the adequacy of performances. In many instances this process has involved "downward" relocation toward subnational groups—toward ethnic minorities, local governments, single-issue organizations, religious and linguistic groupings, political factions, trade unions, and the like. In some instances the relocating process has moved in the opposite direction toward more encompassing collectivities that transcend national boundaries. The beneficiaries of this "upward" relocation of authority range from supranational organizations like the European Union to intergovernmental organizations like the International Labor Organization, from nongovernmental organizations like Greenpeace to professional groups such as Medecins sans Frontiers, from multinational corporations like IBM to inchoate social movements that join together environmentalists or women in different countries, from informal international regimes like those active in different industries to formal associations of political parties like those that share conservative or socialist ideologies—to mention but a few types of larger-than-national entities that have become the focus of legitimacy sentiments. Needless to say, these multiple directions in which authority is being relocated serve to reinforce the tensions between the centralizing and decentralizing dynamics that underlie the turbulence presently at work in world politics.

Associated with the crises that have overcome the macro-micro parameter is an undermining of the principle of national sovereignty. To challenge the authority of the state and to then redirect legitimacy sentiments toward supranational or subnational collectivities is to begin to deny that the state has the ultimate decisional power, including the right to resort to force. Since authority is structurally layered such that many levels of authority may have autonomy within their jurisdictions without also possessing sovereign powers, there is no obvious relationship between the location of authority and sovereignty. Nevertheless, trends toward the relocation of authority are bound to contribute to the erosion of sovereignty. If a state is thwarted in its efforts to mobilize effective armed forces, then its sovereignty is hardly a conspicuous feature of its existence as an independent collectivity. If a state cannot prevent outside actors from calling attention to its human rights record and thereby intervening on behalf of political prisoners, then the reach of its sovereignty is certainly reduced.[6]

The Macro Parameter: A Bifurcation of Global Structures

For more than three centuries the overall structure of world politics has been founded on an anarchic system of sovereign nation-states that did not have to answer to any higher authority and that managed their conflicts through accommodation or war. States were not the only actors on the world stage, but traditionally they were the dominant collectivities who set the rules by which the others had to live. The resulting state-centric world evolved its own hierarchy based on the way in which military, economic, and political power was distributed. Depending on how many states had the greatest concentration of power, at different historical moments the overall system was varyingly marked by hegemonic, bipolar, or multipolar structures.

From the perspective of the postinternational paradigm, however, the state-centric world is no longer predominant. Due to the skill revolution, the worldwide spread of authority crises, and several other sources of turbulence (noted below), it has undergone bifurcation into two increasingly autonomous worlds. Alongside the traditional world of states, a complex multi-centric world of diverse actors has emerged, replete with structures, processes, and decision rules of its own. The sovereignty-free actors (SFAs) of the multi-centric world include multinational corporations, ethnic minorities, subnational governments and bureaucracies, professional societies, political parties, transnational organizations, and the like. Individually, and sometimes jointly, they compete, conflict, cooperate, or otherwise interact with the sovereignty-bound actors (SBAs) of the state-centric world.[7] Table 3.2 delineates the main differences between the multi-centric and state-centric worlds.

Unlike the state-centric world, where most interactions involve events that unfold reciprocally and bilaterally between SBAs, the

TABLE 3.2   Structure and Process in the Two Worlds of World Politics

	State-centric World	*Multi-centric World*
Number of essential actors	Fewer than 200	Hundreds of thousands
Prime dilemma of actors	Security	Autonomy
Principal goals of actors	Preservation of territorial integrity and physical security	Increase in world market shares and maintenance of integration of subsystems
Ultimate resort for realizing goals	Armed force	Withholding of cooperation or compliance
Normative priorities	Processes, especially those that preserve sovereignty and the rule of law	Outcomes, especially those that expand human rights, justice, and wealth
Modes of collaboration	Formal alliances whenever possible	Temporary coalitions
Scope of agenda	Limited	Unlimited
Rules governing interactions among actors	Diplomatic practices	Ad hoc, situational
Distribution of power among actors	Hierarchical by amount of power	Relative equality as far as initiating action is concerned
Interaction patterns among actors	Symmetrical	Asymmetrical
Locus of leadership	Great powers	Innovative actors with extensive resources
Institutionalization	Well established	Emergent
Susceptibility to change	Relatively low	Relatively high
Control over outcomes	Concentrated	Diffused
Bases of decisional structures	Formal authority, law	Various types of authority, effective leadership

Source: James N. Rosenau, *Turbulence in World Politics: A Theory of Change and Continuity* (Princeton: Princeton University Press, 1990), p. 250.

multi-centric world entails sequences of action that take the form of cascades, of fast-moving flows of action that not only precipitate reactions on the part of their immediate targets but that also stimulate new actions on the part of as many SFAs and SBAs as happen to get caught up in the causal networks that crisscross the two worlds of world politics. Cascades, in other words, are the processes whereby the energies of parametric change are sustained and carried through the global system. That the course of cascades can vary from one system or situation to another is amply illustrated in Tables 3.3 and 3.4. Here a sample of decision rules that SFAs and SBAs follow in their interactions with each other are presented, and their diversity and range suggest the intensity that can ensue when actors in the two worlds have occasion to respond to each other.

In sum, although the bifurcation of world politics has not pushed states to the edge of the global stage, they are no longer the only key actors. They are faced with the new task of coping with disparate rivals from another world as well as the challenges posed by counterparts in their own world. The macro parameter is thus perhaps most incisively described as sustaining the two worlds of world politics.

The Sources of Global Turbulence

Given a world with the new parametric values represented by the skill revolution, the relocation of authority, and the bifurcation of global structures, it is hardly surprising that politicians, publics, and pundits speak of a new global order. For it is a new order—not so much because the Cold War has ended or because a successful coalition was mobilized to oust Iraq from Kuwait, but because the fundamental underpinnings of world politics, the parameters that sustain it, have undergone transformation.

Thus far, however, the discussion has been more descriptive than explanatory. We have defined turbulence and indicated the sites at which its consequences are likely to be most extensive and enduring, but we have not accounted for the dynamics that underlie the parametric transformations. What drives the turbulence? This question needs to be clarified, at least briefly, if we are to compare and assess the turbulence and realist paradigms.

Although a variety of factors have contributed to the onset of turbulence, several stand out as particularly salient and worthy of elaboration. As can be seen in the enumeration that follows, some of these sources are external to the processes of world politics and some are internal to them. That is, some of the sources are endogenous in the sense that they are inherent in the political processes, whereas others are exogenous in the sense that they derive from demographic, economic, and cultural processes. Together the endogenous and exoge-

TABLE 3.3   Some Decision Rules Underlying the Conduct of Sovereighty-Bound Actors (SBAs) in the Multi-Centric World

1. States yield jurisdiction, fully or partially, to transnational sovereignty-free actors when

    a. governments in a conflict situation are paralyzed by prior commitments and sovereignty-free actors may be able to break the stalemate;
    b. the initiatives of private actors or transnational collectivities do not intrude upon prior commitments and may yield desirable results;
    c. there is merit in a new course of action, but a public commitment to it prior to a demonstration of its merit runs the risk of public opposition;
    d. an issue has acquired such extensive momentum in a particular direction that to attempt to curb the involvement of multi-centric actors is to risk unacceptable consequences in other policy areas.

2. States allow domestic demands to take precedence over external requirements when

    a. the domestic economy stagnates;
    b. a major subsystem becomes agitated;
    c. domestic opinion coalesces and aggregates around a specific perspective;
    d. internal divisiveness and strife seriously threaten governmental effectiveness.

3. States respond to or seek out relations with sovereignty-free collectivities abroad when

    a. they seek to bring pressure on governments abroad and the collectivities are seen as having potential influence on the issues involved;
    b. they are under pressure to do so from domestic groups at home;
    c. they perceive the foreign actors as helpful in building a policy consensus at home;
    d. they seek to find and promote their shares of foreign markets.

4. States coordinate both with other states and with sovereignty-free actors abroad when

    a. sudden crises or disasters occur in the world economy, the physical universe, or the social world that bear immediately upon the welfare of private groups in several countries.

5. States coordinate with other states as a means of moving more freely in the multi-centric world when

    a. their governments agree on a course to follow, but one or more are severely constrained by the opposition of domestic groups;
    b. transnational interactions among sovereignty-free actors begin to impinge upon the stability of two or more governments.

6. States avoid contacts in the multi-centric world when

    a. their involvement would catch them up in cascades that run counter to their values and policies;
    b. to do so would be to set precedents for future contacts deemed risky.

7. States initiate covert policies and actions when

    a. desired outcomes of international situations are not amenable to action under the norms of the multi-centric system;
    b. private groups or individuals have goals or resources that cannot be mobilized through conventional diplomatic channels or accepted practice in the multi-centric world.

Source: James N. Rosenau, *Turbulence in World Politics: A Theory of Change and Continuity* (Princeton: Princeton University Press, 1990), p. 306.

TABLE 3.4   Some Decision Rules Underlying the Conduct of Sovereignty-Free Actors (SFAs) in the State-Centric World

1. SFAs seek to enhance their relations with states by

   a. being quick to defend the legitimacy of their organizational status and the worthiness of the activities and values from which their existence derives;
   b. avoiding a reputation as an ineffective or unreliable transnational actor;
   c. demonstrating as often as possible a capacity to act independently of the government in which their headquarters are located;
   d. expanding their memberships as widely as possible among citizens and organizations abroad and establishing local affiliates through whom those in other countries can work;
   e. seizing opportunities to intrude themselves into situations where their values and competence can be relevant to the course of events;
   f. maintaining a multiplicity of ties to other transnational actors in their own and related fields.

2. SFAs seek to enhance their internal coherence by

   a. proffering support, financial as well as moral where possible, to affiliates and counterparts abroad whenever the latter get embroiled in conflicts with their own governments or other adversaries;
   b. avoiding situations that may require their memberships to attach a higher priority to their transnational than their national loyalties;
   c. stressing their transnational ties and the benefits derived from them;
   d. resisting efforts by governments to narrow the scope of their activities.

3. SFAs seek to enhance their relationships with the state in which they have their main headquarters by

   a. establishing a multiplicity of links to states and counterparts abroad, thereby increasing the costs to the host state for any effort to curb their activities;
   b. publicizing the contributions their transnational activities make to the welfare of communities in the host state.

Source: James N. Rosenau, *Turbulence in World Politics: A Theory of Change and Continuity* (Princeton: Princeton University Press, 1990), p. 308.

nous sources go a long way toward explaining why what once seemed so anomalous now appears so patterned.

The Proliferation of Actors

Perhaps few facts about world politics are better known than those describing the huge increase in the human population since the end of World War II. Whereas the world's population was in excess of 2.5 billion in 1950, by 1990 the figure had surpassed 5 billion, and it continues to grow at a rapid rate. This demographic explosion lies at the heart of many of the world's problems and is also a continual source of the complexity and dynamism that has overwhelmed the parameters of the global system. Ever greater numbers of people have exerted pressure for technological innovations in a process that has brought about larger, more articulate, and increasingly unwieldy publics. These populations have contributed to the unmanageability of public affairs that has weakened states, stimulated the search for more responsive collectivities, and hastened the advent of paralyzing authority crises. And the sheer weight of numbers has created new and intractable public issues, of which famines and threats to the environment are only the more conspicuous examples.

But the proliferation of relevant actors is not confined to the huge growth in the number of individual citizens. No less important for present purposes is the vast increase in the number and types of collective actors whose leaders can clamber onto the global stage and act on behalf of their memberships. Indeed, this deepening density of the global system is due not so much to the unorganized complexity fostered by the population explosion as it is to the organized complexity consisting of millions of factions, associations, parties, organizations, movements, interest groups, and a host of other kinds of collectivities that share an aspiration to advance their welfare and a sensitivity to the ways in which a rapidly changing world may require them to network with each other.[8]

The dizzying increase in the density of actors that sustain world politics stems, of course, from a variety of sources. In part it is a product of the trend toward ever greater specialization that is the hallmark of industrial and postindustrial economies and the greater interdependence that they foster. In part, too, it is a consequence of widespread dissatisfaction with large-scale collectivities and the performance of existing authorities, a discontent that underlies the turn to less encompassing organizations that are more fully expressive of close-at-hand needs and wants. Relevant here also are the expanded analytic skills of citizens, which enable them to appreciate how they can join in collective actions that serve as avenues for expressing their discontent. Whatever the reasons for the proliferation of collective actors, however, their sheer number has been a prime stimulus to the evolution of the multi-centric world and to the authority crises that have wracked the state-centric world.

Although on a lesser scale, the state-centric world has also under-gone substantial enlargement, with the number of member states in the U.N. having more than tripled since its inception in 1945. Indeed, this growth has contributed to the exponential increase of actors in the multi-centric world, since each new state carved out of the former colonial empires spawned its own array of nongovernmental actors who contribute to the formation of new transnational networks. The organized complexity and deepening density of the global system, in other words, has derived from formal state-making dynamics as well as the multiplication of activities within societies.

The Impact of Dynamic Technologies

The technological explosion since World War II is no less impressive than its demographic counterpart. In a wide number of fields, from ag-riculture to transportation, from communications to medicine, from biogenetics to artificial intelligence, huge leaps have been made in hu-mankind's ability to cope with the laws of nature. As a result, geo-graphic distances have been shortened, social distances narrowed, and economic barriers circumvented. The world gets smaller and smaller as its peoples become more and more interdependent, processes that have had enormous consequences for the skills of individuals, their re-lations with higher authorities, and the macro structures through which their affairs are (or are not) managed. It is highly doubtful, in short, whether world politics would have been overtaken by turbu-lence had major technologies not exploded in the past forty years.

Two of these explosions, the nuclear and communications revolu-tions, stand out as especially relevant to the complexity and dyna-mism that have inundated the three prime parameters. The extraordi-nary advances in military weaponry subsequent to World War II, marked by nuclear warheads and the rocketry to deliver them, im-posed a context on the conduct of world affairs that, in effect, increas-ingly inhibited recourse to military action and reduced the probability of a major global war. The nuclear revolution thus had the ironic con-sequence of depriving states of one of their prime instruments for pur-suing and defending their interests. To be sure, the arms race and events like the Cuban missile crisis (see Chapter 7) infused world af-fairs with a high degree of volatility that often made them seem very fragile indeed. Even as the arms race emphasized the extraordinary capacities several states had acquired, however, so did it point up the limits of state action and thereby open the door for challenges to the authority of states. It is no accident that a series of transnational, large-scale, and powerful social movements—in the realms of peace, ecology, and women's rights—acquired momentum during the same period as states added substantially to their nuclear arsenals.

The communications revolution is hardly less central as a source of global turbulence. The rapidity and clarity with which ideas and information now circulate through television, VCRs, computer networks, fax machines, satellite hook-ups, fiber-optic telephone circuits, and many other microelectronic devices has rendered national boundaries ever more porous and world politics ever more vulnerable to cascading demands. Events that once took weeks and months to unfold now develop within days and hours. Financial transactions that once were mired in long delays can now be consummated in seconds. Diplomats, adversaries, military commanders, and publics who once had to wait long periods before reaching conclusions are now able to act decisively. Today the whole world, its leaders and its citizenries, instantaneously share the same pictures and descriptions, albeit not necessarily the same understandings, of what is transpiring in any situation.[9]

Examples of the cascading effects of the communications revolution abound. Most conspicuous perhaps is the impact of Cable News Network (CNN), which is said to be on and continuously watched in every embassy and every foreign office of every country in the world and which, during the Gulf War, served as the basis for diplomatic and military action on both sides of the conflict.[10] Hardly less telling is the example of the French journal *Actuel,* which was so upset by the crackdown in Tiananmen Square that, having compiled a mock edition of the *People's Daily* that contained numerous accounts that the Chinese leadership did not want their people to read, sent it to every fax machine in China in the fall of 1989.[11] Or consider the explosive implications of the fact that 5 percent of Brazil's households had television receiving sets when its 1960 presidential election was held and that this figure had swollen to 72 percent at the time of the next presidential contest in 1989.

Given the magnitude of these communications dynamics, it is hardly surprising that people everywhere have become more analytically skillful, more ready to challenge authority, and more capable of engaging in collective actions that press their demands. Their information may be skewed and their understanding of the stakes at risk in situations may be loaded with bias, but the stimuli to action are now ever present. Today individuals can literally see the aggregation of demands—that is, the coming together of publics and the acquiescence of governments—and how the participation of their counterparts elsewhere can have meaningful consequences. Likewise, the availability of high-tech communications equipment has enabled leaders in the public and private sectors to turn quickly to their memberships and mobilize them in support of their immediate goals in the multi- and state-centric worlds.[12]

The Globalization of National Economies

If the communications revolution has been a prime stimulus of the tendencies toward decentralization through the empowering of citizens and subnational groups, the dynamics at work in the realm of economics are equally powerful as sources of centralizing tendencies. Starting in the technologically most advanced sectors of the global economy, and following the economic crisis of 1973–1974, a new kind of production organization geared to limited orders for a variety of specialized markets began to replace the large plants that produced standardized goods. Consequently, the products of numerous semi-skilled workers in big plants were no longer competitive with the outputs of a large number of small units that could be tailored to shifting demands, and business became concerned about restructuring capital so as to be more effective in world markets. As capital became increasingly internationalized, so did groups of producers and plants in different territorial jurisdictions become linked in order to supply markets in many countries, all of which fostered and sustained a financial system global in scope and centered in major cities such as New York, Tokyo, and Frankfurt.

In short, capital, production, labor, and markets have all been globalized to the point where financiers, entrepreneurs, workers, and consumers are now deeply enmeshed in networks of the world economy that have superseded the traditional political jurisdictions of national scope. Such a transformation was bound to have an impact upon the established parameters of world politics. Among other things, it served to loosen the ties of producers and workers to their states, to expand the horizons within which citizens pondered their self-interests, and to foster the formation of transnational organizations that could operate on a global scale to protect and advance the economic interests of their members. The rapid growth and maturation of the multi-centric world can in good part be traced to the extraordinary dynamism and expansion of the global economy. And so can the weakening of the state, which is no longer the manager of the national economy and has become, instead, an instrument for adjusting the national economy to the exigencies of an expanding world economy.

The Advent of Interdependence Issues

The evolution of the world economy is not the only source of centralizing tendencies at work in global life. There are also a number of new, transnational problems that are crowding high on the world's agenda and forcing the globalization of certain kinds of issues. Whereas the political agenda used to consist of issues that governments could cope with on their own or through interstate bargaining, conventional issues are now being joined by challenges that by their very nature do not fall exclusively within the jurisdiction of states and their diplomatic institutions. Six current challenges are illustrative: environmental pollution, currency crises, the drug trade, terrorism, AIDS, and the flow of refugees. Each of these issues embraces processes that involve participation by large numbers of citizens and that inherently and inescapably transgress national boundaries—the winds at Chernobyl, for example, carried the pollution into many countries and intruded upon many lives—thus making it impossible for governments to treat them as domestic problems or to address them through conventional diplomatic channels.

Since these challenges are essentially the product of dynamic technologies and the shrinking social and geographic distances that separate peoples, they can appropriately be called "interdependence" issues. And, given their origins and scope, they can also be regarded as important centralizing dynamics in the sense that they impel cooperation on a transnational scale. All six issues, for instance, are the focus of either transnational social movements or ad hoc international institutions forged to ameliorate, if not to resolve, the boundary-crossing problems they have created. To be sure, such issues may originate in local settings that are addressed by local or state authorities, but the fact that their consequences are global in scope means that transnational authorities have to address them as well.

The advent of interdependence issues has contributed to the present era of turbulence in world politics in several ways. First, as in the case of the economic changes, such issues have given citizens pause about their states as the ultimate problem-solvers and, in the case of those who join social movements, the issues have reoriented people to ponder a restructuring of their loyalties. In so doing, interdependence issues have also fostered the notion that transnational cooperation can be as central to world politics as interstate conflict. Equally important, given their diffuse, boundary-crossing structure, these types of issues are spawning a whole range of transnational associations that are furthering the density of the multi-centric world and, as a result, are likely to serve as additional challenges to the authority of states.

The Weakening of States and the Restructuring of Loyalties

Before noting the ways in which states have suffered a loss in their authority, we must stress that we are referring to a relative and not an absolute loss. Postinternationalists do not view states as becoming peripheral to global affairs. On the contrary, states are seen as continuing to maintain their world and its international system and in so doing continuing to infuse that system with vitality and a capacity for adapting to change. More than that, states have been and continue to be a source of the turbulent changes that are at work. After all, it was the state-centric and not the multi-centric world that created multilateral organizations such as the United Nations, that developed the arrangements through which the nuclear revolution has been contained, that responded to the demands for decolonization in such a way as to produce the hierarchical arrangements that have enabled the industrial countries to dominate those in the Third World, and that framed the debate over the distribution of the world's resources—to mention only a few of the more obvious ways in which states have shaped and still shape the ongoing realities of world politics. To discern a decline in the capacity of states, therefore, is not to suggest or in any way imply that they are no longer relevant actors on the world stage.

At the same time, however, it is just as erroneous to treat states as constants as it is to view the skills of citizens as invulnerable to change. States are not eternal verities; they are as susceptible to variability as any other social system, and thus the possibility exists that they could suffer a decline of sovereignty as well as an erosion of their ability to address problems, much less of their ability to come up with satisfactory solutions to them.[13]

Viewed from the perspective of vulnerabilities, the growing density of populations, the expanding complexity of the organized segments of society, the globalization of national economies, the relentless pressure of technological innovations, the challenge of subgroups intent upon achieving greater autonomy, and the endless array of other intractable problems that form the modern political agenda, it seems evident that world politics have cumulated to a severity of circumstances that lessens the capacity of states to be decisive and effective. And added to these difficulties is the fact that citizenries, through the microelectronic revolution, are continuously exposed to scenes of authority crises around the world—scenes that are bound to give rise to doubts and demands in even the most stable of polities and thus to foment a greater readiness to question the legitimacy of governmental policies.[14]

Accordingly, although states may not be about to exit from the political stage, and they may even continue to occupy the center of the stage, they do seem likely to become increasingly vulnerable and impotent. And as such, as ineffective managers of their own affairs, they will also serve as stimuli to turbulence in world politics—as sources of autonomy in the multi-centric world, internal challenges to established authority, and more analytically skillful citizens demanding more effective performances from their leaders.

But this argument for diminished state competence is subtle and depends on intangible processes for which solid indicators are not easily developed. Perhaps most notable in this regard are subtle shifts in loyalties that accompany the globalization of national economies, the decentralizing tendencies toward subgroup autonomy, and the emergence of performance criteria of legitimacy. Such circumstances seem bound to affect loyalties to the state. That is, as transnational and subnational actors in the multi-centric world become increasingly active and effective, as they demonstrate a capacity to deal with problems that states have found intractable or beyond their competence, citizens will begin to look elsewhere than the national capital for assistance. Examples abound. Prior to the dissolution of the Soviet Union, for instance, citizens had to make difficult choices between their long-standing orientations toward Moscow and the "downward" pull of the particular republics or ethnic minorities of which they were also members. With Moscow unable to halt and reverse a steep economic decline, and with subnational attachments being thereby heightened, individuals all over that troubled land are having to face questions about distant attachments that they have long taken for granted. Bankers in Russia, for instance, had to confront a difficult situation in 1990 when the republic's parliament voted to cut its share of the Soviet budget: Normally the taxes for the Soviet Union were deposited in the republic banks and transferred by them to the coffers of the central government, but in this instance the bankers were told not to transfer the full amounts despite pressure from Gorbachev to do so.

It would be a mistake, however, to regard the loyalty problem as confined to multiethnic systems. Relatively homogeneous societies are beset with the same dilemma. Consider the situation of Norway, where the people have a deep emotional and historical attachment to the idea of independence: In 1972 they voted, by a small margin, not to join the European Community (EC), but by 1990 they were faced with the possibility of being the only West European country outside the EC as Sweden, Austria, Finland, and even Switzerland either applied for membership or indicated a readiness to forego their traditional neutrality and seek admission to the EC. Norwegian loyalties, in other words, were being pulled in an "upward" direction as the economic advantages of membership in a supranational organization increasingly seem to outweigh the psychologically satisfying and historically demonstrated virtues of being a member of an autonomous national community.[15] When the decisive vote was held in 1994, however, the upward pull faltered and the Norwegians became, by a vote of 53 to 47 percent, the only nation to reject membership in the European Union.[16] Or ponder the unfolding malaise in France, where a mood of pessimism is widespread and where "many Frenchmen have doubts about the capacity of their country to meet successfully the dangers, opportunities, and uncertainties which the future holds." Put even more succinctly, France is presently marked by a pervasive impression that "something is breaking apart, that society is decomposing," and that, indeed, "all the institutions built over the past 40 years are in crisis and are therefore incapable of responding."[17]

This is not to say that traditional national loyalties are being widely abandoned. Plainly, such attachments do not suddenly collapse. Rather, it is only to take note of subtle processes whereby what was once well established and beyond question is now problematic and undergoing change. Even more relevant, it seems reasonable to presume that the diminished competence of states to act decisively, combined with the processes of loyalty transformation, serves as a significant source of the dynamics that are rendering more complex each of the three prime parameters of world politics. Clearly, the viability of the multi-centric world, the persistence of authority crises, and the analytic skills of individuals are all intensified the more the capabilities of states decline and the more the loyalties of citizens become problematic.

Subgroupism

Since there is a widespread inclination to refer loosely to "nationalism" as a source of the turbulent state of world politics, it is perhaps useful to be more precise about the collective nature of those decentralizing tendencies wherein individuals and groups feel readier to challenge authority and reorient their loyalties. As previously noted, the authority crises that result from such challenges can be either of an "upward" or a "downward" kind, depending on whether the aspiration is to relocate authority in more or less encompassing jurisdictions than those that operate at the national level. In a number of instances of both kinds of relocation, the motivation that sustains the change is not so deeply emotional as to qualify as an "ism." The creation of subnational administrative divisions, for example, can stem from detached efforts to rationalize the work of a governmental agency or private organization, and the process of implementing the decentralized arrangements can occur in the context of reasoned dialogue and calm decisionmaking. Often, however, intense concerns and powerful attachments—feelings and commitments strong enough to justify using terms like "transnationalism," "supranationalism," or "internationalism"—can accompany the press for new arrangements. The downward relocations marked by comparable intensities are perhaps best labeled by the generic term "subgroupism."

The postinternational paradigm posits subgroupism as arising out of those deep affinities that people develop toward the close-at-hand associations, organizations, and subcultures with which they have been historically, professionally, economically, socially, or politically linked and to which they attach their highest priorities. Subgroupism values the in-group over the out-group, sometimes treating the two as adversaries and sometimes positing them as susceptible to extensive cooperation. Subgroupism can derive from and be sustained by a variety of sources, not the least being disappointment in—and alienation from— the performances of the whole system in which the subgroup is located. Most of all perhaps, its intensities are the product of long-standing historical roots that span generations and get reinforced by an accumulated lore surrounding past events in which the subgroup survived trying circumstances.

That subgroupism can be deeply implanted in the consciousness of peoples is manifestly apparent in the resurfacing of strong ethnic identities throughout Eastern Europe and the former Soviet Union when, after decades, the authoritarian domination of Communist parties came to an end. In those cases, the subgroups were historic nations and the accompanying feelings can thus be readily regarded as expressions of nationalism. Not all, or even a preponderance, of decentralizing tendencies attach to nations, however. Governmental subdivisions, political parties, labor unions, professional societies, and a host of other types of subgroups can also evoke intense attachments, and it would grossly understate the relevance of the decentralizing tendencies at work in world politics to ignore these other forms of close-at-hand ties. Accordingly, it seems preferable to regard the emotional dimensions of generic decentralizing tendencies as those of subgroupism and to reserve the concept of nationalism for those subgroup expressions that revolve around nations and feelings of ethnicity.

The Spread of Poverty and the Third World

Underlying the bifurcation of world politics into state- and multi-centric worlds has been another split—between industrially developed and underdeveloped countries—that has also contributed substantially to the onset of turbulence. This regional split between the North and the South—known during the Cold War as the First and Third Worlds—is a gulf that seems destined to widen and sustain, even extend, the processes of turbulence: The terrible problems and thwarted aspirations of peoples in the South are not going to be ameliorated in the foreseeable future and will thus continue to roil global waters. Among other things, the diverse and numerous countries of the South have added to the complexity and dynamism of global structures, sharpened performance criteria of legitimacy, enriched the analytic skills of the underprivileged, hastened the transnationalization of economies, corporations, and social movements, limited the authority of northern states over their production facilities, intensified the flow of people from South to North, lengthened the list of interdependence issues, and strengthened the tendencies toward subgroupism.

The impact of the split fostered by the breakup of Europe's colonial empires is perhaps most obvious with respect to global structures. Not only did decolonialization result in the proliferation of actors in the state-centric world, but it also had the consequence of rigidifying the degree of hierarchy in the state-centric world. The process whereby ever greater power accompanied the emergence of industrial states in the North was not matched when statehood came to Africa and Asia. The newly established states of the South acquired sovereignty and international recognition even though they lacked the internal resources and consensual foundations to provide for their own development, a circumstance that led one astute observer to call them "quasi-states"[18] and led the states themselves into a deep resentment over their dependence on the industrialized world for trade, technology, and many of the other prerequisites necessary to fulfill their desire for industrial development. Their sovereignty, in effect, is "negative" in that it protects them against outside interference but does not empower them to address their problems successfully.[19] The result has been a pervasive global pattern in which the industrial world has continued to prosper while Africa, Latin America, and parts of Asia have languished in a system endlessly reinforcing the inequities underlying the hierarchical structures of world politics.

In addition, resentments in the developing world, the legitimacy problems of quasi-states, and their attempts to use their majority in the General Assembly to alter the U.N.'s agenda and priorities have extended and deepened the global authority crisis. Indeed, the U.N. has become a major site of the authority crisis as the South has challenged the legitimacy of its actions and as the North, fearful of dominance by the sheer number of developing countries, has also questioned its legitimacy by periodically failing to meet its financial obligations to the U.N.

Even as the developing countries have rigidified the hierarchical structure of the state-centric world, so have they added to the decentralizing tendencies in the multi-centric world. Composed of tribes and ethnic groups artificially brought together under state banners by First World decolonizers, besieged by multinational corporations seeking to extend their operations and markets, and plagued with internal divisions and massive socioeconomic problems, Third World countries have added greatly to the breadth and depth of the multi-centric world. Their quasi-sovereignty keeps them active in the state system, but the multi-centric world has been hospitable to their fragmenting dynamics and thereby has contributed to the process wherein subgroup networks are proliferating.

Conclusion

Given the various sources that are fostering and sustaining the dynamic transformations of the basic parameters subsumed by the turbulence model, the question arises as to where world politics may be heading in the foreseeable future. Is the bifurcation of global structures likely to continue? Will it end because states will regain their earlier capabilities and effectiveness? Or might these structures fragment further as the multi-centric world becomes even more central to the course of events? The questions cannot be answered with certainty under present circumstances, but at the same time postinternationalists see no reason to believe that the skill revolution is soon to peter out or that the authority crises are likely to diminish in frequency and intensity. Hence the probabilities seem high that the present bifurcated structures will endure and become more deeply seated with the passage of time. If one subscribes to the turbulence model, one can be assured that more turbulence will, for better or worse, pervade the conduct of world affairs.[20]

4
Realism and Postinternationalism Compared

It does not take a close reading of the two previous chapters to appreciate that one's understanding of world politics is highly dependent on the paradigm one employs to interpret the course of events. This is a profound insight. It highlights, as already noted, that the facts do not speak for themselves, that world affairs are not self-evident, that what we know depends on how we go about organizing all the events and trends to which we attach significance. Moreover, the solutions designed to cope with global challenges are likely to be as sound as one's grasp of how and why world politics unfold as they do.

It follows that both citizens and policymakers will be best equipped to assess and respond to the course of events when they have been explicit about the premises that underlie their understandings of international relations. Thus, it is useful to undertake a comparison of the realist and postinternational paradigms, identifying both their differences and similarities, in order to demonstrate how the same events could have diverse meanings and implications for different observers. Such is the task of this chapter: to contrast the realist and turbulence paradigms without taking a stand as to which of the two approaches is "best." The reader must weigh the validity of the views for himself or herself. There is no "right" paradigm, and we have sought not to load the analysis in favor of one or the other. We care only that readers be sufficiently aware of the differences between the two paradigms to be able to choose between them. The reasons for preferring one or the other—or some variant or combination of them—may vary greatly from reader to reader, but in the end readers will have a preference, and it is important to be conscious of what that preference is.

TABLE 4.1   Comparison of Realist and Postinternationalist Paradigms

	Realist Model	Postinternationalist Model
Global structures	Anarchical interstate system	Bifurcation of state-centric and multi-centric worlds
State sovereignty	Unchanging	Eroding
State structures	Unitary actors	Fragmented
Societal structures	Irrelevant	Central
Role of citizens	Irrelevant	Central
Goals of collectivities	Security dilemma	Concern for internal coherence as well as security dilemma
Conceptions of power	Primarily military	Multiple sources
Use of force	Always possible	Inhibited
Domestic-foreign boundaries	Firm	Porous
Technology and media of communications	Facilitate state controls	Diminish state controls
Law	Positive and exclusionary	Natural and inclusionary
Coalition formation	Alliances	Loose aggregations
Sensitivity to change	Low	High
Appeal of paradigm	Simplicity	Complexity
Form of interaction	Events	Cascades

   The first column of Table 4.1 sets forth the divisions along which the two paradigms may be contrasted. By reading down the other two columns one can discern the coherence of each paradigm, and by reading across the rows one can sense the points at which the realist and turbulence models are similar or different. A quick perusal in this fashion affirms the central thrust of the ensuing discussion, namely, that the differences between the two paradigms are far more pervasive and significant than the similarities.

Global Structures

It is important to stress at the outset a key point at which the realist and turbulence paradigms overlap. Both posit an interstate system in which states possess sovereignty and are not formally responsible to a higher authority. In other words, there is no overarching governmental body empowered to make authoritative decisions with which international actors must comply. In this sense, both paradigms presume an anarchical global structure. To a large extent, however, this similarity is offset by a major structural difference: The realist paradigm allows only for the interstate system and presumes that it pervades and dominates the course of events, whereas the turbulence model delineates a multi-centric system of sovereignty-free actors that exists independently of the interstate system and competes, conflicts, cooperates, or otherwise interacts with it. This bifurcation of world politics adds extensive layers of complexity to the anarchical structure. According to the postinternationalist, power and authority are much more dispersed and decentralized than is presumed by the realist and, under these turbulent conditions, achieving coordinated policies designed to address and alleviate global problems is much more difficult and time consuming.

State Sovereignty

Although both paradigms presume that states possess sovereignty, which accords them the exclusive right to employ coercive force at home and renders them free of higher authority abroad, they differ considerably on the extent to which the principles of sovereignty are carried out in practice. Realists presume that these principles remain intact, that states do not and will not knowingly accept any diminution in their sovereign rights as independent actors. Postinternationalists, in contrast, perceive a continuing erosion in the sovereignty of states. They argue not only that states have lost some control over the inviolability of their borders (as the discussion of the domestic-foreign distinction stresses below), but also that the language of diplomacy has witnessed states interpreting fewer and fewer situations as posing challenges to their sovereign privileges.

State Structures

The difference in the complexity of world politics posed by the two models is extended further by their respective conceptions of how states are constituted. In the realist model states are viewed as strong unitary actors, as so consensual or hierarchical that they speak with only one voice, that of the chiefs of state who occupy the highest positions of authority. Under the turbulence model, in contrast, states are conceived of as weak, fragmented, and undergoing authority crises, with the result that they speak with many voices, of which the chief of state is only one. Indeed, postinternationalists hold that, more often than not, it is unclear whether the official pronouncements of states are reliable guides to their future actions.

Societal Structures

Given the presumption of states as unitary actors, the realist model accords little salience to the internal structures of societies. Realists view states as responding to political and economic challenges and circumstances arising out of the interstate system and, accordingly, it matters little to them what the histories, values, and social structures of any state may be. But the turbulence paradigm proceeds from quite the opposite perspective. Given aroused and active citizens, not to mention extensive subgroupism and weakened governmental authority, postinternationalists perceive states as engaging in external behavior that is very much a consequence of internal tensions and the availability of human and nonhuman resources. According to this view, variability and complexity mark the conduct of states abroad, with the result that domestic variables are often as important as the challenges and circumstances emanating from abroad in forming the sources of states' behavior.

Role of Citizens

It follows that the two paradigms adhere to very different, even exactly contrary, postures toward the role that citizens, both as individuals and as publics, play in world affairs. Inclined to confine causal power to the conduct of states, realists largely ignore individuals who do not occupy high government positions. Either they take publics for granted or they see them as easily manipulated and ever ready to acquiesce to the policies of their state's leaders. Postinternationalists, in contrast, assume that citizens, their skills, and their orientations are consequential, that macro collectivities and institutions derive their sustenance from the individuals they embrace, and that therefore any significant transformation at the micro level is bound to find expression in the aggregated dynamics that give shape and direction to global life. As noted in the previous chapter, moreover, postinternationalists list a number of reasons for concluding that a skill revolution has transformed the way in which citizens everywhere relate to the course of events; thus, theorists taking this view are especially attentive to micro phenomena as they seek to account for the cascading developments that spread erratically through the bifurcated structures of world politics.

Goals of Collectivities

Given its focus on international threats and challenges, the realism paradigm centers on the security dilemma. States are seen as ready to achieve territorial and economic security either through cooperation with other states or, if need be, through a readiness to go to war. Realists do not argue that military preparations are a constant or exclusive preoccupation of the leaders of states. They acknowledge that other policy goals are pursued and that, lately, some security threats—such as the availability of oil imports—have become increasingly economic in nature. At the same time they are also inclined to view war as the ultimate response to threats and thus believe that weapons stockpiles and the readiness of armed forces to enter combat are never far from the center of state concerns. In a turbulence context, however, the goals of states are viewed as marked by much greater variability, with less attention being paid to military considerations and more concern attributed to the achievement and maintenance of domestic coherence and support. Because states are faced with divisive subgroups and skeptical publics, says the postinternationalist, they devote as much energy to sustaining their internal strength as they do to maximizing their external capabilities. State leaders, in this view, are not unmindful of the need for territorial integrity and the dangers of enemy attacks, but their readiness to maintain military preparedness is located in a more encompassing context, one that allows for an equally strong readiness to give primacy to domestic challenges. In addition, and no less important, by positing a diversity of significant actors in the multicentric world, the turbulence model extends the conception of state goals well beyond the security dilemma. Whatever the bases of their organizations, the salient collectivities in the multi-centric world are not so much concerned with security as they are with autonomy, with maximizing the independence of both the state and fellow nonstate actors so that they can realize their aspirations without being hostage to the complexities that mark public affairs. To be sure, like states, the actors in the multi-centric world are ever ready to cooperate with like-minded counterparts, but this readiness does not extend to policies that might result in irremediable jeopardy to their autonomy.

Conceptions of Power

The two paradigms differ considerably in what they regard as the crucial elements of power. Where neorealism stresses the military and tangible dimensions of power, postinternationalism conceives of power more in terms of intangibles—such dimensions as the size and commitment of an organization's membership, the universality of its appeal, the skill of its leaders, and its reputation for keeping promises. Indeed, given the autonomy of its collectivities and the decentralized nature of its structures, the multi-centric world is seen less as an arena of power struggles than as a shifting set of locales in which coalitions are formed and reformed through subtle influence processes. Charts comparing countries in terms of the number of their men in uniform, the size of their agricultural output, and the output of their oil wells are commonplace in realist analyses of international politics, but similar diagrammatic displays are rare in postinternational inquiries. Why? Because, for the postinternationalist, collectivities in the multi-centric world, unlike states, do not rely so much on power bases to affect each other directly as they do on the indirect routes through which they have access to attentive publics, markets, bureaucracies, and other arenas where authority is diffuse and informal. Of course, states are also concerned with influencing these arenas, but most of their policies and actions follow the direct routes to the concentrated and formal centers of decision in other states.

Use of Force

Given different conceptions of power and sovereignty, it is hardly surprising that adherents of the two paradigms take quite different positions on the role of force in world politics. Realists posit that states are always prepared to resort to force to protect or advance their interests. After all, states have the sovereign right to use coercion, and since they are beholden to no higher authority, they must be ready to go to war if their interests cannot be protected in any other way. Postinternationalists do not deny that states work hard at maintaining their war-making potential and indicating a readiness to use it, but they contend that the probability of states actually warring on each other has declined. They perceive states as increasingly inhibited in their readiness to conduct war against other states. The mounting inhibitions are seen as stemming from an appreciation of the devastation that nuclear weapons could wreak as well as from a realization that modern societies are too complex to be easily conquered. In addition, such analysts stress that publics have become increasingly wary of situations involving battle casualties and thus much less mobilizable for war-making purposes.

Domestic-Foreign Boundaries

Virtually by definition, the two paradigms are marked by a wide discrepancy in how they view the boundaries that divide foreign and domestic affairs. For those who subscribe to realism, the boundaries setting off states from their external environments are firm and immutable, guarded by troops, customs officers, tariff walls, and a host of other barriers. Leaders of states thus distinguish between challenges abroad and those at home, and their policymaking arrangements fully reflect this distinction. Thus, foreign and defense departments assume responsibility for the challenges from abroad—and for ensuring that the country responds as a unitary actor—and problems arising at home are handled by interior, labor, transportation, and other such departments.

For postinternationalists concerned with the dynamics at work in the multi-centric world, domestic-foreign boundaries are seen as sufficiently porous to enable a continuous flow of people, goods, money, and ideas to pass through them. Why? Because these collectivities, whether transnational corporations, ethnic minorities, scientific associations, political parties, religious organizations, or subgovernmental bureaucracies, derive much of their purpose and strength from their links and interactions with affiliates or counterparts abroad. Because such groups are not confined within national boundaries, the multi-centric system is in important respects a world without borders—or, more accurately, a world with borders that are traced by the autono-

mous reach of each of its diverse collectivities. Moreover, each collectivity has internal needs and problems but must also function in an external environment. This internal-external balance is far different
from the domestic-foreign boundaries that crisscross the state-centric
world. Among other things, it is a balance that is continuously shifting
as the multi-centric collectivities expand or contract their goals, resources, and activities.

Technology and Media of Communications

Given the importance postinternationalists attach to citizens and their
SFAs, it is hardly surprising that they are sensitive to the role that technology and the mass media of communications play in diminishing
the centrality of states. Indeed, they tend to stress that neither the skill
revolution nor many authority crises would have occurred without the
world's new capacities for transmitting ideas and pictures speedily to
all corners of the earth. Because they are not ready to accord significance to the flow of ideas and their impact on the orientations of publics, realists are not especially attentive to the dynamics of technology
and widening channels of communications. If anything, realists are
inclined to view these factors as facilitating the control of states and
thus as reinforcing the dominance of the state-centric world.

Law

As realists see it, only relatively recently has the scope of international
law broadened beyond a selected range of topics that were of particular
interest to states. Historically, this range was confined mostly to issues
of territory, recognition of other states, treaties, the initiation and conduct of war, and treatment of diplomats, foreign nationals, and dependent peoples (colonies). Not until the latter half of the nineteenth
century did international law begin to include rules on trade and communications. In the twentieth century, other arenas—such as economics, labor standards, and the environment—were touched by international law. Essentially, realists contend, international law is what states
agree it is and only states can use the system directly. Any protection of
citizens (that is, of citizens traveling or stationed abroad) is due to reci-
procity between states. When violations occur, citizens' interests

might be advanced by their respective countries on the grounds that their mistreatment constitutes an "insult" to the country of citizenship.

States are viewed as taking international law seriously, if only because it is one way to manage conflict. But realists note three characteristics of international law to further illustrate the integrity of their argument. First, as noted above, international law embraces only a limited number of topics. Second, by the nineteenth century states generally rejected claims of "justness" in formulating law and instead favored the positive acceptance of rules; in other words, states feel they are bound to abide by only those rules that they have explicitly agreed to (they want to sign on the dotted line, so to speak). Third, international law long excluded citizens, firms, and other organizations from direct access to these rules. This exclusion largely remains the case today. Unless a treaty specifically provides a citizen or nongovernmental organization "standing," only international organizations and states are subjects of public international law. Indeed, it took a 1949 advisory opinion by the International Court of Justice to give international organizations the right to bring a claim against a state. The decision (for the United Nations) was considered a landmark change and provoked a dissenting opinion by J. Hackworth, who argued, "There is no specific provision in the United Nations Charter, nor is there any provision in any other agreement conferring upon the United Nations authority to assume the role of a state."[1]

The strict boundary between domestic and international actions is very much present in the legal realm. National courts (called "municipal" under international law) will defer making a judgment on many topics until they have received guidance from the foreign office. In some cases, courts (in Anglo-American systems) have refused a case on the grounds that it is a political question beyond the competence of a national court.

In contrast, the postinternational paradigm emphasizes four aspects of the law in world politics. First, there has been a vast growth of rule making by international organizations. Second, advocacy groups advance their aims through a proliferating set of legal strategies. Third, many actors in world politics now couch their legal claims in language emphasizing an underlying normative base of "justness" and reason. This philosophical orientation, in essence, draws on natural rather than positive legal traditions. Last, citizens, firms, and other organizations are increasingly successful in gaining direct access to the rule making that has been traditionally left to states alone.

States may well set up international organizations, but once in place, these organizations often set the rules for states. Postinternationalists stress that one need not even turn to the most dramatic instance of this process, the European Community, which lies somewhere between an international organization and a territorial state. Rather, they note, one need only consider how the rules for civil air travel, trade, labor, and a host of other functional areas are deeply structured by international organizations. Obligations set out by international organizations often lead to changes inside states as new departments are created to meet the obligations. Viewed from a postinternational perspective, therefore, international rule-making can serve as an important source of internal political change.

The same perspective, moreover, stresses that advocacy groups such as Amnesty International or Greenpeace now have sophisticated strategies for using domestic and international legal fora to advance their organizational interests. Human rights organizations in developing nations—which are not yet as important as those in developed countries—exemplify this point. Human rights organizations take cases into national courts primarily to educate judges on international law regarding human rights. In the United States, they also lobby Congress to influence the shape of the law. In Europe, the European Court of Human Rights, although still closely tied to states, hears complaints. In many Latin American countries, grassroots groups of mothers formed in the 1980s to protest "disappearances"; human rights organizations from other countries often supplied information to these groups and carried their message to the world. A number of regional international organizations concerned with human rights now solicit reports from nongovernmental organizations (NGOs).

Claims on behalf of human rights, the environment, or economic justice (and the NGOs in these areas increasingly go into "alliance" with each other) often lie outside existing international treaty frameworks. As postinternationalists see it, however, such organizations also tend to threaten the authority of states in general by basing their claims on natural law, which says that there is a law beyond anything written that can be accessed in order to reason about social problems. The essence of the theory of natural law, one observer notes, is that "law was derived from justice."[2] By appealing to justice, actors in the multi-centric world can begin to challenge existing rules.

The fact that SFAs have increasingly gained access to the organizations used by states to solve problems highlights the important roles they can play in decisionmaking on global problems. As consultative NGOs to the United Nations and its specialized agencies, they may be actively consulted by U.N. members in their areas of expertise. At home, these same groups can pressure both for legal and policy changes. Thus, the postinternationalist concludes that subgroups are using a combination of legal strategies and newly won access to state and international organizations to form a complex web of legal processes and thus expand their influence in shaping world politics.

Coalition Formation

At times it is in the interests of a single actor to associate with others or to build a following. In the realist view, alliance between states is a solid basis for advancing interests when going it alone will not suffice. An alliance is a formal pact, usually concluded after lengthy negotiations, between two or more states that outlines a relationship between the contracting parties and is generally directed against specified actions by other states. States would prefer to pursue their interests by themselves, using solely their power base. Alliances are thus a second-best strategy. Generally, states use alliances to maintain the balance of power. Very powerful states, especially in bipolar structural situations, may weave a web of alliances, thereby creating a followership of states.

Viewed from a postinternational perspective, coalition processes are far less formal and much more spontaneous than the realist would concede. Indeed, sometimes the processes are virtually out of control as members join, bargain, defect, or use other unpredictable strategies. This informality derives, in other words, from the involvement of numerous groups and the participation of individual citizens, all of whom associate with the coalition for their own reasons and thus have varying degrees of commitment and may remain involved for as long or as short a time as they wish. Accordingly, coalitions in the multi-centric world undergo continual transformations as issues come and go, whereas alliances in the state-centric world are ordinarily enduring and fixed features of the relationships among their members.

Sensitivity to Change

Perhaps the sharpest difference between the realist and turbulence models concerns the role each ascribes to change dynamics. Realists cite the centuries-long history of the interstate system to bulwark their premise that institutions are firmly in place and essentially impervious to any major changes that could recast fundamental structures. They readily acknowledge that war, revolution, and shifting alliance formations have periodically altered the degree to which the interstate system is organized along bipolar or multipolar lines, but such alterations, they say, occur in the context of an unchanging system rooted in the anarchical arrangements wherein states seek to maximize their interests in terms of the power available to them. Neorealists concede that transnational organizations have become increasingly relevant to the day-to-day developments that mark world politics, but at the same time they presume that this greater relevance is not so great as to alter the underlying nature and predominance of the interstate system. In the words of one leading realist, states "may choose to interfere little in the affairs of nonstate actors for long periods of time," but they "nevertheless set the terms of the intercourse. ... When the crunch comes, states remake the rules by which other actors operate"[3]—which is another way of asserting that states are capable of resisting change dynamics and thereby maintaining the continuities on which their system rests.

In contrast, the turbulence paradigm is highly sensitive to the forces of change that are unfolding at local, national, and global levels. Since it locates the sources of transformation in underlying processes, such as those driven by new technologies and restructured authority relations, rather than in events such as war and revolution, the turbulence approach posits a number of points at which change can be initiated, the more so as the dynamics of technology and authority relations quicken in pace and broaden in scope. To be sure, those who employ a postinternational perspective do not ignore the pervasiveness of continuities and historical patterns in global life. They acknowledge that people are rooted in habitual ways and that organizational inertia is widespread. Still, on balance, they conceive of the continuities as under constant siege by a variety of forces that turn people, institutions, and societies in new directions. Indeed, it is the uncertainties that attach to the multiplicity of change dynamics that are conceived to render world affairs so turbulent.

Conclusion

In short, it matters a great deal which paradigm one chooses to infuse order into the welter of phenomena that make up world politics. The realism model is compelling in its simplicity, whereas the turbulence approach forces one to come to grips with the complexities of global life. Each thus has its virtues and its drawbacks even as they both offer a coherent means for advancing understanding. As a result, readers must make their own choices as they ponder the world in which they live, choices that are bound to shape what they regard as salient and crucial in the course of events. And as stressed at the outset, the more self-conscious they can be about the paradigmatic choices they make, the more they are likely to grasp and clarify what is at work in world politics as the twentieth century draws to a close.

5
The Politics of the Antarctic

The continent of Antarctica (see Figure 5.1) belongs to no nation, although a number of states have made claims on sections of it. This unusual state of affairs was created by the 1959 Antarctic Treaty, which came into full force in 1961 and is often referred to as the Antarctic Treaty System (ATS). Australia, Argentina, Belgium, Japan, Norway, South Africa, France, Chile, Great Britain, the Soviet Union, New Zealand, and the United States negotiated the original treaty, and since then forty-one nations have signed it, thereby showing approval of the treaty's aims and committing themselves to its execution. For the first thirty years of the agreement, the treaty could only be revised through unanimous agreement of the voting members. After thirty years, any voting member could call a conference to review the treaty.

The treaty has five unusual features:

1. It was the first arms control agreement of the Cold War—it stipulated that neither military forces nor nuclear weapons could be placed in the Antarctic (although armed services personnel and equipment could be used to move scientists there).
2. The agreement set aside territorial claims for the duration of the treaty; claims over territorial waters were left unaffected. Thus, it did not solve the territorial question, it just put it on hold.
3. It set aside the continent as a preserve for science.
4. It permitted researchers to visit any area at any time.
5. It established procedures for coordinating research and solving any new problems that might arise.

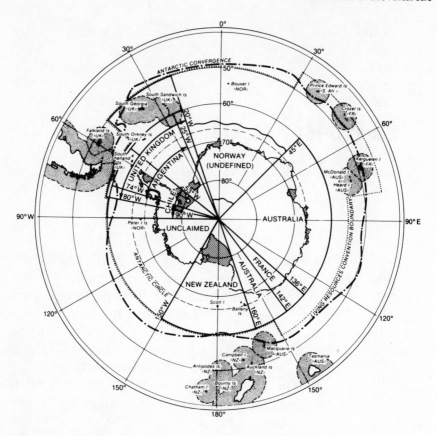

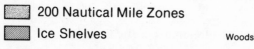
200 Nautical Mile Zones

Ice Shelves

© Christopher C. Joyner
Woods Hole Oceanographic Institution, 1987

FIGURE 5.1   Map of Antarctica

Source: David B. Newsom, ed., *The Diplomatic Record, 1989–1990* (Boulder: Westview Press, 1991), p. 157.

States that have signed the treaty do not automatically get to make decisions about the management of the Antarctic. Voting on Antarctic issues is confined to the Antarctic Treaty Consultative Parties (ATCPs). Originally, to become a consultative party, a state had to demonstrate that it was capable of conducting substantial scientific research in the

Antarctic through expeditions or the establishment of stations. Due to the rigorous climate, this was no small matter; thus, the agreement tended to favor wealthier states with fairly extensive scientific capacities over smaller, weaker ones. This voting arrangement, over the years, came under increasing attack by Third World nations in the General Assembly of the United Nations. In 1990 Greenpeace further complicated the scene by "wintering over" and doing research. Since Greenpeace is not a state, it cannot sign the treaty or vote on matters pertaining to the Antarctic. It did, however, strengthen its argument that it should be allowed to observe meetings of the consultative parties.

The original consultative parties, for their part, sought to address the criticisms of elitism leveled by Third World states by admitting new states to full voting status, even though these countries are barely involved in research.[1] New voting members include Brazil, China, India, South Korea, Peru, Ecuador, and Uruguay, making a total of twenty-six consultative parties. The group has only recently begun to invite nonstate organizations to its meetings.

As the treaty anticipated, scientific work produced information and raised new issues about the continent and the waters around it. Two issues, living resources and mineral resources, are of particular interest because they led to new international agreements. The living resources question is largely covered by the Convention on Antarctic Seals and the 1980 Convention on the Conservation of Antarctic Marine Living Resources (CCAMLR).[2] Minerals were to be covered by the Convention on the Regulation of Antarctic Mineral Resource Activities (CRAMRA), but this convention has never come into force. These agreements, along with other international treaties that touch on matters related to Antarctic resources (e.g., whaling), now form the legal core for the management of Antarctica.

In this chapter we pose four questions about the political management of the Antarctic. First, why did the Antarctic Treaty come into being in the first place? Second, why was the minerals convention (CRAMRA) negotiated? Third, why did CRAMRA fail to go into effect? And fourth, what predictions can we make about the likely future of the Antarctic Treaty System?

Responses to these questions are offered from the realist and postinternationalist perspectives. As can be seen in Table 5.1, which presents an overview of the responses elicited by each of the four ques-

TABLE 5.1   Theoretical Overview of the Antarctic Treaty

Question 1: Why Was the Antarctic Treaty Negotiated and Put into Effect?

Realism	Postinternationalism
Mutual fears of a widening nuclear arms race—in an area that had not experienced U.S.-Soviet rivalry—led the two powers to cooperate.	A research structure designed by the scientific community provided a convenient framework for states to use in resolving disputes.
All states with active territorial claims in the Antarctic followed the hegemonic leadership of the United States.	The normative (value) priorities of the scientific community helped states escape the dictates of sovereignty.
The strong bipolarity of the international system made it easy to put the treaty in place.	
The United States structured the problem so that states were not likely to be penalized for cooperation.	

Question 2: Why Was the Minerals Agreement Negotiated?

Realism	Postinternationalism
Mineral exploitation could destroy the entire security regime of the ATS.	Activities by the scientists (SFAs) put minerals on the agendas of states (SBAs).
	The 'delegation of rule' to the scientific community would be threatened if negotiations occurred outside the ATS.

Question 3: Why Did CRAMRA Fail to Go into Effect?

Realism	Postinternationalism
Conflicts over different state interests were likely to surface if CRAMRA went into operation; this outcome might have threatened the security regime.	The ability of the ATCPs to enact the agreement had been weakened by authority crises among states and within ATCP states.

Question 4: What Is the Likely Future of the Antarctic Treaty System?

Realism	Postinternationalism
No change is likely.	The centralizing tendencies in global politics will lead to the subordination of Antarctic governance to multi-centric actors and more encompassing environmental rules.

tions, the two theories tell a very different story about the origins and workings of the ATS.

The Realist Interpretation

Question 1: Why was the Antarctic Treaty negotiated and put into effect?

Realist Response 1: Mutual fears of a widening nuclear arms race—in an area that had not experienced U.S.-Soviet rivalry—led the two powers to co-operate.

The highest concern of states is the preservation of sovereignty, followed by the maintenance of security from military threats. The mid-1950s was perhaps the most intense period of the Cold War as relations between the USSR and the United States were bitter and characterized by high levels of distrust. Both nations "fought" the Cold War through arms racing—getting more and better weapons—and through gaining allies.

The arms race had been limited to internal acquisition of weapons, the placement of nuclear-capable bombers in Eastern Europe by the Soviets, and the establishment of a string of U.S. bases along Soviet and Warsaw Pact borders. Despite this show of strength and willingness to "go nuclear" if necessary, neither side actually wanted a nuclear war. Thus, a mutual concern over the danger of nuclear war constrained both nations.

During World War II, Britain and Germany had used some of the sub-Antarctic islands for their submarines and had lost some shipping from these operations. Norway had asserted its territorial claim in 1939 to forestall a claim by Nazi Germany.[3] With this history, it took little imagination for both the United States and the Soviet Union to see that Antarctica could become yet another spot where the Cold War might be contested. No nuclear weapons were deployed in the Antarctic, nor were any planned (indeed, until the mid-1950s the Soviets had expressed little interest in the region). If the Antarctic remained a contested area, however, those plans could change. The two states were faced, in essence, with a prisoner's dilemma situation. For the Soviets, the best security outcome would be for it, but not the United States, to place military systems on the continent. The reverse was true for the

United States. If each acted as though it expected the other to do nothing, they would both end up with the second worst outcome: both nations with military systems in the area. A second-best option was also available: Keep the arms race out of the region entirely.

Even leaving aside the threat of nuclear deployments, the potential for direct conflict remained. If the United States decided to assert territorial claims or to counteract a Soviet move in the region, the Soviets would encounter trouble. The U.S. Navy and its airlift capacities would serve the United States well as it built and supplied military operations in the Antarctic.

Soviet capacity to project power and build expensive bases in the Antarctic was less than that possessed by the United States. It could be done, of course, but such a project would stretch Soviet capacity and divert its still small navy and airlift forces from the main threat in Europe posed by the North Atlantic Treaty Organization (NATO). At the same time, although the United States did not discount Soviet power, it recognized that sending U.S. forces to Antarctica would divert resources from Europe and the Pacific, where deterring the Soviet threat was essential.

Realist Response 2: All states with active territorial claims in the Antarctic followed the hegemonic leadership of the United States.

Sovereignty is such a crucial aspect of international relations that the answer to why the treaty was negotiated must also explain why those states with territorial claims were willing to set them aside. The United States wanted to maintain allied unity and prevent the Soviets from exploiting any dissention between the allies, and the allies were also unwilling to have Soviet interference. Therefore, the United States was willing and able to exercise its power and leadership toward those states with claims.

The United States announced that it recognized no claims in the Antarctic and reserved the right to make its own—which continues to be U.S. policy in the 1990s. This approach created a "level" field for the allies; no nation's claim was singled out as better or worse than any other. At the same time, since great powers set the tone for the development and operation of international law, the U.S. stance cast all claims into doubt. Uncertainty and ambiguity now dominated the calculations of Britain, Argentina, and the other states with territorial ambitions. Any attempt by a claimant state to assert strongly its territorial claim might have evoked either a countervailing territorial claim by the United States or U.S. actions designed to show the imperfections of the other nation's territorial claim.

If the United States had asserted its own territorial claim, the legal situation would have become impossibly muddled. Moreover, the allies could easily see that if the United States made a territorial claim, so would the Soviet Union. The conflict this scenario would engender could cost all claimants their existing stakes in the Antarctic or even draw them into a military conflict with the Soviet Union.

If the United States took actions to show that another nation's claim was invalid, the results were not likely to turn out any better for the claimants. The claimant states in the Antarctic might find U.S. personnel acting in a claimed zone as though there were no legal claim; indeed, actions by U.S. personnel in Antarctica prior to the treaty were designed with precisely this attitude. At the very least, such behavior would weaken the international legal claims of the claimant states. At worst, it could lead to direct confrontation between the United States and its allies.

Although the United States strongly preferred not to have any direct conflict with its allies, the outcome would not have been in doubt: U.S. power would prevail. Argentina and Chile, for instance, would not be able to overpower the United States in the area; indeed, not even Britain could hope to win such a contest of wills and capabilities. And, as noted in the previous section, the allies would have little inclination to switch sides to the Soviet-led bloc (for example, Chile and the Soviet Union did not even have diplomatic relations in the 1950s).

Thus, the allies found it acceptable to follow the leadership offered by the United States once it was provided. Since the United States tried to act impartially toward all nations with territorial claims in the region, never actually threatening these states with force but instead engaging in continuous, sensitive diplomacy, it gained a measure of legitimacy. In sum, it exercised hegemonic and not coercive leadership, even taking up and expanding an idea Chilean diplomats had suggested: setting aside claims for a period of time.

Realist Response 3: The strong bipolarity of the international system made it easy to put the treaty in place.

The evidence of U.S. leadership among states with territorial claims underscores the strong bipolarity of the international system at the time. This structure clarified matters for the Soviets and disciplined U.S. options. Essentially, the United States and the Soviet Union had, in addition to conducting an arms race, divided the world into two camps. The United States had its allies, who would generally follow the U.S. lead. So did the Soviets. The bipolarity colored the two superpowers' consideration of the mixed sovereignty questions of the region.

Seven states—Chile, Argentina, Britain, France, Norway, New Zealand, and Australia—had made definite territorial claims to parts of the Antarctic. The claims of Chile, Argentina, and Britain overlapped. Other areas of the continent were claimed by no nation or were in a hazy situation where nations reserved the right to assert territorial claims. Neither the United States nor the Soviet Union had (or have) asserted claims, but both could do so under the legal doctrine of discovery.[4]

From the Soviet perspective, the nations that had long-standing claims in the Antarctic were solid U.S. allies. Even without asserting a direct claim, the United States might well have been able to convince its allies to provide bases to U.S. forces. Certainly, the ring of U.S. bases around the Soviet Union and elsewhere indicated that the Americans viewed this option as an efficacious method of expanding and projecting U.S. power.

Things did not look so sanguine from the American perspective. The overlapping claims, especially between Argentina and Great Britain, could weaken the allies' resolve. Conflict between Argentina and Britain could provoke an unwanted war in the Western Hemisphere, thereby necessitating a choice between the long-standing relationship with Britain and the newer, but still valuable, relationships with members of the Organization of American States (OAS) like Argentina. (This possibility, of course, became reality in 1982 with the Falklands War.)[5]

Two official statements illustrate the concern of U.S. policymakers. The Policy Planning Staff in the State Department circulated a paper in June 1948 that commented:

[That allies had conflicting claims] is a source of embarrassment to the U.S. because of our close relations to Great Britain and our commitments in the Western Hemisphere. This embarrassment is susceptible of exploitation by

the USSR to the further disadvantage of the U.S. Our national interest requires that a settlement of this dispute be reached which will be acceptable
to the three countries involved.[6]

A few years later, a National Security Council memorandum argued
for the following:

Orderly progress toward a solution of the territorial problem of Antarctica,
which would ensure control by the U.S. and friendly parties, ... freedom of
exploration and scientific research for the U.S. and friendly parties ... and
access by the U.S. and friendly parties to natural resources discovered in Antarctica.[7]

Still, the clarity of the division of allies (and the Soviets had no allies
with important Antarctic interests) made it easier for the Soviets to assess the dangers it faced. For reasons discussed in the next section,
there was little likelihood that U.S. allies could be detached and induced to support Soviet claims. Had the division been murkier, the Soviets might have tried to woo, say, the Argentinians to their side. To
avoid being left out in the cold or facing the combined strength of the
United States and all other claimant states, a negotiated outcome was
in order. The United States, rightly or wrongly, placed a high value on
the threat to bloc coherence. Although for different reasons, the
United States thus had reason to negotiate on this count as well.

Clearly, cogent power politics arguments for demilitarizing the Antarctic could be made on all sides. The sovereignty question gave the
United States leverage over its allies, and the combined threat of the
arms race and new assertions of territorial claims pressed the United
States and the USSR into accommodation.

Realist Response 4: The United States structured the problem so that states
were not likely to be penalized for cooperation.

Still another reason realists might offer for the successful completion
of the Antarctic Treaty is that the United States created a context in
which states could risk cooperation. It cut the sovereignty Gordian
knot by an artful device: No state's claims could be asserted, but neither could a state's claims be denied for the duration of the treaty. A
similar idea had been proposed in the 1940s by Chile, which further legitimated the suggestion among states with an interest in the Antarc-

tic. Moreover, the nations had agreed to let scientific exploration occur without concern about territorial claims during the International Geophysical Year (1957–1958).

At the same time, all the parties pledged not to put any nuclear or military forces in the area. Thus, states with claims did not actually have to forego them, and because military forces were banned, their cooperation would not likely prove foolish. The United States and the Soviet Union also benefited from the combination: Both could threaten each other with the prospect of a sovereignty claim if the other failed to live up to its disarmament obligations. No state came out worse off than it had been going into the negotiations, and the Soviet Union and the United States came out better off than they had been prior to the treaty. British diplomat John Heap said of the 1959 treaty that although science was the beneficiary, no one "should ... believe that such altruism was in the minds of the negotiators; it was not. The parties gained little from it but what they all, variously, stood to lose without it made the exercise worthwhile."[8]

One other element of the treaty bolstered the confidence that the obligations undertaken would be observed. Article VII, the inspection provision, said that the parties could freely travel anywhere in the Antarctic and could visit the installations of any nation. Thus, the monitoring problem of the treaty was solved. If the United States, the Soviet Union, Chile, or any other party cheated, everyone else would soon notice.

So it was that this treaty came into force at the height of the Cold War. The security of the United States and the Soviet Union were in potential jeopardy if the arms race were to extend to the Antarctic. Lack of clarity over sovereignty claims provided each nation with a lever of influence over the other and proved a means of disciplining America's claimant allies. These factors were finessed in the treaty through its "setting aside" of claims and disarmament rules.

Question 2: Why was the minerals agreement negotiated?

Realist Response 1: Mineral exploitation could destroy the entire security regime of the ATS.

Detailed negotiations for what would be called the Convention on the Regulation of Antarctic Mineral Resource Activities (CRAMRA) began in Buenos Aires in 1981 at the eleventh consultative meeting. Negotiations continued until 1988, when a treaty was agreed upon by the ATCPs, then numbering twenty, at Wellington, New Zealand. The ATCPs stipulated that for the treaty to go into effect, at least sixteen of the original twenty states would have to ratify it. That number would have to include all the claimant states, the United States and the USSR, and at least three developing countries.[9] None of the nations, however, formally ratified the agreement, and as we shall see in the next section, it seems unlikely that the treaty will ever go into effect. On May 1, 1990, many of the signatory parties decided to forego any exploration (even though the regime permitted it) for fifty years; in summer 1991, all parties agreed to the Antarctic Environmental Protocol, which imposes a fifty-year ban on mining.

New Zealand was the first to raise the issue of a need for a regime for nonliving resources. Its reason for doing so was not that exploitation was about to begin. On the contrary, the logistics and exploration costs, not to mention remoteness from markets, made (and still make) exploitation entirely prohibitive. Instead, New Zealand was concerned about the ATS as a whole. "In the worst case," commented Christopher Beeby, who would chair the discussions, "the result could be a breakdown of the treaty, the loss of the disarmament regime that it contains, and more generally, of the stabilizing effect that it has had on the entire area south of 60 S latitude."[10]

Unlike the case of exploiting living resources, the prospect of using mineral and other nonliving resources could have a direct impact on the entire ATS:

> Mineral resources (with the notable exception of floating icebergs) cannot move through national zones: they are fixed in place. These resources are thus inherently more capable of being exploited by a single national entity if uncontested jurisdiction over them can be established. Hence, the claims issue is more difficult to avoid for fixed mineral resources than it is for the living resources of the Southern Ocean.[11]

Rather than face renewed conflict on the question of sovereignty, the parties sought to solve the problem before it became one. They negotiated under the same formula as the Antarctic Treaty itself: No sovereignty could be gained or lost through the agreement. In effect, the negotiations were made subservient to the major rules of the game that had so successfully reduced international conflict.

The centrality of the ATS itself was underscored by the fact that the parties did not choose some other context in which to negotiate the minerals regime. The consultative parties chose to keep the minerals question directly under the authority of the ATS. This was not the only option available to the players. As will be seen, they could have chosen the approach in the Convention on the Conservation of Antarctic Marine Living Resources (CCAMLR) or used the U.N. Law of the Sea.

The CCAMLR covered animals that came and went into different claimed areas and into areas of the Southern Ocean that were not covered by the ATS at all.[12] Because of the nature of the marine resources, claimant/nonclaimant status was relatively unimportant (although it is instructive that in the CCAMLR negotiations, Chile, the only claimant and fishing state, defended its claim and not its fishing interests). Moreover, because the Southern Ocean is considered the high seas and could be fished by anyone, nations outside the ATS had a legal right to join the negotiations. Some fishing states did. These considerations did not hold in the minerals problem. Minerals stay in one place and could be in a claimant state's territory, thus posing a direct threat to the ATS. As a result, it was easy to exclude non-ATCPs from talks on minerals.

Another potential approach might have been to apply the Law of the Sea (LOS) convention. That document set out boundaries and established a procedure for mining resources not generally thought to be under any one nation's control. This was a most unlikely strategy, however, for the minerals agreement. First, the United States and a number of European allies had just refused to sign the LOS agreement precisely because it gave credence to the idea that areas deemed "the common heritage of mankind" should be controlled internationally and that wealth generated from such areas ought to be shared with poorer nations. Second, even though claimant states might have wanted new international economic rules, they did not want to give up the potential of asserting territorial claims sometime in the future. The Law of the Sea convention was not an option.[13]

Question 3: Why did CRAMRA fail to go into effect?

Realist Response 1: Conflicts over different state interests were likely to surface if CRAMRA went into operation; this outcome might have threatened the ATS security regime.

The evidence for this response lies primarily in the discord generated by the negotiations themselves. As negotiations for CRAMRA went on, disturbing divergent interests among states were revealed. Non-claimant and claimant states wanted to ensure that the balance of power on regulatory committees in CRAMRA did not favor interests opposed to theirs. Nonclaimants said that "regulation would have to be undertaken by the parties to the regime, acting collectively and without distinctions of any kind, through [the regime's] institutions."[14] Claimants, in general, sought a primary regulatory role.

The states opted to use consensus rather than majoritarian voting. Unlike the consensus procedure in CCAMLR, however, consensus in the context of the mining agreement would have been very difficult to achieve. CCAMLR did not have regulatory committees; the proposed mining agreement did have them. Each committee would have representatives from claimant states and from states that wanted to start mining; the United States and the USSR were guaranteed seats. In itself, this arrangement was not a bad idea, since all interested parties had a say. The critical difference between CCAMLR and CRAMRA consensus lay in this: Under CCAMLR, fishing was permitted until forbidden; in CRAMRA, mining was forbidden until permitted.[15] This stipulation would create a delay in mining because consensus to start something is harder to come by than consensus to stop an activity.[16]

In this setting, states concerned about the environment could stop the exploiting states and exploiting states could brake any further development of environmental rules. Such delays would aggravate existing tensions. Those more interested in preserving the continent for scientific or environmental reasons might decide, for example, that the ATS rule of setting aside, yet preserving, territorial claims was unworkable. Similarly, claimant states, desirous of economic gain from their "territory," might decide that the ATS was holding them back.

Question 4: What is the likely future of the Antarctic Treaty System?

Realist Response 1: No change is likely.

The interests of states are well protected by the ATS; therefore, no change is likely in the future. States, like people and organizations, are often creatures of habit.[17] They will persist in maintaining things that work even though there may be leaks and inefficiencies. The ATS pro-

tects important security interests of the different states, and so it is satisfactory. In some respects, one can even view the fifty-year ban on
mining as an example of this conservatism. Rather than solve a problem and engender more points for conflicts, states chose to "let sleep-
ing dogs lie."

This expectation, however, should be checked against the reasoning
used to explain the creation of ATS itself. If the fundamental reasons
for the ATS have changed, then business as usual may not continue.

Important changes have, of course, occurred, especially since 1989.
The end of the Cold War also substantially reduced the prospect of extending the arms race to Antarctica. Thus the United States and Russia
are likely to have far less strategic interest in Antarctic matters than in
the past. Yet, if the United States were to put Antarctica far down on its
strategic, economic, or even environmental agendas, other parties
might press their interests more strongly; thus, the prospects for military confrontation by the claimant states still lurk in the background.
The Cold War may have ended, but U.S. interests in a stable political
environment and in good relations with Britain and the nations of
South America still remain. It thus seems quite doubtful that the
United States will lose interest in the southern polar region. And since
it is the only nation currently capable of sustained military action on a
global scale, it is reasonable to anticipate that the United States can
maintain the Antarctic Treaty System if it prefers to do so.

The uncertainty in the power structure of the international system
surely will influence the political calculations of the claimant states.
The United States could still assert a territorial claim if any of the
claimant states sought to change the agreement significantly. Moreover, there is no other power with which to ally for support against
such U.S. action. Last, other states, already somewhat dissatisfied with
the way the ATCPs manage the Antarctic, might become even more
vocal and active if claimant states did anything to assert sovereignty
over their territorial claims.

This point brings us to the willingness of other states to follow U.S.
hegemonic leadership. In today's international environment, even the
former states of the Soviet Union are willing to take leadership cues
from the United States. It is true that the Southern Cone states of South
America are more powerful than they were in the 1950s, but all of
them face daunting economic conditions (which could militate
against their taking cues from the United States). They remain, however unhappily, dependent in large measure on U.S. markets and capi-

tal. This dependence may reduce the legitimacy of the United States as a leader, but there is a countervailing tendency as well. The United States also serves as a shield against those states outside of the ATS that would somehow internationalize the region. Follow the leader still seems the best course.

In sum, the important changes in the international environment are not so great as to obviate the original reasons for the Antarctic Treaty. The power of the United States still holds. The conditions of unreconcilable differences if national preferences are pressed still remain. States remain better off with the treaty than without it.

The Postinternationalist View

Postinternational theory leads to different kinds of evidence and answers relevant to the questions we just examined from a realist perspective. The turbulence that now engulfs world politics had barely begun when the Antarctic Treaty went into effect. The decision to negotiate this agreement, however, does provide evidence of the early rumblings of turbulent change. The fraying of the agreement over time further illustrates how turbulent world politics has become. To be sure, the state-centric world, with its concerns about sovereignty and security, dominated in the first years, but over time its importance has declined. Instead, the multi-centric world of sovereignty-free actors (SFAs), including the scientific community, has come to share center stage with the sovereignty-bound actors (SBAs). The scientific community recognized early the danger of nuclear war and the need to build cooperative relationships. Thus the pressure for a continent for science, free of security problems and borderless, came not from states but from the sovereignty-free scientific community. In a sense, the scientists who promoted the Antarctic Treaty were precursors to the widening array of competent groups and thoughtful individuals who now are active in the Antarctic and other political arenas.

Question 1: Why was the Antarctic Treaty negotiated and put into effect?

Postinternational Response 1: A research structure designed by the scientific community provided a convenient framework for states to use in resolving disputes.

The idea behind the International Geophysical Year (IGY) of 1957–1958 was to advance understanding of the physical world.[18] Scientific organizations around the world designed projects to investigate a host of geophysical phenomena. On the nongovernmental side in the United States, the prestigious National Academy of Sciences[19] and its operational arm, the National Research Board, organized university work. The National Science Foundation, a government agency, funded many IGY efforts and was the lead government agency for the U.S. contribution to the project. The Soviet Academy of Sciences coordinated Soviet activities, as did national academies of science in other nations. These national activities, as well as the results of the IGY, were further coordinated by the International Council of Scientific Unions (ICSU), a specialized agency of the United Nations.

Given its centrality to atmospheric and ocean phenomena, the Antarctic received much attention during the IGY. Very little was known about the region; hence, for the duration of the IGY, nations interested in the region were allowed to set up scientific stations in the area without worrying about territorial claims. Eventually, more than forty stations were put into operation. They were run by scientists from the aforementioned twelve nations that would ultimately sign the Antarctic Treaty. Since it was very costly to do research in the Antarctic, the scientists created the Scientific Committee on Antarctic Research (SCAR) to coordinate the Antarctic work. SCAR shared information with the Scientific Committee on Oceanic Research (SCOR), which had links to the ICSU.[20]

IGY research emphasized how very little was known about Antarctica and underscored how much could be learned about the Earth from stations located on the continent. Thus, scientists from the twelve nations who had done research in Antarctica during the IGY went home and started pushing the idea of making the Antarctic a "continent for science." The grip of the scientific community on subsequent political choices shows in the role SCAR played in shaping the formal Antarctic Treaty. First, the countries invited to participate in the negotiations were selected from those that had been represented in SCAR during the IGY. Second, when Poland asked for a seat at the negotiating table, SCAR handled the problem. Poland was told it would be welcome once it had undertaken year-round research.[21] That meant it could join, but it also meant that its application came too late to participate in the treaty negotiations. A situation that could have caused a political conflict between the United States and the Soviet Union was resolved fairly and amicably through the scientific community. Indeed, the rule on year-round research as the basis on which consultative status is determined ended up in the treaty and technically remains in effect to this day.

Domestic science agencies also continued to dominate Antarctic discussions. A good example comes from the United States, where, in 1959, as states were discussing the possibility of an Antarctic Treaty, a dispute arose over who should coordinate U.S. Antarctic research. On one hand, the Department of Defense (DOD) thought it should be the lead government agency, arguing that science was "but one of this country's interests in Antarctica." The department's argument was supported by members of the House Armed Services Committee, who claimed that putting the research under the NSF would "emphasize science 'at the expense of the political, economic, and military considerations.'" The suggestion that the DOD should be the lead government agency "produced dismay among a number of civilian scientists" as well as the State Department. In order to counteract this trend, the scientific community worked to ensure NSF's dominance. The National Academy of Sciences formed the University Committee on Polar Research to get more scholars involved in Antarctic research. This committee claimed it was uninterested in politics, but *New York Times* science writer Walter Sullivan thought otherwise, saying, "Its formation is, in effect, an emphasis on the scientific approach" to the management of the continent.[22] In sum, the Antarctic Treaty shows the imprint of IGY activity. SCAR became a permanent mechanism for coordinating scientific research; the national academies of science remain active; in the United States, the NSF won out over the DOD and continues to be the lead U.S. government agency for work on the region; and the stations stayed in place. Last, the treaty contains provisions for linking SCAR to SCOR and ultimately to ICSU.

States had been hung up on how to resolve territorial claims without engendering military conflict. Moreover, they needed low-conflict mechanisms for coordinating Antarctic management problems. The decision by states (caused at least partially by domestic and international scientific pressure) to set aside claims so that research could ensue opened the door to the scientists. Their research coordination devices were appropriate not only for their own work but also for the world of states. One scholar put it this way: "Antarctic science is the key to international credibility both for a nation within the Antarctic Treaty System and for the Antarctic Treaty System within the broader international community of nations."[23]

The postinternational model notes that states often yield jurisdiction to SFAs when "governments are paralyzed by prior commitments and SFAs may be able to break the stalemate and when the initiatives of SFAs do not intrude upon prior commitments and may yield desirable results."[24] Living with the IGY status quo would reduce state paralysis, and using the coordination devices of the scientists hardly intruded on the perquisites of states.

A mirror of the states' interests in the scientific solution shows up in the ways the scientific community benefited from collaboration with the SBAs. Here the postinternational model says that SFAs work with SBAs to defend the worthiness of their activities and values and when they can intrude themselves into a situation where their values and competence can affect the course of events.[25] What could better secure the worthiness of the scientific project than a state commitment to their organizations and values? Without a doubt, the most relevant use of Antarctica at the time was for research; thus, the scientists could readily "intrude" themselves into SBA activities without generating SBA resistance.

Postinternational Response 2: The normative (value) priorities of the scientific community helped states escape the dictates of sovereignty.

Organization was not the only factor that accorded a prominent role to science. The global scientific community valued free communication and unfettered research. In its own affairs, consensus decision-making was the norm. Many scientists believed they had a special, positive role to play in reducing the dangers of nuclear war in the midst of Cold War distrust and had started to seek ways to reduce the threat. The community was able to bring these values to bear in the governance of Antarctica.

Many of the same scientists who had applied their talents to the war effort during World War II were now trying to find avenues to arms control and disarmament. Demilitarizing the Antarctic and banning nuclear weapons from the continent fit in nicely with this normative priority in the scientific community.

Two efforts illustrate the value the community put on preventing nuclear war: Pugwash conferences and the *Bulletin of Atomic Scientists*. In 1957, the first of the International Conferences on Science and

World Affairs brought scientists from the United States, the Soviet Union, and other nations to Pugwash, Nova Scotia. The meetings, now called the Pugwash conferences, continue to this day. The idea came from an appeal by Bertrand Russell and Albert Einstein in 1955 to discuss, as objectively as possible, problems science might address. The initial conferences paved "the way for serious negotiation on controlling nuclear armaments, ending the cold war, solving the Vietnam question, and on opening talks on European Security and Cooperation."[26] Each participating nation has a national Pugwash committee that tries to influence its government and international organizations. The *Bulletin of Atomic Scientists* (created before Pugwash), which flowed from the post–World War II "scientists' movement," focused on the danger of atomic (nuclear) warfare.[27]

The scientific community had yet another concern. It viewed the emphasis on secrecy as one of the most disconcerting aspects of the Cold War. Science advances by building on the efforts of others; if important results of work are muzzled in the name of national security, the scientific enterprise itself can be jeopardized. If knowledge gleaned from Antarctic research were classified, many fields of basic science would be hampered. Thus, it was clearly in the interests of the community to advocate freedom of information.

This value accounts for the freedom-of-movement and exchange-of-information clauses found in the treaty. Members of the scientific community were able to locate their interests in the stream of world events and press for outcomes consonant with those interests and values. That the values could also be cast in terms comprehensible to states was all to the good. Both multi-centric and state-centric actors could advance their values and interests.

The character of scientific decisionmaking also lent itself to the political needs of states. As we have seen, typically scientists use committee structures to achieve consensus. They consider the available data, assess the unknowns, reach conclusions about the evidence, and make decisions about what to do next. When everyone agrees on the next step, the decision is "made." Consensus decisionmaking is also used by states—but for rather different reasons. Consensus insures a state against decisions that would impair its interests. Any state can stop a decision, or force important changes, by simply not agreeing. This approach allows every state to retain its cloak of sovereignty; it can also slow decisions down dramatically and thus perpetuate the status quo.

Until recently, most decisions about Antarctica were so scientifically based that the science version of consensus dominated; that is, decisions were generally quiet and only nominally contentious. Only as issues have become more politicized owing to the minerals agreement has the disjuncture between the two meanings of consensus grown.

The result of this confluence of multi-centric and state-centric interests was a novel form of governance: Sovereignty exists only at the periphery, held in abeyance, so to speak. Freedom to speak and travel freely, and freedom from the fear of war and nuclearization, exist at levels not experienced anywhere else on the globe. The scientists rule Antarctica, although states may believe they retain ultimate control over the rulers. Over time, however, this unusual form of "separation of powers" between scientific rule in an international politico-legal context would yield unanticipated, complex political problems for actors in both the state-centric and multi-centric worlds.

Question 2: Why was the minerals agreement negotiated?

Postinternational Response 1: Activities by the scientists (SFAs) put minerals on the agendas of states (SBAs).

The need for CRAMRA would not have arisen at all had it not been for the efforts of scientists. Years of coordinated scientific research produced excellent evidence of mineral wealth on the continent itself and in offshore areas. The character of this information, however, created considerable uncertainty about the economic value of the resources. Thus, scientists "caused" the problem for states by producing highly uncertain information about the actual scale and scope of minerals.

The presence of minerals had been mere speculation at the outset of the treaty. The speculation gained a measure of reality as fossil evidence built up indicating that the climate of Antarctica had once been quite warm. Scientists were interested in how this effect had come about. Had the Earth possessed a much warmer climate all over the globe? Or, as the theory of plate tectonics claimed, had the Antarctic once been located somewhere else?

The answer came in December 1967 when a New Zealand geologist, Peter J. Barrett, found a fragment of what would be identified as a Labyrinthodont in the Trans Antarctic Mountains. The Labyrinthodont fossil looked virtually the same as similar ones found in Africa and Australia; it was unlikely that the Labyrinthodonts "arose independently here and there. It is much more likely that they arose in one center and then spread out."[28] That likelihood would argue for the plate tectonic theory—Antarctica had once been elsewhere. This possibility was further enhanced by another characteristic of the fossil animal: It only lived in freshwater areas. It could not have swum over an ocean of saltwater to reach Antarctica.

With this information and field samples, geologists could reasonably claim that the Antarctic had once been connected to the landmasses that now form Africa, Australia, Madagascar, and South America. If these regions contained minerals, then surely the Antarctic did too. Since the fossil evidence showed a lush, tropical, wet climate, the chances were good that oil and natural gas reserves lay offshore and perhaps also buried under the ice.

Thus, it was the everyday operation of science in Antarctica that raised the prospect of mining. But the information science had provided was not the kind that would normally be collected prior to making a mining decision. According to one author, Bernard P. Herber, "Science has generally given the sort of information that formal prospecting would have provided, but not the more detailed and definitive information which could be provided by formal minerals exploration inclusive of drilling, blasting, and similar procedures."[29]

In the realist discussion of why CRAMRA was negotiated, we set out a subquestion that asked why the ATS was the umbrella for the minerals negotiations. Other options—a new international conference; linkage to other treaties; a stand-alone treaty (like CCAMLR) between interested parties—were available. Postinternational theory suggests a rather different line of reasoning for answering the question, although, as the realist interpretation argued, preservation of the status quo was clearly a value. The difference arose from the nature of the status quo.

Postinternational Response 2: The 'delegation of rule' to the scientific community would be threatened if negotiations occurred outside the ATS.

Gathering information suitable for actual mining decisions would have subverted the rule of "science" in Antarctica by generating information that required different legal rules. According to Herber:

An important difference exists ... between mineral deposit information obtained from scientists and that which would have been obtained via formal commercial prospecting and exploration in that the latter information bestows proprietary rights of ownership while the former does not. In fact, such proprietary rights would be technically impossible to establish under the "free exchange of knowledge" requirement of the Antarctic Treaty.[30]

Antarctic scientists feared that their work would be hampered by efforts to assess the economic viability of Antarctic nonliving resources. Two matters concerned them. First, the limited funding for basic science in the area could be diverted to applied research into prospecting and mining engineering under extreme conditions. Second, even limited commercial efforts—never mind actual exploitation—would endanger the environment, disrupt many field efforts, and indeed, remove the special reasons for setting the continent aside for science. By placing the issue inside the ATS regime, scientists could control much of the information through SCAR and their special relationships at home with the official policy establishment.

Had there been a genuine interest in mining, the CRAMRA would not have looked the way it did. It would have been easier to get permission to mine, just as it is relatively easy to fish under the Convention on the Conservation of Antarctic Marine Living Resources. For instance, the special regulatory committees that would have been set up for "certain aspects of the regulation of mining" would have been avoided, as they are in the CCAMLR.[31] But by emphasizing the environmental aspects over the economic ones, science could retain its leading role as steward of the continent.

The scientists succeeded in keeping the mining issue well within their sphere of "governance." As in the past, the scientific community benefited from the impasse over sovereignty in the world of states. Any change that would facilitate mining would pose security and sovereignty challenges to the states. The CRAMRA would have imposed minimal changes on this status quo. As we shall see, however, the very fact of the negotiations almost radically altered the governance of the region.

Question 3: Why did CRAMRA fail to go into effect?

Postinternational Response 1: The ability of the ATCPs to enact the agreement had been weakened by authority crises among states and within ATCP states.

Authority crises permeate world politics. Whether expressed at local levels or played out in the United Nations, states can no longer assume their decisions will be followed. This point can readily be seen in two ways through the Antarctica case. First, Third World states pressured for more openness in decisionmaking and even for placing Antarctic activities under direct U.N. auspices. Second, as part of their efforts to stop the exploitation of Antarctica, environmental groups employed two strategies. They allied themselves with states in the General Assembly, and they agitated for changes in policy within the territorial boundaries of the ATCPs. U.N. pressure and environmental group activism combined to reshape what was possible for the states that were to be party to CRAMRA. What looked like a "done deal" in 1988 had unraveled by 1991.

That there had been a change in the ability of the ATCPs to control Antarctic matters can be seen by the initial failures of the U.N. to put the region on the agenda. The General Assembly attempted on a number of occasions to schedule a discussion of the governance of Antarctica.[32] During the International Geophysical Year, India asked that Antarctica be discussed in the General Assembly; the issue was withdrawn, however, after Chile and Argentina vehemently opposed it. In 1958 the proposal was made again, but by then the treaty negotiations were well on their way, so the proposal failed. In 1974 the Food and Agriculture Organization considered Antarctic questions regularly, and it ultimately came to play a role in the CCAMLR (in monitoring krill). In 1976 the first major speech about the region was made in the General Assembly.[33] Soon after the ATCPs began serious negotiations on minerals in 1981, activity in the U.N. on Antarctica increased. But it was not until 1983 that the General Assembly made Antarctica a regular item of discussion. The questions the General Assembly debated fell into two primary areas: the "property status" of the region and its development, and second, the perceived elitism of the ATS.

A number of developing states in the U.N. General Assembly wanted to designate the Antarctic as the "common heritage of mankind."[34] This term, first used by Arvid Pardo of Malta in connection with the Law of the Sea, refers to those areas of the world—the high seas and outer space, for example—that are not or should not be considered the property of any single state but rather belong to all of mankind. This formulation had been strongly resisted (and continues to be resisted) by the consultative parties. Antarctica, they claim, is not *res nullius* (the property of nobody), and the U.N. cannot just ignore the past. More important, the common heritage principle implies development. "Since this purpose," argued Australian diplomats, "has never been dominant in Antarctica, where the environment is extremely vulnerable to the activities of man, ... it would not be appropriate to apply the concept to Antarctica."[35]

The problem of elitism seems mostly to have been a misunderstanding. Early in the 1983–1984 General Assembly debates, non-ATS states thought the voting was too secret and the full voting membership rule too elitist. U.N. critics called for open meetings and access to the treaty, whereas ATS members pointed out that all decisions from consultative party meetings were made public; surely there was no need to have open meetings, since this was not common practice in negotiation. They also noted that any state could accede to the treaty (as a number of states had done); the rule on voting reflected the fact that ATCPs bore the costs of Antarctic work and were the ones directly affected by problems in management.

Other SFAs, notably environmental organizations, used the General Assembly discussions as an entry into Antarctic affairs. Greenpeace provided information to the United Nations, as did other groups. To make use of the elitism attack, Greenpeace wintered over in Antarctica and conducted its own research, then demanded the right to participate in Antarctic decisionmaking; the ATCPs, however, rejected the proposal.[36]

The efforts of the General Assembly did have an effect, however. The ATCPs opened up their proceedings a bit in order to counter charges of elitism on the part of developing states, and acceding countries were invited to observe much of the CRAMRA's work and make comments about the proceedings. Continued U.N. pressure may also have prompted the ATCPs to admit a number of major Third World countries, notably China and India, to full voting status. Now 80 percent of the world's population is "represented" in Antarctic decisionmaking. The ATCPs have also begun to invite some nongovernmental organizations to observe meetings or to serve on individual delegations of the ATCPs.[37]

The effects of these responses to U.N. pressures proved to be double-edged. On the one hand, the wind was knocked out of the sails of those who said the governance of Antarctica was largely a rich-country affair enhanced by secret proceedings. Once India and China were made voting members, they acted like typical ATCPs. Neither of those states has advocated U.N. control of Antarctica.

On the other hand, the greater availability of information about decisions and problems increased demands for good performance by these self-appointed stewards of Antarctica. Quite simply, everyone knew more about the decisions of the consultative parties, so critics could focus on continuing problems even more effectively. One can already detect a shift in emphasis: The critics are focusing less on the role of states and more on the governance provided by scientists.

Even as these efforts went on, the internal capacity of states to control outcomes was thwarted by environmental activism within their borders and on Antarctica itself. Sheer bad luck may also have hurt the states while helping the environmentalists. For example, an oil spill caused by an Argentine Navy ship off the coast of Antarctica in January 1989 had horrendous ecological results for animal populations—even worse, said some, than oil spills elsewhere.[38]

In December 1988, Greenpeace sent a ship to the Antarctic to protest the construction of a runway at the French Antarctic base, Dumont d'Urville. The runway would have split a penguin rookery in two and forced part of the rookery to cross the runway to get to the ocean.[39] Greenpeace, therefore, claimed the construction was interfering with the habitats of animals, a violation of the Antarctic Treaty. A fight between the construction workers and Greenpeace crew members ensued, and construction stopped. This small incident shows how different the power of SFAs is from that of states. Had a state's warship interfered in such a way, there would have been a major diplomatic crisis, recriminations, perhaps even war. But SFAs do not threaten sovereignty in the same way that states can—even though in this case, the action, as we shall see, certainly stopped states dead in their tracks.

While the "action" at the French base was taking place, Greenpeace was also protesting to the Australian government that the provision of port facilities to the French in Hobart, Tasmania, constituted complicity with France's illegal acts. Accompanying the protest in the Antarctic was an effort to persuade Australia not to agree to CRAMRA.

Greenpeace was not the only active environmental force. Jacques Cousteau lobbied the French government. According to the *New York Times*, he "persuaded the French Government to back out of the agreement," and his efforts were rewarded when, in September 1989, the prime ministers of France and Australia made a joint announcement stating that any mining in Antarctica was unacceptable. Said the August 18 communiqué, "Mining in Antarctica is not compatible with protection for the fragile Antarctic environment."[40] Having succeeded with France and Australia, Cousteau then turned his efforts to other countries.

The withdrawal of France and Australia, two of the key signers of CRAMRA, meant that the whole agreement was now in doubt. The two countries had proposed a long moratorium on any mining. As a result, the floodgates of activism were opened in states not yet convinced that CRAMRA was a bad agreement. This result can clearly be seen in what happened next in the United States, where the process of coalition building became unstable.

U.S. Antarctic policy emerges from consultations within and among government agencies and nongovernmental groups. The Antarctic Policy Group (APG) represents intragovernmental bargaining, while the nongovernmental organizations express their views through the Antarctic Public Advisory Committee (APAC). One description of how the United States reached its negotiating stand for CRAMRA reported, "The negotiating position of the U.S. on Antarctic mineral issues was derived from a set of instructions drawn up by an interagency task force, the Antarctic Policy Group (APG)."[41] The process began with intra–Department of State bargaining between the Bureau of Ocean and International Environmental and Scientific Affairs and the Economic Bureau. That draft document went to the APG proper, which has representatives from the "Departments of State, Interior (especially the U.S. Geological Survey), Energy, Defense and Commerce (the National Oceanic and Atmospheric Administration), as well as the Marine Mammals Commission, the Environmental Protection Agency, the National Science Foundation, and the Arms Control and Disarmament Agency."[42] The APG was then advised by nongovernmental entities via the Antarctic Public Advisory Committee, "a group drawn from public international organization, industry, and academic community. The APAC meets two or three times each year with the APG and various congressional staff to discuss Antarctic issues and U.S. policies. ... The Antarctic mineral delegation consisted of a public interest representative from the International Institute for Environment and Development, an industry representative from the American Petroleum

Institute, and a private technical advisor from the academic community, as well as APG members."[43]

Very probably, the separate elements in this melange of interests had
failed to reach genuine consensus on the U.S. position. When the
French and the Australians withdrew their support for CRAMRA,
American environmental groups opposed to the minerals agreement
stepped up their actions, making an end run around the Antarctic advisory process to reach the U.S. Congress. These groups, especially
Greenpeace, the Antarctic and Southern Oceans Coalition, and the National Wildlife Federation, wanted no mining in the region. Their preferred option was to create a world park and to emphasize environmental protection.[44] Greenpeace wanted the U.N. to take over the
management of Antarctica. These preferences made their way into
Congress. Some proposed bills would have had the Secretary of the Interior prepare plans for a world park; others asked for amendment of
the Antarctic Conservation Act of 1978 that would have required environmental impact statements for any U.S. activity. In the end, on October 26, 1990, the House and Senate agreed on wording for HR 3977.
This bill prohibited "U.S. citizens from engaging in mineral resource
activities in Antarctica" and called "on the Secretary of State to negotiate a new agreement banning mineral development."[45]

Following the congressional action, the State Department notified
other Antarctic parties that the United States, too, would have to discuss CRAMRA again. In Madrid in 1991, the United States eventually
agreed to a fifty-year moratorium on mining activities.[46] The moratorium succeeded in delaying the park (although de facto it created one),
while addressing the interest group and legislative pressures at home.

The end runs around the Antarctic negotiators that produced the
ban did satisfy the environmental activists. As one report put it, "Environmental groups were delighted with the results of the Madrid meeting. Greenpeace, speaking in quite moderate tones, said the compromise has been hard for the states to make, but was a good one. The
World Wildlife Fund 'said ... that if the draft protocol was endorsed by
the Antarctic Treaty nations it would be a major step toward setting up
a world park in Antarctica.'"[47]

The United States at first refused to approve the moratorium proposal. But in early July 1991, the Bush administration reversed its earlier position and agreed to sign provided that a three-fourths agree-

ment of states would replace unanimity as the prerequisite for allowing mining to start. That stipulation was approved, and in October 1991 the moratorium went into effect. What prompted the Bush reversal? Some claimed that it was pressure from Congress, environmentalists, and foreign governments: Both realms of world politics squeezed the president's administration, and he gave in.[48]

The difficulty the consultative parties had in controlling outcomes was thus closely associated with changes in legitimacy afforded them to manage the Antarctic. Gillian Triggs put it this way: "The law-making agenda changes, it seems, not because of carefully articulated government policy and interstate consensus, but because of public opinion which has formed and developed at a transnational level, irrespective of perceived national priorities and interests."[49] This fundamental change, one stemming from alterations in the basic parameters of world politics, may play out in surprising ways in the future.

Question 4: What is the likely future of the Antarctic Treaty System?

Postinternational Response 1: The centralizing tendencies in global politics will lead to the subordination of Antarctic governance to multi-centric actors and more encompassing environmental rules.

Although decentralizing authority crises have shaped current debates over the future of Antarctica, two factors augur for centralization. First, environmental issues encompass large, integrated systems. Or, more correctly, environmental issues form a network of overlapping systems that tend toward the creation of a single system. Second, the existing structures of worldwide scientific communication are likely to grow stronger and denser as environmental research progresses. This could mean that the management of such communications will have to dovetail with global environmental agreements.

Antarctica, already the beneficiary of scientific organization and values, is likely to be folded in with other scientific structures because of its critical role in governing the global climate. It would be unwise to engage in any activity that might alter Antarctica's climate because of the possible cascading effects it might have on the larger climate. Preserving Antarctica would also ensure that scientists had access to excellent bio- and eco-indicators of changes in pollution and their effects.

Agreements on recent atmospheric problems (ozone depletion agreements are the most notable, but global warming agreements look probable as well) often curtail industrial activities even as they increase the role of scientific research, monitoring, and assessment. Thus, it is unlikely that Antarctica will be opened to minerals development or even offshore drilling. Stricter rules on scientific activities and tourism will likely emerge (and, indeed, at the same time the parties announced the official moratorium, they also set out stricter rules on uses). If this future unfolds, it probably means that the World Park idea will not quite take hold—at least in the sense that visitors to Yosemite or Banff might imagine. Parks often get overused and overdeveloped to the detriment of their ecosystems. Antarctica's ecosystem is so fragile that very little visiting could be permitted beyond strictly controlled scientific stays.

Whether the current formal treaty system of voting continues or the U.N. takes over depends on the outcome of a future conflict between economic development and environmental issues.[50] The idea that some areas may be a common heritage of mankind, the reader may recall, has a development basis. Developing countries do not want the industrialized world to gain all the product and profits from using areas previously inaccessible and unowned, such as the seabed floor. In the U.N. Law of the Sea negotiations, arrangements were made to share any wealth from seabed minerals development. (The United States refused to ratify the convention until 1994, when changes were made in these provisions.) One way of criticizing this seabed arrangement is that it pays too little attention to the environment. Preserving the environment is not at all like redistributing the wealth.[51]

In an effort to preserve the Antarctic status quo, consultative states might simply continue to argue that the General Assembly of the U.N. could not possibly be a steward for the environment, since its interest would largely be in developing the area. Similar arguments might be used to delay almost any U.N. initiative to manage a global resource. The cost of such a tactic, however, would be more and more use of the values and structures of the scientific community.[52] Under that scenario, we might find increased centralization of environmental issues in the multi-centric half of the world political system. States would, in effect, extend the rule that science governs from Antarctica to other areas.

How would this scenario come about? Developing states that attempted to use the General Assembly to redress global inequities could find themselves without plausible allies. They would probably be deserted by their erstwhile environmental allies: When the moratorium was announced, the environmentalists applauded and dropped the U.N. management rhetoric. Environmentalists work in developing countries where they sometimes undermine existing internal power relations (a pattern that is not necessarily bad, since the links among sustainable development, human rights, and the environment may foster a rise in standards of living). Among states, environmentalism—until recently an industrial, middle-class phenomenon—ends up providing issues on which industrial states can maintain their power advantages over developing countries. Thus, rather like the Bush administration at the time of the moratorium, these states may find that environmental arguments are hard to resist at home or abroad and that such arguments are likely to win out against development ones. The best option for a developing country is to support management by scientists, because that route would facilitate participation by their own scientific communities.

Very likely, Antarctica will come increasingly under the sway of actors in the multi-centric world. Even though these actors are not hierarchically ordered and possess vast differences in goals and interests, this direction of change suggests more centralized management of Antarctica. The reasons for the centralization lie in two areas: First, as we have noted, the character of the issue warrants increasing integration. Second, the specific history of Antarctica as a continent for science argues for centralization. The scientific community, though hardly of one cloth, is quite well interconnected and informationally hierarchical. That is, reports flow up and down from local researchers to the larger community and, in the case of Antarctic research, from the individual to SCAR and from there throughout the relevant U.N. agencies and national scientific organizations.

Performance criteria, which in a postinternational world are used to give and withdraw legitimacy to those who would govern, fit nicely with science. Research is (for the most part, but not always) peer evaluated; it is open to others. One must be careful here. Scientific advice on difficult sociopolitical questions can degenerate into the "hired gun" phenomenon, where my expert takes on the views of your expert and everyone ends up more confused than when they started. But so far, SCAR has succeeded in directing the scientific work in Antarctica.

SCAR and the consultative parties acting in their political roles did almost drop the legitimacy ball over CRAMRA. But they seem to have learned that a "no regrets" policy of environmental preservation is the safest course. By shielding the continent through careful and environmentally sound research rules, and by linking the region with larger agreements, the scientific community may gain even more control over the area than it now has.

Conclusion

In this chapter we sought to show how a reasonable interpretation of the Antarctic Treaty, its history, and its future is readily provided by both realism and postinternationalism. The question of which of the two interpretations is the more sound and incisive can only be answered by the reader. The reader could decide that the relative simplicity (parsimony) of the realist view is preferable to the more complex and "thick" view offered by postinternationalism. Or, the reader may decide that, at least for this case, the complexity of the postinternational perspective offers the analyst a stronger grip over relevant variables.

6
The United Nations

Most case studies describe processes wherein actors conflict as they seek contrary goals in an evolving situation. As such, they are narratives of how problems arise, persist, or get resolved with the passage of time. In this case, however, the focus is on an institution, the United Nations, and how it is adjusting to a wide range of challenges. Our concern is less with a single issue moving through time and more with the dynamics whereby numerous overlapping and simultaneous issues are addressed by a multipurpose organization at roughly a single point in time. Stated differently, we are interested in multiple narratives and how they interact to shape the authority, stability, resources, and structures of a vital instrument for the maintenance of international order.

Although postinternationalism presumes that the onset of turbulence in global affairs began well before the end of the Cold War in 1989, it also recognizes that this significant turn in world affairs served to bring to the fore the question of what roles the U.N. can and should play in the course of events. The U.N.'s peacekeeping activities had been hidden deeply within the shadows of superpower rivalry during the prior four decades; the collapse of the rivalry, along with the appearance of clear-cut indications that the world had become too complex for any country to predominate as a superpower, meant that the U.N. could no longer be viewed as a peripheral institution. A vacuum had been created. The demise of the Soviet empire and the surge of domestic preoccupations in the United States meant that the long-established mechanisms for preventing or coping with conflicts around the world were no longer available. And there were many trouble spots. Iraq invaded and conquered Kuwait. Ethnic groups in the former Yugoslavia resorted to civil war. Somalia was struck by famine and intense tribal warfare. A democratic election was overturned by a military coup in Haiti. Cambodia's warring factions quarreled over the format for a nationwide election. And so it went all around the globe as the world groped for a new order to replace the Cold War system to which it had become so accustomed. Under these circumstances the U.N. loomed as an institution suitable for generating the cooperation necessary to address many of the crises that were erupting within and between countries. Perhaps more accurately, in the absence of any alternatives, the world turned to the U.N. for remedial actions. By the mid-1990s this trend seemed likely to result in a condition of system overload whereby the U.N. would be committed to remedying more conflict situations than it could manage or finance.

Given the U.N.'s expanded involvement in a multiplicity of conflicts, it is hardly surprising that the organization has become the focus of considerable controversy among governments, within bureaucracies, between political parties, in newspaper columns, and in the U.N. itself. And as each situation involving the U.N. develops, so do affirmations of its importance or criticisms of its role intensify. As will be seen, these varied reactions to the U.N.'s performances are partly dependent on whether a situation appears to be improving or worsening, but they are even more profoundly a consequence of whether the critic is looking at the situation from a realist or a postinternationalist paradigm. Perhaps never before, in fact, have the distinctions between the two paradigms been more evident in the course of events. The differences can readily be discerned in conceptions of the U.N.'s history and development, in reactions to the question of an appropriate role for the U.N. in the many civil wars that have evolved since the end of the Cold War, in the policies pursued by the new secretary general of the U.N., in the issue of whether U.S. troops should serve under foreign commanders in U.N. peacekeeping operations, in the emergent global concern with protecting and extending human rights, in the monitoring of domestic elections, and in the difficult problem of providing adequate financing for all the U.N.'s new assignments—to mention only the more prominent of the controversies that have surrounded the organization since 1990.

History and Development

Viewed from a realist perspective, the sudden burst of U.N. activity in recent years reflects the undoing of bipolarity in the international system. The civil wars in which the U.N. now tries to interject its peacekeepers were there before 1989. Indeed, they were enhanced and prolonged by the U.S.-Soviet rivalry for spheres of influence. Once the Soviets decided not to compete, either the problems were soon corrected (as was the case in Namibia) or they flared out of control (as in Somalia and Bosnia). Thus it follows, the realists would stress, that it is only because the present period is one in which the polarity of the system remains in doubt that the U.N. gives the illusion of playing its own game. But further reflection suggests a different line of reasoning. Realists contend that underlying the illusion is a developmental process wherein parts of the international system are becoming multipolar, thus allowing for the assertion of regional leadership, while other parts are tending toward unipolarity, thus enabling the United States to operate as first among equals in the security realm. The European Union's (EU's) effort to take the lead in bringing peace to the former Yugoslavia is offered as one case of regional leadership, and the continuing amenability of the Cambodian situation to Chinese policies is cited as another. For realists, the fact that the EU did not on its own succeed in bringing peace to Bosnia provides confirmation of the fact that multipolar arrangements were at work, especially since the EU's efforts suffered from disputes among its members and not from any inherent inability to resolve the situation. The continuing centrality of the role of states in the international system's developing structure is further validated by the method by which at least a tentative measure of peace came to Bosnia: The bombing of the central market in Sarajevo brought an end to the disputes among the EU's members and, reinforced by coordinated threats by the United States and NATO to bomb Serbian guns surrounding the city, led to the withdrawal of the weaponry around that beleaguered city.

Realists might also argue that the same situation highlights the unipolarity inherent in the relative power position held by the United States: The uncertainty that marks many of the more severe conflict situations around the world can be traced to U.S. confusion over what to do and what to fight for as it reviews its core interests, but chances for a peaceful resolution of the Bosnian situation were increased considerably once the United States decided to join the threats of military action. Put more succinctly, recent disputes on the role of the U.N.—on how and where it should operate—have been led by U.S. concerns. Given the relative strength of the United States, the sensitivity of the U.N. to U.S. preoccupations will continue well into the future.

Irrespective of the degree to which the system is evolving in unipolar directions, realists would reason that the United States is unlikely to lose interest in the U.N.—for the latter helps the former play its role as hegemon. That was the case in the early years of the U.N. and it remains the case today. Hegemons would not last long if they had to apply raw power at every turn. It is far better that they find ways of legitimating their power so that others will accept it more readily. The costs of the limited constraints placed on U.S. action due to membership in the U.N. are minor compared to the gains. U.N. procedures facilitate discussion, reduce the costs of information about what matters to other states, and provide a mechanism for military leadership that does not force other states to choose the United States as their leader. In short, as it has from the outset, the U.N. must still proceed cautiously when U.S. interests and concerns are at stake.

Indeed, the realist historical perspective concludes, the U.N.'s original structure, especially its grant of the veto to the great powers, continues to underlie the organization's viability. The fact that the veto has not been used lately is a measure not of the U.N.'s transformation but of changes in the world that have dissuaded the five permanent members of the Security Council from resorting to the veto. After all, it was the availability of the veto that encouraged the major powers to join the U.N. in the first place. And there is every reason to believe that the United States and all the other permanent members of the Security Council would not hesitate to use their veto power again if they deemed circumstances to warrant its exercise.

Postinternationalists have a very different perspective on the origins and development of the U.N. since 1945. As they see it, the U.N. has undergone a transformation that corresponds to the changes occurring in the world. For them the evolution of the U.N. and its present conditions bordering on system overload are part of a long-term process of international institutionalization. This process includes the evolution of norms favoring multilateralism, the development of the habit of cooperation, the building of new formal governmental organizations and the expansion of old ones, and the increasing legitimization of nongovernmental organizations as role players within these organizations and institutions—all of which have added to the pace of change that marks U.N. structures and processes.[1] Admittedly, say the postinternationalists, the original purpose of the U.N. was to provide a league of states that would protect states' interests and make up for their deficiencies. But today, sometimes subtly and sometimes quite obviously, the purpose has shifted in the direction of using international institutions to deal not only with the burgeoning transnational and global problems that cannot be managed through cooperation among states alone but also with the problems faced by peoples, by individuals whose needs and wants far exceed what they have. Postinternationalists are quick to note that the U.N.'s Charter opens by referring to "We the peoples," a conception that anticipated well the transformation of the micro parameter posited by the turbulence model. And the transformation of this and the other two parameters, a postinternationalist might conclude, is precisely why the veto has not recently been exercised in the Security Council: The evolution of global norms relevant to international cooperation and the pressure of publics for their maintenance has made it increasingly difficult for any of the permanent members to take on the opprobrium that would result from negating the council's will.

As will be seen, the notion of institutionalization at the international level is a key to grasping the role of the U.N. in today's world. The theme is foremost in the postinternationalist interpretation of the U.N.'s new peacekeeping roles and the evolution of the secretary general's position. The continuation of this institutionalization process also affirms the notion that the roots of turbulence did not begin with the end of the Cold War.

State Sovereignty and U.N. Autonomy

At the core of the controversies over the U.N.'s expanding roles is the question of whether it remains the servant of the states that created it in 1945 or, instead, is becoming an autonomous actor with its own authority. Although realists acknowledge that the U.N. has become more central to the course of events than it was in the past, they contend that its expanded activities have been undertaken in response to Articles 7 and 99 of the U.N. Charter and to the wishes of its members as these have been expressed in resolutions adopted by the General Assembly or the Security Council and subsequently implemented by the secretary general or any of the numerous agencies that make up the U.N. system.[2] Accordingly, they argue, states have the capacity in any situation to curb or end the activities of U.N. officials deemed to have exceeded the authority granted them by the Security Council. Postinternationalists, in contrast, discern in many of the very same actions a measure of independent autonomy. They view the situations in which the U.N. becomes involved as so complex and urgent that the U.N. officials on the scene must perforce make quick decisions and initiate actions that cannot possibly be monitored by, or referred back to, the Security Council. In turn, such actions are seen as becoming precedents for future responses to a variety of situations. Consequently, it is contended, U.N. officials have a wide leeway that, for all practical purposes, is essentially free of supervision and thus amounts to an independent, autonomous authority.

In other words, whereas realists view U.N. officials and agencies as servants and instruments of states, postinternationalists see them as independent actors. Put more elaborately, whereas the realists interpret U.N. actions as occurring at the convenience of states and thus always being subject to reversal or cessation by a vote of (or veto in) the Security Council, postinternationalists argue that in subtle but substantial ways the convenience-of-states mentality has given way to a states-are-obliged-to-go-along attitude. They claim the latter attitude is so pervasive as to result in states not reversing or bringing to a halt U.N. actions even though they continue to retain the formal right to do so.

Whichever of these perspectives one might find most compelling, clearly the question of where authority is located with respect to the U.N. is not a simple either-or matter. States may regard their sovereignty as indivisible, as a set of rights they either have or do not have, but it does not require much reflection to realize that sovereignty is a variable, that a state's authority may vary from one issue area to another, and that states may pay lip service to their sovereignty even as they accept unilateral actions by the U.N., nongovernmental organizations, multinational corporations, or other actors central to the course of events. Realists may stress that such unilateral actions are always conditional upon the continual acceptance of states, but at the same time they appear to recognize that changing circumstances make it extremely unlikely that any state will, on its own, defy the will of the international community and insist that, say, the U.N.'s unilateral actions be ended. Such a state might contend that the U.N. has exceeded the authority granted it by the Security Council, or it might seek the support of other states in calling for a reconvening of the council, but the norms of international governance no longer encourage it to stand on ceremony, to justify rejection of the U.N.'s action on the grounds that the sovereignty of states is inviolable.

In focusing on the legal rights of states to exercise their sovereignty, realists are led to stress the difficulties and failures the U.N. has experienced in taking on a host of new obligations. As they see it, multilateral efforts can, at best, enjoy limited success because the U.N. lacks the power, the resources, and the decisiveness to cope with conflicts in which the adversaries pit their military forces against each other. Why? Because U.N. officials derive their authority from agreements reached by states and, since states are ever mindful of their own interests, such agreements are bound to reflect the contradictory perspectives of the states that sign them. That is, they are bound to be watered down by the reluctance of states to set precedents that might undermine their own sovereignty, by states' unwillingness to commit their own citizens to battle, and by their need to cope with the constraints of their domestic economies. Despite their inclination to emphasize the continuing viability of state sovereignty, however, realists seem ready to acknowledge that the structures of global affairs have undergone considerable change and that the concept of sovereignty is thus in flux. Put differently, they still view international relations as unfolding at the convenience of states, but they acknowledge the existence of a number of new situations in which states appear to feel obliged to go along with certain kinds of U.N. actions, especially in those situations where humanitarian intervention in the domestic affairs of tension-ridden states seems warranted.

If realists are preoccupied with the unchanging dimensions of sovereignty, their postinternational counterparts are inclined toward the opposite extreme of the continuum and the notion that sovereignty has changed to the point where its relevance is questionable. They see the readiness of the Security Council to intrude the U.N. into the domestic affairs of member states as a fundamental normative transformation signifying a continuing erosion of the sovereignty principle. Yes, states accept and vote for such intrusions, they argue, but in so doing they accord the secretary general and other U.N. officials considerable leeway to cope with situations, a leeway that amounts to nothing less than an independent autonomy running counter to, and even negating, the principle that states have ultimate authority. Sure, states remain powerful and can get the Security Council to negate or reverse the actions of officials in the field, but the likelihood of this occurring is seen as minimal since the members of the Security Council have a stake in not emasculating the U.N.'s prestige.

The U.N. as an Actor

Given the readiness of realists to acknowledge that world politics have undergone transformation and that the sovereignty principle may be in flux, and given the inclination of postinternationalists to concede that states remain powerful, it might be asked whether the two schools of thought are converging on each other and whether, in effect, we are raising a false set of issues, or at least overemphasizing the differences, by the ensuing analyses, which contrast the two in rather stark terms. Our answer is no. Whatever the degrees of overlap between the realist and postinternationalist perspectives, the remaining differences that separate them are considerable and lead to very different interpretations of what drives the course of events. More than mere nuance differentiates the convenience-of-states and states-are-obliged-to-go-along orientations. As will be seen, profoundly different consequences follow from adhering to one or the other approach. Accordingly, in order to more fully assess these conflicting perspectives, we turn to an examination of several dimensions of the U.N. that have recently become highly salient. The pace and scope of the U.N.'s activities, its peacekeeping efforts, its intrusion into the elections and human rights policies of its members, its work on development and environmental issues, its organizational structures, and its financing have all become the focus of controversies that put in sharp relief how adherents of the two perspectives vary in their perceptions and evaluations of the organization's emergent roles.

Pace and Scope

It is not difficult to demonstrate the large extent to which the U.N.'s activities have expanded since the end of the Cold War. In 1987 the U.N. assigned some 10,000 peacekeepers—mostly troops in blue helmets who were supposed to resort to force only if attacked—to five operations around the world on an annual budget of about $233 million. Over the next seven years the number of troops rose to 72,000 in eighteen different situations at an annual cost of more than $3 billion. Similarly, where the Security Council used to meet once a month, by 1994 its schedule involved meeting every day and often twice a day. In 1993 alone, the Security Council adopted more than 181 resolutions and statements, all of them high-minded in tone (such as a demand for the end of ethnic cleansing in the former Yugoslavia) but few of them enforceable.

Although these new patterns represent a dramatic increase in the U.N.'s role since the end of superpower competition and highlight the need for new modes of cooperation, the extent of the hastened pace and widened scope can be interpreted in several ways depending on whether one is inclined to view history from a realist or a post-internationalist perspective. Some analysts, including realists who worry about the U.N. exceeding its mandate and capabilities, stress that the appointment of an activist, Boutros Boutros-Ghali, as the U.N.'s new secretary general in January 1992 contributed to the accelerated involvement of the organization in diverse conflict situations around the world. Knowing of Boutros-Ghali's aspiration to turn the U.N. into "a new instrument in the public opinion, a new instrument for the member states,"[3] such analysts view the Security Council as being too quick to follow his lead into new conflict situations. Not so, say postinternationalists; rather, the pace and scope of the U.N.'s missions accelerated because the processes of fragmentation quickened in a turbulent world no longer readily manageable by interstate cooperation, leaving the U.N. with the opportunity to respond to demands for expanding its activities as new situations evolved to threaten the well-being and stability of people in various parts of the world. Indeed, even Boutros-Ghali is quoted as saying that the structure of world politics, and not personalities, accounts for the broadened scope of the organization's activities:

> Very often people like to compare [secretaries general as less active than me]. I say, "No, let us speak very justly. If I would have been [in office in earlier periods], I would have done exactly the same [as my predecessors did]. And if [they were in the office now, they] would have been compelled, even if [they] did not want to do it, to be more active. So, very often it is the period that creates the man."[4]

Furthermore, whereas realists may ascribe the acceleration of the U.N.'s pace and scope to the onset of multipolarity, those who subscribe to the turbulence model are likely to interpret the acceleration as deriving from the changing, postinternational structure of world politics. In their view, Boutros-Ghali's immediate predecessor, Javier Perez de Cuellar, left the office at a time when the U.N. had succeeded in helping to bring about an end to violent conflict in a number of diverse situations—Afghanistan, Iran-Iraq, Namibia, Nicaragua, and El Salvador[5]—with the result that "people went from thinking the U.N. could do nothing to thinking it could do everything."[6] These actions supported the momentum that led the Security Council to hasten the pace and expand the scope of the organization's activities.

In short, although states may still view themselves as possessed of the sovereign rights that enable them to slow and narrow, even negate, U.N. activities, the likelihood of their exercising these rights in crucial world situations is more complicated than realism suggests. Yet, as noted below, the structure of world politics is not evolving so quickly as to prevent states from contesting U.N. policies and, in some instances, backing away from them.

Peacekeeping, Peacemaking, and Peace Enforcing

Various stages mark the processes whereby peace is established and maintained within and between societies. Violent conflict may be ended through negotiations, or peace may be enforced by preventing adversaries from resuming hostilities while the foundations of a lasting peace are laid. During the Cold War the U.N.'s participation in these processes was highly circumscribed. As was the case in Cyprus or on the Golan Heights, it intervened only when invited by the adversaries to police previously agreed-upon cease-fire lines, thereby giving the politicians time to negotiate a solution. As the political vacuum widened with the end of the Cold War and superpower competition, however, so did the tasks assigned to U.N. peacekeeping forces. Recently the U.N. has been asked, not always by the adversaries, to become involved in what Secretary General Boutros-Ghali has called "second-generation operations"[7]—that is, to intervene directly in unfolding situations and to steer them to a desired outcome. The goal may be to convince an aggressor country to give up its conquered lands (as in the case of Iraq in Kuwait), to manage and oversee elections following the end of bitter conflicts (as in Angola, Cambodia, El Salvador, and South Africa), to deliver food and medicine in war zones (such as Bosnia), to restore order and stability (as in Haiti), or to escort relief convoys and reverse massive social disintegration (as in Somalia).

Put differently, participation by intervention has replaced participation by invitation as the basis for U.N. action in many situations. And underlying this shift, a postinternationalist might note, has been a readiness of states to recognize their declining competence and thus to accept U.N. missions that extend beyond the organization's long-standing commitment to impartial peacekeeping and require it, instead, to engage in enforcement actions.

The most successful instance of peace enforcement, and one that probably served to encourage many of the other second-generation operations that followed, occurred shortly after the end of the Cold War. In August 1990, Iraq invaded and conquered Kuwait, an action so blatant as to stimulate the United States to mobilize a coalition of thirty-two countries to force Saddam Hussein's Iraqi troops out of Kuwait. At virtually every stage, the United States submitted its proposals to the U.N. Security Council for approval before the U.S.-led coalition took action. For the first time, the Security Council made full use of the collective security provisions of the U.N. Charter (Chapter VII). Early in 1991 the Gulf War was launched, and the U.N.-sponsored coalition defeated the Iraqis in but a few weeks. And the newly discovered capacities of the U.N. did not end with the cessation of hostilities. Confronted with hundreds of thousands of Iraqi Kurds and Shiite Muslim Arabs fleeing Saddam Hussein's brutal repression at the war's end, the horrors of which were captured and repeatedly displayed over global television, the Security Council approved Resolution 688, which condemned the repression and asked the secretary general to investigate the plight of the refugees. The council dismissed Iraq's objection that its handling of the problem was an internal affair and that any U.N. action was "blatant interference," asserting instead that the wave of refugees flowing toward Turkey and Iran threatened "international peace and security." This action was not merely an extension of the peacekeeping obligations that the U.N. took on at the end of the war. Resolution 688 was, rather, an entirely new intrusion into the sovereignty principle.

But the breakthrough into uncharted areas of the sovereignty principle was not clear-cut and unqualified, for Resolution 688 did not back up its statement of concern for the refugees with action to protect them. That came from the United States, which was in large part moved by European pressures and by the television scenes of human suffering to undertake to establish, supply, and protect sanctuary sites for Kurdish refugees in northern Iraq. The United States contended that the building of sanctuaries came under Resolution 688, but Secretary General Javier Perez de Cuellar questioned whether the United States could lawfully intervene on Iraqi soil without a new and explicit authorization by the Security Council. When the United States subsequently sought approval for a U.N. police force to replace its forces in northern Iraq, the secretary general sent an envoy to Baghdad to ask for Iraq's approval of the idea. Iraq rejected the request, claiming it involved an illegal violation of Iraqi sovereignty, and the secretary general reiterated that new Security Council authorization was needed for the U.N. to take over the policing process. Reluctant to use its veto, the United States was reported not to have sought the new authority, on the grounds that both the Soviet Union and China opposed U.N. intervention without Iraq's consent. Their opposition had its roots in the multi-centric world, with the Chinese being fearful that the Tibetans could theoretically appeal for the same sort of U.N. protection and the Soviets having the same fear with respect to the Baltic republics. With respect to Iraq's aspiration to develop nuclear weapons, in contrast, the Security Council continued to govern the course of events and refused to remove economic sanctions until Saddam Hussein allowed U.N. inspectors to monitor its possible nuclear sites and to destroy any materials that could be used to build nuclear weapons.

So in the period extending from late 1990 through early 1991, the tipping of the balance against the sovereignty principle was halting and spasmodic. But it did tip, and the U.N.'s actions were followed not by an outcry in defense of the sovereignty principle but by considerable criticism of the U.N.'s inaction on the sanctuary issue. More than a few editorials and columnists praised the United States for its compassionate actions and denounced the U.N. for being mired in the sovereignty principle. Humanitarian imperatives, many argued, take precedence over those affirming nonintervention, thus justifying relaxation of the sovereignty principle.[8] And this line of reasoning, along with the success of the coalition in the Gulf War, was surely one source of the U.N.'s subsequent shift to a rash of second-generation operations in Cambodia, Haiti, Bosnia, Somalia, and elsewhere.

The U.N.'s involvement in Somalia is perhaps particularly revealing of the difficulties encountered by the second-generation operations. In December 1992, the United States led a twenty-seven-nation coalition of 28,000 troops to protect deliveries of humanitarian aid in a country bordering on starvation as a result of feuding among warlords. Five months later the original goal of providing security so that relief agencies could supply food to starving Somalis was attained as both the famine and the civil war outside the capital, Mogadishu, were brought under control. Hence, the United States withdrew the bulk of its troops and handed over command of the operation to the U.N., which was then given the mandate of turning from peacekeeping to the much more complex task of peacemaking—that is, helping the Somalis reconstruct, rehabilitate, and rebuild their social and political system. But pursuit of this goal was greatly complicated by a continuing armed struggle in Mogadishu between U.N. troops and a recalcitrant warlord, General Mohammad Farah Aidid. In mid-June 1993 General Aidid's forces ambushed and killed twenty-four Pakistani peacekeeping troops, and as a result, the U.N. launched a huge military campaign aimed at destroying Aidid's political and military base. A reward of $25,000 was offered for the general's capture, but this ploy was unsuccessful and the general's supporters went on killing peacekeeping troops.

As the U.N. became more aggressive and escalated the war with Aidid, so did its policies become more controversial. Some argued that negotiations with Aidid were the only way to bring an end to the conflict; others felt that only his capture would bring hostilities to a halt. An Italian general in command of the 2,442-man Italian force in Mogadishu favored negotiations so strongly that, insisting he had to wait for instructions from Rome, he refused to carry out orders from the U.N. commander to wage a more vigorous campaign against Aidid. The Italian general was immediately removed from his post despite a huge outcry from politicians in Rome.

In early August four U.S. soldiers were killed by a remote-controlled bomb set off by Aidid's forces, an action that contributed to a U.S. decision to send a Special Force of commando troops to assist in the search for General Aidid. On October 3, 1993, eighteen of the commandos were killed in a U.N.-led battle with Aidid's forces. There followed a flood of American opinion opposing the U.S. (but not the U.N.) presence in Somalia and a decision by President Clinton to place American troops under U.S. rather than U.N. command and to withdraw them by April 1, 1994. France and Belgium soon announced that they would also withdraw their troops. The same decision was interpreted by a gang of toughs in Haiti as a sign the United States lacked the will to carry out its intentions of landing troops and other advisers to help Haiti's transition to democracy. They were right: A week later, by creating a commotion at the dock as the first ship sought to leave its load, they got the White House to order a suspension of the U.S. military effort in Haiti.

Thus, supplemented by a record of comparable vacillation and inaction in the former Yugoslavia that allowed horrendous atrocities to occur in Bosnia, the optimism that surrounded the U.N. after the Gulf War petered out and yielded two years later to much skepticism—among publics as well as elites in all parts of the world—as to the organization's peacekeeping capacities in the face of many simultaneous challenges that were undermining the world's post–Cold War order.[9] Some said the U.N. was taking on more than it could handle, given the limits on its finances and the availability of trained personnel. Others stressed that the very countries that had come to rely on the U.N. as a peacekeeper were not ready to put their soldiers' lives at risk in situations that did not clearly fall within their national interests. The continuing indecision with respect to the unfolding horrors in the former Yugoslavia served, along with Somalia and Haiti, as a major source of this conclusion:

> One of the lessons driven home with a vengeance by the Western response to the war in Bosnia is that the liberal Western democracies feel themselves politically weak. The political cost of fighting war is high in a democracy. Peacemaking forces are subject to casualties. Leaders avoid risks unless direct interests are at stake. ... But support for collective security still seems to be too amorphous, too watery a concept to serve as fuel. So UN members steer clear of peacemaking where it is obviously needed. They do so for a compelling domestic reason—the fear of body bags. Perhaps they are right to do this. Yet until they do otherwise, the UN idea may remain a fig leaf disguising the reality that in the new order as in the old, the great powers do and take what they want, when they want it.[10]

A former U.N. undersecretary in charge of peacekeeping put the same thought in a broader historical context: "After a brief post-cold-war honeymoon, the United Nations is once again suffering from the inability to enforce its decision in critical situations, this time without the excuse of the obstacles created by the Cold War."[11] And the activist Secretary General Boutros Boutros-Ghali concurred with this perspective: "I am firmly committed to the concept of peace enforcement. It is essential if we are to strengthen international peace and security. But there is a new reality: member states are not ready for it. I must accept reality. I also most continue to give you my view."[12] And perhaps the most incisive insight into the problem was provided by the reaction of a U.S. senator, Robert Byrd, to his country's involvement in Somalia: "I do not see in the front of this chamber the U.N. flag. I have never saluted the U.N. flag. I salute Old Glory, the American flag."[13]

At first glance, the foregoing account of the U.N.'s peacekeeping missions would appear a vivid vindication of the realist perspective. Adherents of this approach can readily argue that the Gulf War was a quintessential case of how the main actors in the state-centric world cope with disturbances in their established order: Thirty-two states collaborated on behalf of their national interests and in response to the leadership of the world's hegemon to preserve the integrity of one of their kind and restore the status quo ante. Sure, acknowledge the realists, the thirty-two-state coalition proceeded under the auspices of the U.N., and yes, the Security Council did dare to intrude upon Iraq's sovereignty; but in these actions the U.N. simply served as a vehicle of the coordination of states intent upon preventing the spread of nuclear weapons and maintaining the viability of their long-standing system. Put differently, from a realist point of view, the U.N. is an instrument of the state system and did exactly what it was designed to do, namely, carry out the policies of its members. To quote the secretary general again, "What is going on in places like Angola, Cambodia, El Salvador, Georgia, Haiti, Somalia, Tajikistan and the former Yugoslavia is nothing less than an effort to preserve the foundations of the state system while beginning to shape a post-cold-war structure of peace and security."[14]

Those who subscribe to a postinternationalist approach view this realist affirmation as misguided and inaccurate. They can readily interpret the same sequence of events as still further evidence of the underlying soundness of the postinternationalist approach. First, they would be quick to point out, the realist presumption that states are solitary actors is clearly revealed by these events to be fallacious. The dynamics surrounding the U.N.'s vacillation in Bosnia and its retreat from Somalia and Haiti were driven not by governments pursuing their national interests but by publics unwilling to support peacekeeping operations that involve troop casualties. Even the Gulf War, it might be said, can be interpreted as a state-centric operation only because extensive casualties did not occur on the U.N. side of the battle line. Had there been large numbers of battle deaths, it seems very doubtful indeed whether the coalition would have held together and a prolonged war fought to the finish. In sum, the very same skill revolution at the micro level that served to support the multilateralism that led to so many tasks being assigned to the U.N. also operated to foster a retreat from the tasks when their noxious side became predominant.

Furthermore, postinternationalists might well contend that the overloading of the U.N. with peacekeeping tasks is in itself a measure of the extent to which state authority has undergone erosion. Some of this authority, the postinternationalist would say, is being subtly transferred to the U.N., which is not serving as an instrument of states but as an autonomous actor that reflects the needs of the multi-centric world and its more empowered peoples and thus straddles the grand divide of a bifurcated world. The very fact that ambiguity surrounds a number of peacekeeping questions—such as when the U.N. should intrude its blue-helmeted troops into a situation, whose troops will be sent, under whose command, at whose expense, to enforce terms of the peace decided by what authority—suggests the insufficiency of traditional peacekeeping norms enunciated in the 1960s and the emergence of a new world order in which states may not have the final say. Or, perhaps more accurately, although the postinternational model may have no ready-made answers to such questions, certainly it is also the case that realism offers no clear-cut guidelines to help the theorist through this thicket of new questions posed by the onrush of many new peacekeeping roles assigned to the U.N.

For some analysts, the word "multilateralism" fills this analytic gap and offers a modicum of clarity about the new global order by emphasizing that collective action can be taken in a world of weak states and a weak U.N.[15] For realists, "multilateralism" refers to collective actions undertaken by states; for postinternationalists, the term connotes the involvement of publics, the dispersion of authority, and the activity of nongovernmental as well as governmental actors—that is, the presence of the multi-centric as well as the state-centric world. As Boutros-

Ghali put it, "Multilateralism is the democracy of international society."[16] But whatever label may be appropriate, it seems clear that a transformation of the world's prime authority structures is underway. Blue-helmeted troops now exercise force on behalf of goals that are better characterized as those of the global community than as those of states. Senator Byrd may never have saluted the U.N. flag, but the fact that he felt the need to contrast it with the American flag suggests that it symbolizes the presence of a critical actor on the world stage. Indeed, the fact that the U.N. has acquired enemies (as distinguished from those who bear it no ill will but are simply pessimistic about its peacekeeping capacities)[17]—publics and governments that blame the organization for their problems (as has happened in Somalia and Bosnia)— is perhaps the surest measure of the large extent to which the U.N. has made the transition from an idealistic visionary of world order to a major player in the processes whereby some form of order is fashioned in this turbulent era.[18]

Command of Troops

That the changing world scene has given rise to confusion over the question of the U.N.'s authority can be readily seen in the issue of who commands the blue-helmeted troops stationed in eighteen situations around the world. The U.N. has a command structure with officers who, though obviously having a particular nationality, are U.N. commanders both in name and in fact. The question is, Whose command counts when the countries providing the troops give orders that are contrary to those issued by the U.N. commanders? As previously noted, such a clash occurred in Somalia when an Italian general was sent back to Rome because he awaited instructions from the Italian government rather than carrying out the orders of his U.N. commanders on the scene. Less clear-cut is the outcome of the controversy surrounding U.S. policies toward the issue. Early in the Clinton administration, word spread that the president, inclined to support a multilateralist policy and eager to scale back the United States's role as a global policeman, was prepared to back away from a long-standing policy that required U.S. troops to be under U.S. commanders in combat situations.[19] Ever mindful of the political pitfalls such a shift would encounter in Congress, the projected new policy was to be hedged in a number of ways, including allowing the heads of U.S. military units to disregard orders from U.N. commanders that they considered to be illegal or questionable.[20] But strenuous objections from Secretary General Boutros-Ghali, based on the fact that such a veto could lead other nations to retain the right to ignore U.N. commands, led to the removal of this clause from the draft of a presidential directive on peacekeeping operations.[21] Then, in early October 1993, after eighteen U.S. soldiers were killed in a bungled raid in Mogadishu, President Clinton announced that the United States would send combat reinforcements to Somalia and that these forces would be placed under U.S. rather than U.N. command until the United States finally withdrew from Somalia (which occurred the following April).

However, clear-cut lines of authority did not prove easy to work out. The need for close coordination with U.N. forces confounded the drawing of such lines of command. U.S. troops were committed to clearing roadblocks from the streets of Mogadishu and purifying the water for troops in Somalia, for example, and these tasks could only be executed through such extensive contacts with U.N. forces as to blur the chain of authority. Indeed, interviews with military officials both on the scene and in Washington "portrayed the relationship between United States and United Nations forces as too intertwined to be easily separated. Despite the effort by the Administration to put distance between itself and the United Nations, they said there were reasons that the relationship may grow even closer before the American withdrawal."[22] The United States is the primary state reluctant to put its forces under U.N. command, but its resistance to such an arrangement is not readily implemented.

Nor is the United States alone in rethinking peacekeeping arrangements. Although deeply committed to involvement in peacekeeping operations, for example, Canada is reevaluating its policies in this regard. Canadian troops experienced severe hardships in Bosnia, thus eroding domestic support for Canada's long-standing tradition of participation in U.N. peacekeeping missions.

In sum, the more the U.N. gets involved in second-generation missions that necessitate it to engage in enforcement activities, the more is its authority likely to get evoked and challenged. The conduct of field operations, whether in military or nonmilitary matters, involves too intricate a set of tasks for state officials to reserve to themselves the final word on issues that urgently require resolution. Whether they want to or not, officials seem bound to cede some authority to those on the scene even if they are wearing blue helmets. Realists might stress that states continue to retain the sovereign prerogative of having the last word, but for all practical purposes such a conclusion runs counter to the actual experience of those who have to relate to the U.N. in the daily crises that mark the course of world affairs.

Election Monitoring

Where ambiguity and resistance characterize the U.N.'s involvement in peacekeeping operations, quite the opposite can be said with respect to its newly emergent monitoring role in domestic elections. Along with human rights issues, elections constitute one domestic arena that appears to be increasingly accepting of the idea that the U.N.—as well as numerous transnational nongovernmental organizations—should take on major responsibilities.[23] And here it is also clear that the postinternational perspective fits the evolving pattern more exactly than does the realist approach. Neither model fully explains the dynamism of the many peacekeeping operations, but in the case of recent elections all three parameters of the postinternational model contribute to an explanation of why the sovereignty principle has been so extensively breached in the case of that most precious of domestic institutions, the national election. Perhaps the most realists have to offer as an explanation is that the state-centric system has a stake in the domestic stability of its members and thus is ready to authorize its prime intergovernmental organization's participation in their internal affairs. Such an interpretation is undermined, however, by the fact that interventions in domestic elections have not been confined just to the system's prime intergovernmental organization. Upwards of 200 transnational organizations, for example, observed and monitored the 1989 Nicaraguan election, a fact that is not easily accounted for by the realist perspective.

But all three parametric transformations of the postinternational model are consistent with the U.N. playing an enhanced role in domestic elections. Consider the macro parameter. There are at least two ways in which its transformation seems likely to have contributed to the emergent pattern. For one, the bifurcation of global structures has weakened the sovereignty, competence, and legitimacy of national governments and made them more ready to accept, if not more dependent upon, collective action by international organizations as a means of coping with the world's trouble spots. Second, initially spurred by a series of U.N.-sponsored covenants on human rights in the 1960s and subsequently promoted mainly by actors in the multi-centric world, the spread of norms protective of human rights on a global scale has fostered a climate of world opinion that serves to legitimate and encourage U.N. participation in the domestic elections of members whose democratic institutions are not firmly in place.

The transformation of the macro-micro parameter has also boosted the U.N.'s role as an election monitor. States that are still governed by highly authoritarian regimes are being put on the defensive in this era marked by a trend toward democratic procedures, and many other states are facing the possibility of a crisis of their authority structures because of the trend toward performance criteria of legitimacy. Thus, during elections, the U.N.'s monitoring teams enter, as it were, an authority vacuum in which their activities stand out as having been sanctioned by the international community as well as the government holding the election. The U.N.'s insistence that it be involved in all stages of the electoral process and that its presence be approved by all major political groups adds further to its authority. Needless to say, the U.N. monitoring teams are also subjected to performance criteria and thus must maintain an impeccable reputation for impartiality in the conduct of their responsibilities if they are to retain their legitimacy. Since all the incentives are conducive to helping the U.N. teams maintain an even-handed approach in carrying out their monitoring tasks, the teams are unlikely to act in such a way as to undermine the expanding authority that attaches to their presence as arbiters of fairness. Indeed, given a record of irreproachable conduct and steadfast unwillingness to approve fraudulent or otherwise flawed elections, the U.N.'s authority in this regard will probably remain untarnished even in those instances when controversy accompanies the election outcome or when the losing regime prevents a freely elected government from taking the reins of power. For then the opprobrium will fall on those individuals or factions who thwart the democratic process.

In short, although the ultimate outcome of elections in developing countries may negate the efforts of outside monitoring teams, the U.N. cannot fail but add to its electoral authority if it adheres to the strict standards of equity it has set for itself as an outside observer of the domestic politics of its members.[24] It has going for it the "politics of

shame," which, in effect, attaches blame to those who thwart democratic values rather than to those who seek to implement them.

Turning to the micro parameter, one is led to wonder whether the
enlarged analytic skills of citizens will increase their responsiveness to
the presence of the U.N. monitoring teams and, if so, whether new
habits of compliance will evolve that incrementally add to the organization's authority vis-à-vis that of its member states. Put more generally, is the skill revolution, supplemented by a growing record of successful international involvement in domestic elections, likely to
reinforce the global norms that allow for external intervention in the
internal affairs of countries? Other things being equal—that is, in the
absence of direct confrontations between the monitoring teams and
state authorities at polling sites—the question can readily be answered
in the affirmative. Citizens will not need to ponder transferring any
loyalties or habits of compliance to the U.N., but their expanded analytic skills are likely to enable them to assess the consequences for
themselves of international observers being present during the campaign and on election day. Leaving aside those who do not want their
authoritarian regime toppled, most citizens seem bound to appreciate
that the monitoring teams are present because the teams' sponsors
used the politics of shame to persuade the regime to accept them and
that they subsequently made it possible for the election to be conducted fairly. Accordingly, it seems probable that the more the analytic
skills of citizens undergo expansion, the more likely citizens are to
modify any skepticism they may have about the U.N. as an actor in
world politics—or, at the very least, the more likely they are to accord
salience to the U.N. and move it toward the center of their perceptual
range.

These derivations from the turbulence model are supported by recent events. Viewed in the context of the transformative changes that
have slowly but steadily accelerated since the end of World War II,[25]
the U.N.'s incremental evolution toward readiness to participate in domestic elections, and the recent surge in acceptance of the external
monitoring process, is hardly surprising. More accurately, it is not difficult to explain why the first U.N. monitored election, in Korea in 1952,
"failed to create momentum for further election monitoring"[26] and
why thirty-eight years then ensued before the organization monitored
another election in an independent nation. The initial monitoring sit-

uation was a consequence of circumstances that attended the Korean War; indeed, it was the only time in the history of the U.N. that it observed an election without the host country's official permission. In so doing it ignored members of the Korean National Assembly who protested that the country's sovereignty was being violated, but such reasoning soon became worldwide as the Cold War deepened and fostered intensified claims of national sovereignty. Consequently, in the ensuing decades the U.N. declined a number of requests from member states to monitor their elections.[27] Indeed, the sovereignty principle was still intact late in the 1980s when the U.N. secretary general denied a Nicaraguan request for monitoring on the grounds that there was no "precedent whatsoever for carrying out such supervision in an independent country."[28]

During the same period, however, in subtle and incremental ways U.N. organs did move toward a resolution of the clash between the sovereignty principle and the idea of monitoring elections in troubled situations. Not only did they acquire expertise and lay the groundwork for a new precedent by observing or supervising thirty plebiscites and elections in non-self-governing territories between 1956 and 1990, but the issue surfaced in their debates with increasing frequency as time passed, spurred by the global authority crisis that underlay the worldwide proliferation of democratic movements and generated pressures on governments to hold elections. These pressures led governments to look abroad for monitoring teams that, in turn, would add to their domestic legitimacy by sanctioning election outcomes.[29] Wide cracks in the armor of national sovereignty began to appear in 1989, when the U.N. broke its unblemished "hands-off" record by sending an election team to Nicaragua. In taking this action, the U.N. maintained deference toward the sovereignty concept by using wording that allowed and encouraged such missions "in well-defined circumstances ... primarily in situations with a clear international dimension."[30] Involvement in the Nicaraguan election was viewed as justifiable because it helped to protect the international peace of the region and had come about not only as a consequence of a Sandinista request but also in response to the Esquipulas II initiative of Central American presidents. Then, with the Observer Mission to Verify the Electoral Process in Haiti in October 1990, the U.N. undertook a precedent-setting involvement in a situation without a clear threat to the maintenance of international peace.[31] By 1992 the U.N. had "provided technical assistance for elections in Albania, the Congo, El Salvador, Ethiopia, Guinea, Guyana, Liberia, Madagascar, Mali, Rwanda and Togo, and ... Angola [and had assisted] in preparations for referendums planned for Eritrea and Western Sahara."[32]

Again, the shift in U.N. policies coincided with a change in the identity and orientations of the secretary general: In 1988 Javier Perez de Cuellar commented that the U.N. "does not send observers to elections ... [or] take part in political elections," whereas at the end of 1991 his successor-elect, Boutros Boutros-Ghali, was reported to expect "the United Nations to take a wider role in encouraging democracy by helping to organize and monitor elections in developing countries."[33] It would be a mistake, however, to view this shift as resulting simply from the idiosyncratic perspectives of different leaders. Such an interpretation overlooks the parametric transformations outlined above and the way in which they surged forward with the end of the Cold War. The new secretary general could not have made election verification a top priority if the world and its organizations, polities, and peoples had not come to appreciate the limits of the sovereignty principle and the virtues of collective intervention on behalf of an emerging right of political participation. If the impulse to support fair elections ever was subject to the idiosyncratic preferences of a particular secretary general, it is no longer; today it has become embedded as a requirement of the office if the pending electoral situation can be defined as having an "international dimension." And even then, given a bifurcated, ever more interdependent world, the definition of "international dimension" will steadily broaden, and thus the presence of U.N. teams in critical elections will occur with increasing frequency. Indeed, the U.N.'s role in the Cambodian election of May 1993 was deemed "a remarkable success," given that nearly 90 percent of the country's more than 4.7 million eligible voters turned out over six days of polling in the face of repeated threats of violence on the part of the dreaded Khmer Rouge guerrilla organization.[34] No less of a success marked the activities of the 1,800 civilian observers sent by the U.N. to help monitor South Africa's first open elections in April 1994.

Human Rights

The same rationale underlying U.N. involvement in domestic elections—that protection of peoples' rights is not subject to national boundaries—has also become increasingly central to the organization's readiness to intrude upon the sovereignty of states with respect to the rights of women, children, indigenous peoples, and minorities as well as the free expression of speech and assembly away from the ballot box. As with election monitoring, the U.N.'s movement in the human rights field came to a halt for a long period during the Cold War. To be sure, its Human Rights Commission and NGOs kept such issues alive during this period, but it was not until the end of superpower hostilities that momentum began to grow. Despite the Universal Declaration of Human Rights that the U.N. adopted in 1948, nothing substantial was done to implement its principles until 1991. In the intervening years, the Western democracies, espousing the universality of human rights, had sponsored resolutions condemning violations of human rights in certain developing countries, but these had been blocked by China and other Asian states on the grounds that such rights existed only as a function of a country's history, level of economic development, and cultural and religious traditions.

For example, intensive debate focused on Myanmar, formerly Burma, where military rulers had refused to hand over power to a democratically elected parliament and had placed Daw Aung San Sou Kyi, the opposition leader and (subsequently) winner of the Nobel Peace Prize, under house arrest. At first Myanmar's Asian neighbors blocked passage of U.N. critical resolutions in the hope that they could promote a change of policies in Myanmar through other means, but by 1991 the other Asian countries tacitly acknowledged failure to budge the military rulers, and from that year onward the General Assembly adopted a series of increasingly harsh rebukes of Myanmar. In 1993 the General Assembly adopted a resolution unanimously and went so far as to ask Secretary General Boutros-Ghali to intervene with the Myanmar government. At the same time, the assembly's Third Committee adopted critical human rights resolutions on Iraq, Iran, Cuba, the Sudan, and the former Yugoslavia.[35]

Resolutions of the General Assembly were not the only sign that the U.N.'s concern with human rights was accelerating. In June 1993, a U.N.-sponsored World Conference on Human Rights concluded with a call for the organization to play a larger role in denouncing abuses. Although the conference had no legislative authority, it broke new ground by extolling an extended definition of human rights to include those of children, minorities, indigenous people, and (with a particularly strong emphasis) women. It is noteworthy from a postinternational perspective that much of the success of the conference was attributed to extensive lobbying activities undertaken by nongovernmental organizations in the human rights field.[36]

A further sign that the sovereignty principle is undergoing transformation occurred at the end of 1993 when the General Assembly resolved one of its most long-standing contentious issues and agreed to the proposal establishing a U.N. high commissioner for human rights who would have the capacity to intervene wherever basic freedoms were being suppressed. The new post had first been proposed by Uruguay in 1952 and was subsequently pressed hard by the United States, but it could not previously win a majority, much less a unanimous vote, for forty-one years, or—as postinternationalists would put it—until the basic parameters of world affairs underwent transformations that heightened global sensitivities to the fundamental rights of individuals. Under the agreement the high commissioner is charged with "promoting and protecting the effective enjoyment by all of all civil, cultural, economic, political and social rights." The position's duties include "preventing the continuation of human rights violations throughout the world," and the commissioner is authorized to "dialogue with all the governments in the implementation of his/her mandate with a view to securing respect for human rights." Yet, to some extent the sovereignty principle retained its vitality in the human rights field despite the creation of the new post: The power to force governments accused of abuses to change their ways was not accorded the new high commissioner, although proponents of the agreement noted that the official could try to shame the abusers by publicizing violations and reporting them to the General Assembly or to the fifty-three-nation Human Rights Commission in Geneva.[37]

There are other indicators that emergent global norms pertaining to human rights have not fully replaced those that affirm the sovereignty principle. In the votes rebuking Iraq for its human rights violations, for example, the number of countries abstaining rose from twenty-six in 1992 to forty-one in 1993, a difference that suggests a broadening sympathy with Iraq's plight vis-à-vis the U.N. Similarly, although the governments represented at the World Conference on Human Rights yielded to some of the pressures exerted by nongovernmental organizations, they resisted the anger of the NGOs and refused to allow them to participate in the deliberations that shaped the final declaration.

Perhaps even more telling, when the U.N. Correspondents Association invited a leading Chinese dissident, Shen Tong, to speak and hold a news conference at U.N. headquarters in New York, Boutros-Ghali ordered the press room to be locked, posted guards outside the door, and prevented the news conference from being held in the U.N. because the Chinese government had protested the invitation. "In view of its apparent purpose as an act of political opposition to a member state of the United Nations," Boutros-Ghali said, "it would not be appropriate for this event to take place on the premises of the Secretariat." Accordingly, although the press room had been the scene of many presentations by Afghan, Iranian, Iraqi, Guatemalan, El Salvadoran, Irish, and Kashmiri dissidents despite the opposition of their governments, Shen's news conference was held on the First Avenue sidewalk, just outside the U.N. visitors' entrance.[38]

While those who adhere to a realist approach might well be heartened by the secretary general's firmness about the press conference and by the other indicators that sovereignty considerations are still operative in world politics, they may also want to consider the fact that Boutros-Ghali apparently feels that in some situations he is free to resolve conflicts over the sovereignty principle on his own without recourse to the Security Council or the General Assembly for policy guidance.[39] For if this decisional freedom is framed in the context of other observations the secretary general has made about the limits of state action—for example, "The time of absolute and exclusive sovereignty ... has passed; its theory was never matched by reality"[40]—his refusal to permit the press conference can be interpreted as a temporary expedient on an issue of transitory importance.

As in everything else during a transformative period, in short, the trendline depicting the U.N.'s evolution is anything but smooth. On the one hand, in some respects the realist perspective is alive and well in the conduct of U.N. affairs, and changes in the interpretation of the sovereignty principle are halting and marked by a two-steps-forward-one-step-back kind of rhythm. On the other hand, the central tendency in these turbulent times appears to favor collective intervention into the domestic affairs of countries when democratic and humanitarian values are under assault.[41] The predominance of the new interventionary norms may not always lead to humanitarian values prevailing over nationalistic ones—as indicated by the failure of externally observed elections to establish freely elected and enduring governments in Panama and Haiti, not to mention the U.N.'s failed efforts to prevent the self-destruction of the former Yugoslavia—but the evolution of the norms, erratic and circuitous as it may be, seems bound to continue as the complex bifurcation of world affairs becomes ever more ingrained.

Development and Environment Issues

If realists stress the continuing importance of the state-centric world's mechanisms for handling issues of war and peace, postinternationalists counter with the cruciality of the multi-centric world to development and environment issues. It is in the latter realms, after all, that NGOs are especially active and effective. They tend to define the issues and to mobilize publics eager for new environmental and developmental departures. Although that may be the case, realists respond, the influence of the NGOs is possible only because the priorities of the state-centric world allow for the central presence of multi-centric actors in the development and environment arenas. Such matters are simply less important to states and thus they tolerate significant U.N. activities in these areas.

Whatever roles actors in the two worlds may play with respect to the U.N.'s activities in the fields of economic development and environmental protection, these activities are of considerable importance even though they rarely capture headlines comparable to those that accompany the U.N.'s work in the peacekeeping, domestic elections, and human rights areas. Indeed, in terms of long-run impact, the former activities may be even more significant. Time and space do not permit here an intensive analysis of the U.N.'s diverse programs in the realms of economics, health, population, and related fields, but suffice it to say that the organization has an extensive worldwide network that carries forward the research and assistance required by these programs. It is a network with offices in a majority of the developing countries and is managed by the U.N.'s Development Programme, its Population Fund, its Children's Fund, its International Drug Control Programme, its World Food Programme, and many other agencies that are part of the U.N. system. And it is also a network that generates problem-solving ideas that often propose radically new approaches and subsequently generate widespread interest and culminate in global conferences and recommendations that arrest the attention of

officials and publics around the world. Thus has the world been ap-
prised of long-term problems associated with the environment, climate change, biological diversity, sustainable development, and a host
of other situations that have come to occupy high places on the global
agenda.

The U.N. as an Organization

Like any large-scale organization, over the years the U.N. has been
plagued by internal problems that have fostered numerous recommendations and efforts designed to bring about structural reforms—
changes that would render the organization less subject to bureaucratic inefficiency and corruption and, accordingly, more capable of
adapting to the changing nature of world politics. But the reform process has moved slowly, not only because large bureaucracies tend to be
pervaded with inertia, but also because each proposed change has political ramifications that tend to evoke opposition from member states
that fear the change will curtail their access to or influence in the policymaking process. Criticism of the management or budgetary practices of one or another subagency of the Secretariat, for example, was
long considered an attack on the countries from which the subagency
heads came, with the result that often inefficient managers and practices were kept in place longer than would be the case in a less politicized organization. This problem was especially prominent during the
U.N.'s early years, when officials occupied their positions through the
recommendations of their governments well before the emergence of
a tradition in which international civil servants regard themselves as
impartial and not beholden to their country of origin. With the Cold
War receding into the past, however, and with the U.N. now in its sixth
decade and led by still another generation of administrators, the values
of a truly international civil service have begun to win more adherents,
thus making it easier for, say, the secretary general to merge sub-
agencies, eliminate bureaucratic layers deemed to be unnecessary, clarify the chains of responsibility, remove aides regarded as inefficient,
and otherwise streamline the Secretariat.[42]

It seems likely that history will judge the U.N. trendline of administrative efficiency as being in an upswing in the present era. The advo-
cates of the realist and postinternationalist approaches would interpret such a pattern in very different ways. The latter would probably

contend that the emergence of an international civil service tradition and the secretary general's increased capacity to reshuffle responsibilities, bureaus, and personnel reflect the declining competence and sovereignty of states. Member states need the services of the U.N. more than ever, the postinternationalists might argue, and thus they will become more and more unlikely to intervene in the streamlining process and more and more prepared to accept its consequences. Nonsense, the realist might reply—the administrative trendline is consistent with the natural evolution of any large organization that manages to persist through time and has little to do with the capabilities or rights of states. After all, it is states—and, most notably, the United States—that are failing to keep up with their financial commitments to the U.N., and there is not much the secretary general can do about it other than continuously press them to meet their obligations. Recall too, such incidents as the secretary general's cancellation of a press conference at the request of China or his refusal to move against Iraq's treatment of the Kurds without renewed authorization from the Security Council. Surely, the realist might conclude, these are not examples of states yielding the center of the international stage. To such affirmations of realism the postinternationalist might respond by quoting a complaint of a leading realist whose objection is precisely that the secretary general is exercising increasing degrees of independent authority: "Although the U.N. Charter vests all executive power in the Security Council, so far the governments of member states have passively accepted Boutros-Ghali's reinterpretation of his role and theirs. The member states have adopted the secretary general's priorities and programs as if he were the chief executive in a presidential system and the Security Council were a rubber-stamp legislature."[43]

Enlarged Security Council

Whatever progress may have occurred with respect to improving the quality and quantity of the work performed by the Secretariat, it is the Security Council and its adaptation to the changing nature of world affairs that many observers regard as the first priority on the list of organizational reforms deemed urgent. The core of one argument, advanced most vigorously by the United States, is that membership in the Security Council needs to be altered to reflect the ways in which the distribution of power in the world today is different from what it was when the U.N. was founded in 1945. The issue is a delicate one and, accordingly, hotly contested. Some states argue that Germany and Japan should replace France and Great Britain as permanent members of the Security Council—thus gaining the right to veto any action by voting in the negative—in order to bring the council into closer alignment with the present distribution of power. Others insist that such a proposal would go nowhere because France or Britain would veto it and that therefore the number of permanent members should be increased to include Germany and Japan. Still others contend that major developing countries from the Third World should also be given permanent membership to more accurately represent present-day realities. And although most countries want to preserve the veto and add to the ranks of the Security Council, some of the smaller ones want to abolish permanent seats and vetoes altogether.

At present, the most likely compromise, if one is to occur, would involve maintaining the veto and expanding the ranks of the permanent members of the council by adding those countries that have become major actors on either the world stage or within a particular region. Most experts would agree that Germany and Japan qualify as major actors and that the major regional powers include India, Brazil, and Nigeria. Such an arrangement, moreover, would help to ameliorate the U.N.'s dire financial straits by virtue of the fact that Germany and Japan have enjoyed considerable economic prosperity and could thus be asked to shoulder substantial increases in their financial contribution to the organization if they were to assume permanent council membership.

The matter is further complicated by the expectation that new permanent members should significantly increase their security contributions to the U.N.'s peacekeeping operations. This expectation is controversial because both Germany and Japan are constitutionally prevented from sending troops into combat abroad and because, for some, the idea of remilitarizing these countries is threatening. Others insist that the two countries be required to make the necessary constitutional revisions to ensure full military participation, while still others, fearful that, owing to domestic opposition, such a requirement could never get adopted in one or both countries,[44] are willing to settle for an arrangement in which Germany and Japan would participate by contributing medical and logistical support to future peacekeeping missions.

In any event, whatever changes may be made in the structure of the Security Council and the obligations of its permanent members, the proposals to alter it and thereby make the U.N. more adaptive would appear to rest on the realist premise that the U.N. is a state organization run by and for states. However, to propose rendering the organization more adaptive to a changing world is possibly to acknowledge that sovereignty has eroded somewhat and that some sovereignty-free actors have become at least as important as many states. Those who are inclined to take a postinternational approach would focus on the adaptation idea as consistent with their worldviews. And, indeed, this difference of perspective on the restructuring of the U.N. has proven to be divisive. In the United States, upon the invitation of President Bush and congressional leaders to assess what changes should be recommended, the sixteen-member Commission on Improving the Usefulness of the United Nations took two years to reach a divided set of recommendations. The majority argued that the end of the Cold War created "a unique chance for a U.S.-led United Nations to fashion common responses to mankind's common problems," whereas a minority of six contended it was "far from clear whether the United Nations is ready for the post–Cold War world and urged the U.S. to defend its interests alone where necessary."[45]

Financing Problems

Because many member states fall behind in their financial obligations to the U.N., it is regularly in dire financial straits, especially now as the organization takes on more and more missions. In late 1993, in fact, the U.N. was deemed to be on the brink of bankruptcy. In September it would have been unable to meet its payroll had the Japanese not made a $194 million peacekeeping payment. So dire was the situation that heads of state and foreign ministers were asked to finish their speeches by 6:00 P.M. so that the building could be closed and overtime costs avoided. Similarly, each delegation was limited to just two copies of official documents—one in English and one in French—and had to purchase translations in any other language.[46]

The ironies and contradictions are staggering: The member states have committed the U.N. to extensive peacekeeping missions in the absence of any other means of addressing festering situations in Bosnia, Somalia, and elsewhere—thereby increasing peacekeeping costs tenfold between 1987 and 1993—but then have fallen behind in their payments, largely because they feel the U.N. is not up to the tasks they assign it. Only eighteen countries met the payment deadline on January 31, 1993,[47] but the United States is the most conspicuous culprit: By late 1993 it had fallen behind by $1 billion in its obligations to the U.N., or half the debt the organization was owed. Equally important, although the Clinton administration has been especially vigorous in championing multilateralism through the U.N., the United States has not exercised the leadership in the various situations that could ensure the success of the peacekeeping missions. Thus, it is little wonder that the secretary general, faced with a large and continuing gap between the U.N.'s peacekeeping commitments and the resources to carry them out, recurs continuously to the financial problem: "Money, money, money," he is quoted as reiterating, "that is the prerequisite for the United Nations playing the role it could play after the Cold War."[48]

Part of the explanation for the vast numbers of member states that fall behind in their payments, of course, lies in the financial difficulties that are plaguing many of them. There are limits to this explanation, however, since the same states spend considerable sums for their own national defense. The United States, for example, spends $2,016 on defense for every dollar it contributes to peacekeeping,[49] and "on average, the nations of the world invest only $1.40 in peacekeeping for every $1,000 they devote to their own armed forces."[50] No, the explanation must go deeper, and for both realists and postinternationalists a more fundamental analysis is readily available. The former can easily argue that, of course, multilateralism cannot work. States are too committed to their own narrow interests to be ready to pay for operations far removed from their immediate concerns. And postinternationalists can again focus on the authority crises that have overtaken most states and their subsequent inability to suffer battlefield casualties, which in turn serves as a disincentive to pay their share of the peacekeeping operations. The reasoning follows different paths, but both schools of thought come to the same negative conclusion with respect to the U.N.'s ability to generate the resources it needs to adequately shoulder its responsibilities.

The Secretary General

Earlier it was suggested that the dynamics presently at work in world politics are too powerful to be significantly shaped by the individual occupying the role of U.N. secretary general, that different persons in the job would make different decisions but that the variability in this regard would not be very great. It does not contradict this insight to also assert that the demands on the secretary general are enormous and the holder of the post has become a critical actor on the world scene. To be sure, other top officials of the U.N. play key roles, but they are not in the public limelight and thus their actions do not have the same extensive consequences as do those of the organization's head. The U.N. secretary general is perhaps the only official on the global scene whose activities and responsibilities are deeply embedded in both the state-centric and multi-centric worlds. Realists would likely claim that the secretary general's role is confined to the former world and that servicing its need for preventive diplomacy and for a respected intermediary who can ameliorate conflicts takes priority, whereas postinternationalists would doubtless stress the secretary general's role in refugee, human rights, development, environment, and elections problems. Both schools of thought, however, uncover an essential truth about the centrality of the position. Consider, for example, the secretary general's activities in the state-centric world: Not only does the official have to manage a gigantic bureaucracy and preside over a vast system of agencies, but there is also the time-consuming task of negotiating with the states that make up the U.N.'s membership. Boutros-Ghali succinctly described this latter task in the course of explaining the difficulties he encounters in launching peacekeeping operations authorized by the Security Council:

As a good pragmatist, I must work as well as I can within the current reality that our only power is persuasion. In each case I must begin from Square One. I must telephone the president of a country and say, "Mr. President, please can't you help me? Can you send me some troops? Can you send me two planes? Can you advance the dates on which we will get this help?"

Then I must phone his minister of defense to work out the details. It can take five or six weeks. Then countries change their minds. That has happened in Bosnia and in Somalia. They change the dates on which their help will be available. They promise free transportation and then come back and say we must pay some kind of low-cost price.

Three months, four months go by. Eventually we are able to overcome these difficulties. But rather than doing it in two weeks, we are doing it in months. In the meantime, a lot of people die. This is the price.[51]

This picture of the secretary general's lack of authority with respect to enlarging peacekeeping operations does not obtain, however, with respect to his or her authority over the forces already assigned to the U.N. and the policies they follow in the field. Or at least it would appear that Boutros-Ghali has prevailed each time a conflict arises between his strategies and those of the U.N.'s battlefield commanders. This factor has already been noted with respect to the operations in Somalia, but even more recently the same pattern surfaced in Bosnia. The French general, Jean Cot, who commands the 26,000 peacekeeping troops in the former Yugoslavia complained publicly that the troops were dangerously exposed because the Security Council failed to match its words with actions—that is, with air strikes that would combat snipers and artillery fire. General Cot said he had twice asked the secretary general for authority to call for air strikes but had been rebuffed. Thus, he said, the peacekeeping forces were like "a goat tethered to a fence." Boutros-Ghali was said to respond to this remark with "outrage and anger," and he insisted to top French officials that General Cot be removed from the post.[52] Shortly thereafter, the *New York Times* reported, "The French Defense Ministry said today that it would recall Gen. Jean Cot ... at the request of Secretary General Boutros Boutros-Ghali."[53]

Conclusion

What does this analysis of the U.N. tell us about the present state of the organization and its future? What does it tell us about the prospects for cooperation on a global scale that would make the world a better, more hospitable place in which to live, with fewer conflicts and a more equitable future? Is it possible that twenty years from now the global community, through the U.N., will still be unable to address head-on atrocities, such as those that have occurred in the former Yugoslavia, and the breakdown of community and continued squalor that presently marks life in Haiti, Somalia, and elsewhere? What light does the discussion shed on whether the realist or the postinternationalist perspective is better suited to generating appropriate answers to these large questions? Is the U.N. likely to continue to be essentially an institution and instrument of the state-centric world? Or does the trendline suggest that has it begun to acquire an autonomy of its own that locates its authority astride the bifurcation that separates the state-centric and multi-centric worlds?

Readers will have to answer these questions for themselves. And, clearly, it will not be easy to do so. The evidence is mixed, causation is extremely difficult to sort out, the world is in turmoil, nothing is static, and the U.N. may well be in a period of dynamic transformation. Yet, although no one ever said the world was an orderly place, that does not mean it is unfathomable. If readers are to come to terms with the global disorder and locate points in the process where some leverage can be exercised on behalf of desirable change, they have no choice but to ponder the questions and use one or the other perspective to develop responses to them. Or, if neither the realist nor the post-internationalist perspective seems to provide satisfactory answers, then readers must self-consciously develop an alternative approach that provides a modicum of coherence to their grasp of an incoherent world.

7
Missiles in Cuba, Protests in Tiananmen Square, and Other Crises

Perhaps no sequence of events is more challenging to one's theoretical perspective than those that fall under the general heading of "crisis." Such situations arise suddenly; they collapse the time frame for decision; they transform nuanced differences into raw clashes of power over crucial values; they move relentlessly toward deadlines; and at some point they may well elude or slip beyond the control of high-level officials. Thus, crises are often described as putting their participants on a seemingly uncompromisable "collision course." The actors differ so intensely over the disputed issues that they feel obligated to press for outcomes that can be neither avoided nor postponed.

These attributes of crises challenge our theories because they unfold so quickly that many of the variables out of which our models are constructed may not appear to be operative, thereby seeming to deprive us of our theoretical perspectives and confounding our grasp of what is transpiring. To be sure, decisionmaking theorists allow for choices made under crisis conditions and thus can readily analyze the key turning points and outcomes of crises. But such theories are concerned primarily with policymaking processes and do not attempt to account for the dynamics of more fundamental societal and systemic variables. The realist and postinternational models, in contrast, are more encompassing. They sweep across longer time spans and they concentrate on the ways in which conflicts derive from underlying forces at work within the competing societies and the larger international systems of which the adversaries are a part. Such models are best suited to explain the patterning of events rather than the specific event, so that normally they do not address particular actions that are taken when time is short and deadlines loom.

What, then, can realist and postinternational analysts do when confronted with crises that evolve quickly and culminate soon thereafter? Do they hold off undertaking interpretations until the more fundamental forces at work can be retrospectively assessed long after the crisis has ended and normal patterns have been restored? Or do they conclude that waiting for the advantages of hindsight suggests their theories are profoundly flawed and that thus they had better cope as best they can by fitting whatever dynamics are manifested by the crisis into their theoretical framework? Do some situations lend themselves more readily to realism while others are more conducive to probing through application of the postinternational model? If the actions and interactions observable in the crisis do not seem to be explicable by their preferred theory, can theorists shift to another model that appears to fit better within the contours of the crisis? Or, given the ability of theories to account for any form behavior may take, are we not so locked into our preferred theory that it is virtually impossible to shift back and forth between models as circumstances warrant and our interests change?

That these questions amount to a serious and vigorous challenge to theorists is readily evident in our conviction that the last question requires an affirmative answer. Yes, virtually at all times we are locked into a particular way of looking at the world. Only through self-deception can an analyst anticipate shifting back and forth among models of world politics in order to explain different types of crises. Fluctuations of this sort are not ordinarily possible. Analysts might well change to another model as their understanding deepens and their existing perspectives seem obsolete. But such shifts tend to be enduring and thus occur rarely rather than repeatedly. Given the thoroughgoing nature of theories as systems of thought—especially their capacity to account for virtually any event or trend that may arise in a situation—normally we do not have reason to look to another model for guidance. Put more emphatically, usually we are locked into the theory with which we are most comfortable. It gives meaning to any and all discrepancies. It infuses order into seemingly disparate developments, highlights the central actors, clarifies their motives, and explains their successes and failures. It accentuates the relationships that matter and anticipates their likely evolution. Thus it is hardly surprising that analysts ordinarily adhere to a single model as they observe, ponder, and interpret the unfolding world scene.

Crises in world politics, in short, are also crises for theorists. At the most basic level crises test the premises, logic, and flexibility of our theories, and the more severe, intense, and abbreviated the crises are, the more stringently do they test our understanding. Hence it is important that the challenge of interpreting crises be addressed by determining how well realism and postinternationalism do in offering meaningful accounts of specific crisis situations. Such is the purpose of this chapter. We shall take on the challenge in three stages, first by inquiring further into the general characteristics of crises that render them theoretically difficult; second, by outlining the turning points of several recent crises; and third, by using these cases to explore the difficulties they pose for realists and postinternationalists.

Crisis Conditions

In addition to shortening the time frame so sharply as to inhibit or (in some cases) prevent the discernment of key underlying variables, crises are distinguished by several other characteristics that hinder the effort of theorists to fit the flow of events into their models. One involves the large degree to which crises revolve around deadlines. The specific day and hour at which the collision course will come to an end may not become clear until a crisis is well along—though sometimes it is set well in advance—but the fact that the actors are bound to collide in the near future is known to all concerned. Why? Because one or the other (or both) of the parties to the crisis has specified that the adversary has to undertake certain actions in the near future, or else remedial and (usually) violent steps will be taken to resolve the situation. Whether it be the removal of missiles from Cuba, the cessation of protest rallies in Tiananmen Square, or the halting of unmanageable flows of refugees—to mention only a few of the more conspicuous demands that have marked modern crises—deadlines for specified actions are set in the immediate future and it only remains to determine whether the challenging adversary will carry through on the threat or the challenged party will comply before the deadline expires. If no deadline is set, or if no remedial actions are specified as having to be taken by a target date—as is the case in a preponderance of the situations on any political agenda—then the parties interact as they must to resolve their differences in due time without recourse to the urgent rhetoric of crisis. But deadlines render situations into tests of will and thereby generate last-minute negotiations or otherwise intensify the unfolding conflict.

Put differently, it is not until a call for a specified action is set in an immediate time frame—or an unexpected flow of events creates an urgent time frame that must be met if untoward outcomes are to be avoided—that officials, publics, journalists, academics, and other interested parties are inclined to attach the word "crisis" to a situation. Consider, for example, the British agreement to turn Hong Kong over to the People's Republic of China on July 1, 1997. In the mid-1990s that date was still felt to be so far off that tensions associated with the takeover had yet to reach crisis proportions, but it is reasonable to anticipate that as the date gets closer and closer, so will the situation be increasingly characterized as one of crisis. No matter that the outcome is predetermined; it will be viewed as a crisis because it will be far from clear how much change the Chinese will impose on Hong Kong and how far the residents of that city will go in accepting or protesting any new policies the Chinese may adopt when they take over. Similarly, although there may have been good reasons to regard the overthrow of a democratically elected president and the subsequent efforts of thousands of Haitian refugees to flee by boat to the United States as being of crisis proportions, the more the situation dragged on across several years without the United States casting its threat to restore President Aristide in a specified time frame through armed invasion, the harder it became to describe the problems posed by that troubled country as a crisis. Once the flow of refugees mounted to the point of severely overcrowding the hastily erected shelters for them, however, the situation quickly escalated. An invasion was projected for the near future through an extensive troop buildup, and President Clinton made a nationwide television appeal for support. As a result, the situation was quickly upgraded to a crisis by leaders, the press, and publics throughout the Western Hemisphere.

It follows that uncertainty is another characteristic of crises. No political situation is free of some degree of uncertainty, of course, but given the immediacy of the time frame within which action must be taken, uncertainty about the outcome of a crisis is especially intense and fully experienced by all concerned. Of course, uncertainty is no stranger to theorists. It is, rather, a pervasive condition with which they must endlessly cope and serves, in effect, to infuse their theorizing with probabilistic forms of reasoning. Knowing that there can be no assurances as to how events will turn out, good theorists have long been accustomed to allowing for uncertainty by founding their hypotheses on likelihoods, on central tendencies from which deviations can be expected to occur.

Most crises are also marked by the adversaries having opposite goals in a situation, with one favoring the status quo and the other eager to alter it. Their conflict may appear to be over land, rights, privileges, procedures, or security. The main gulf that separates them, however, has to do exclusively with change. Are new arrangements with respect to land, rights, privileges, procedures, or security to be welcomed or prevented? Needless to say, the parties start down the collision course when the one seeking to alter the status quo—whether it be missiles in Cuba, freedom of speech in China, or freedom from fear in Haiti, Cuba, and Rwanda—initiates actions on behalf of the desired changes. The actions may or may not be justified, depending on the perspective employed, and they may or may not be recognized as initiating a crisis (since the initiating party does not know whether the adversary will contest or yield to the actions), but the first step on the road to collision is discernible when the status quo is challenged.

Once the first step is taken and a counterreaction evoked, the long-run goals of transforming or preserving the status quo recede into the background and, as noted, the situation becomes a test of wills, a test of which party to the crisis has the greater power to prevail. Indeed, it is axiomatic that there can be no crisis unless efforts to exercise power are involved. The act of implementing a law is not considered a crisis because authority is evoked to achieve compliance. Authority is legitimate power; people accept the application of what might, in other circumstances, be called power because they think they ought to or because they believe the person or agency asking for a given behavior has the right to do so. Nor are the day-to-day decisions of states and other collectivities regarded as exercises in crisis decisionmaking. Again, legitimate authority may be involved or simple bargaining among the players may be at work. But what about situations where a legislative majority adopts a new law that is subsequently implemented by the government? Is not the implementation of the law an exercise of power even though administrative routines of this sort are standard governmental operations and not the first step toward crisis conditions? How, then, to distinguish situations in which the exercise of power can give rise to crises? If the newly enacted law dramatically alters the status quo, why is it not regarded as provoking a crisis?

A useful way of responding to these questions is to differentiate between situations in which the risks and benefits of a particular change are distributed among all (as is the case when laws are adopted by accepted constitutional procedures) and those in which one or more groups perceive an impending and unfair shift in who will bear the new risks and who will enjoy the new benefits (which may give rise to crises).[1] Examples abound. A family may experience a "crisis" when a child or spouse suddenly wants to do things not done before. Business firms often reach a fever pitch during a crisis over leadership. States consider themselves in crises when impending changes seem likely to increase their risks and lessen their benefits in substantial ways. In everyday political life, much can be achieved and many can be "empowered" to take action, but in a crisis the actors are dominated by the sense that an impending loss may lie ahead.

Still another attribute of crises is that they can culminate in calamitous outcomes and often in violence and death. Having become ever more committed to the exercise of power as they move down the collision course on behalf of cherished values, the adversaries can be too committed to back off and end the crisis. Like the game of chicken, one party may veer off and accept defeat by calling for negotiations, but sometimes neither party changes course, with the result that violent conflict will ensue when the deadline is reached.

It follows that if the adversaries in a crisis are institutional structures—such as states, the U.N., corporations, or terrorist organizations—then analysts will be encouraged to focus on decisionmaking processes. At every point along the collision course, not to mention a number of points during the earlier interactions that gave rise to the crisis conditions, the parties to the situation are faced with choices— with having to decide what demands to make, what resources to mobilize, what compromises are feasible, what alternative courses of action are possible, and so on across a multitude of choice points. For those who employ decisionmaking theories, therefore, crises offer marvelous opportunities for testing and revising propositions. And this is especially so when—as happened in the case of the Cuban missile crisis—subsequent years witnessed the publication of memoirs and interviews in which the participants recalled what they did and why they did it.

Crises seem to look solely like decisionmaking problems because they collapse the time in which the key variables interact. In this abbreviated "space," they highlight decisionmaking processes while masking the underlying systemic dynamics that brought about the collision course. Indeed, it is not far-fetched to observe that often crises are seen as emphasizing the salience of choice to the virtual exclusion of everything else. But treating crises as though they were unique and not susceptible to broad theorizing is like saying we should ignore words if punctuation occurs in a sentence. It is the logic of the string of words that demands the punctuation, not the other way around.

In short, it would be surprising if systemic theories like realism or postinternationalism, both of which focus on big structures, large processes, and huge comparisons,[2] drew a blank in their effort to interpret crises. Curiously, however, crises have rarely been thought of in terms of systemic variables. Rather, given the short time frame in which they are conceived, they are usually depicted in terms and logics drawn from psychological theory or bureaucratic politics.[3] The focus of this chapter is thus hardly characteristic of most writing about crises.

The first task is to confront the fact that realist and postinternationalist theories are far more encompassing than those that focus on decision phenomena. Rather than anticipating the behavior of individuals in choice situations, the theories of concern here seek to explain large societal and systemic patterns that subsume the underlying dynamics that narrow and guide the choices open to decisionmakers. What, then, do these broader theoretical perspectives have going for them when crises arise? The answer is provocative: At first glance crises appear to offer very little that facilitates theorizing by realists and postinternationalists, which is why earlier we stressed that crises amount to severe tests for these more systemic approaches.

Good theorists, however, are not prepared to back away from severe tests. Not only are their frameworks abstract and thoroughgoing enough to permit explanation of any development, but their commitments to their theories are also so strong that they are unlikely to abandon them just because, at first glance, only decisional phenomena are discernible or because much seems otherwise unfamiliar. On the contrary, the challenge of severe empirical tests enlivens theorists to stretch their imaginations and clarify theoretical nuances that they had not previously recognized. Consequently, and more important, when they turn to a close inspection of a crisis, they find that appearances can be deceiving, that both the actions and attributes that characterize the crisis—as well as those that are conspicuously absent as the collision course evolves—can be interpreted as indicative of the dynamics on which their theories are founded.

Missiles, Massacres, and Migrants

In order to facilitate comparisons of the capacity of realists and post-internationalists to interpret and explain crises, we turn now to outlining briefly the major stages of several types of collision courses the world has witnessed in recent decades. One focuses on the sudden introduction of missiles into Cuba in 1962, another depicts the crisis that followed the advent of huge protests around Beijing's Tiananmen Square in 1989, and a third portrays the circumstances surrounding the flight of refugees from Rwanda, Haiti, and Cuba in 1994. Taken together, these cases are sufficiently differentiated to serve as good tests for any systemic theorist.

Missiles in Cuba

Following a routine flight over Cuba on October 14, 1962, a U.S. U-2 aircraft with advanced equipment for aerial photography returned with clear pictures that indicated the Soviets were building missile sites on the island of their Communist ally. The pictures disclosed missile launching pads capable of delivering their nuclear loads well beyond the 90 miles that separated Cuba from the U.S. mainland. Whether the United States would have accepted the presence of nuclear missiles in Cuba had the plan to install them been publicly and matter-of-factly announced by Moscow is a matter of some dispute, but having come upon the pending installation under conditions of secrecy and surprise, U.S. officials found the presence of the launching pads to be clearly unacceptable from the moment of their discovery.

Within forty-eight hours after they were taken, the photographs were on the desk of President John F. Kennedy, who immediately recognized that the interests of the United States were such that not only would the erection of the launching sites have to be halted, but indeed that they would have to be dismantled and removed from Cuba at once. To allow them to be in place for any length of time would not only amount to permitting a dangerous threat but would also accord the missiles a legitimacy in Soviet and Cuban eyes that would heighten their resistance to removing them. In other words, time was of the essence; a crisis had suddenly evolved that, for the next thirteen days, occupied center stage in international affairs as the world's most dangerous nuclear confrontation, one that might well have collapsed into a nuclear holocaust.

One of the major turning points of the Cold War, what is called the "Cuban missile crisis" in the United States, the "Caribbean crisis" in the former Soviet Union, and the "October crisis" in Cuba has become the subject of a vast literature. Virtually every minute of the thirteen days has been recounted and analyzed by those who participated in the crisis[4] as well as by numerous journalists and academics.[5] Indeed, more than two decades later, conferences of the surviving U.S., Soviet, and Cuban participants were held as part of a continuing effort to comprehend how the world could come so dangerously close to destroying itself.[6] The following paragraphs summarize this literature to tell briefly the story of the Cuban missile crisis.

The crisis had its origins some months earlier when the Soviet leader, Nikita Khrushchev, had the idea of deploying the missiles while planning for a trip to Bulgaria, where he made several speeches in May 1962 strongly complaining about the presence of U.S. missile sites close to his country's borders in Turkey. In addition to having a desire to redress the huge imbalance with the United States in deliverable strategic nuclear weapons, the Soviets were also motivated to install the missiles in Cuba by a perceived—and understandable[7]—need to prevent a U.S. invasion of the island that would have brought an end to the Cuban revolution and the successful expansion of Communist influence into the Western Hemisphere. Although judged to be less important, a third motive for the Soviet action involved national pride and prestige, the aspiration not to be outdone as a superpower by having a lesser nuclear capability.

The subsequent accounts of Soviet and Cuban decisionmaking during the summer of 1962 indicate that various officials and agencies in the two countries differed over the mix of reasons for installing the missiles,[8] but no traces of those differences surfaced publicly during the planning of the installation. Indeed, implementation of the plan was carried out under such strict conditions of secrecy that the 40,000 Soviet troops who were sent by ship to install, guard, and operate the missile sites thought they were being assigned to duties in a cold clime and "reportedly brought with them full winter gear, and were only told where they were going after their ships had passed the Strait of Gibraltar."[9]

This is not to say, however, that the decisionmaking process through which the Soviet and Cuban officials planned the installation of missiles was marked by a high degree of rational calculation. They did manage to conduct their deliberations in secret and to transport the men and materials necessary to build and operate the missile sites without being detected, although they erred in failing to camouflage the sites as the launching pads neared completion. But during the intense negotiations as the crisis reached a climax, there were a number of indications that various officials and agencies in the Soviet policymaking process interpreted the purposes of the project differently and that, consequently, the operation was not shaped by rigorous debate or well-thought-out ramifications. Nor did the retrospective discussions decades later provide any "reason for revising the common wisdom that the venture was, in important respects, ill-conceived and subject to insufficient critical examination."[10]

A plenitude of data suggests that U.S. officials proceeded with considerable caution and much deliberation. Although faced with little time in which to decide how to respond to the evidence of missile sites being erected 90 miles off the coast of Florida, President Kennedy did not act immediately. Instead he turned to his closest advisers, an ad hoc group of some fourteen officials—later formalized as the Executive Committee of the National Security Council (or ExCom for short)—who met almost continuously for six days and proceeded systematically to frame, ponder, amend, reject, and revise a variety of alternative proposals for counteraction to bring about the dismantling of the launching pads and the removal of the missiles from Cuba. Illustrative of the many efforts to maximize rationality was a self-conscious decision for President Kennedy not to attend all the ExCom meetings so that its deliberations would not be unduly influenced by the aura of the presidency.[11]

Even as it struggled with the pros and cons of one or another strategy, however, the ExCom was extremely cautious in calling upon policymaking agencies for information and analysis. So as to increase the chances of successfully implementing their eventual course of action, all concerned were committed to secrecy, it being reasoned that in this way the United States would have an advantage when the situation became public knowledge. So secret were the committee's deliberations, in fact, that at one point President Kennedy went ahead with a previously announced political trip to Chicago in order not to tip his hand to the Soviets (shortly after he arrived, it was announced that he had a cold and was returning to Washington). Similarly, when Soviet Foreign Minister Andrei Gromyko paid a visit to the White House on October 18, Kennedy did not ask about the possibility of missiles being installed in Cuba and Gromyko made no mention of the subject, apparently "to the relief of both" men.[12]

Nearly a week passed while the ExCom agonizingly framed, pondered, revised, and chose among six possible courses of action: (1) do nothing, (2) pursue diplomatic pressures, (3) secretly approach Castro, (4) invade, (5) conduct a surgical air strike, and (6) establish a naval blockade in which any ships entering Cuban waters would be boarded and searched, with those carrying missiles being prevented from unloading their cargo. In the end it was decided to pursue the blockade option on the grounds that the first three plans would not achieve a removal of the missiles and that the fourth and fifth could be employed if the blockade failed and the situation escalated to a more dangerous level of confrontation.[13]

The intensive, round-the-clock processes of decisionmaking culminated at 7:00 P.M. eastern standard time on October 22, at which point President Kennedy went on national television to inform the American people that the Soviets were installing missiles in Cuba and that the United States was demanding their removal and imposing a naval blockade on all offensive weapons destined for the island as of 10:00 A.M. on October 24. Newly available evidence suggests that Khrushchev was angered by Kennedy's speech and ordered acceleration of the building of the missile sites. Even more important, he ordered Soviet ships to ignore the naval quarantine, with the result that the next two days were mired in stalemate as neither side publicly altered its position. At the same time, neither side provoked a confrontation, and there is some evidence that sixteen of the eighteen ships sailing toward Cuba turned back during the night of October 23. The other two ships, however, continued toward Cuba with submarine support and stopped just outside the quarantine area at 10:25 A.M. on October 24.

The stalemate began to unravel on October 26. There is some uncertainty as to exactly how the ensuing sequence of events started—whether it began with a letter that Khrushchev sent to Kennedy or with a luncheon conversation between a Soviet embassy official and an ABC State Department correspondent—but that evening Khrushchev's letter arrived and it "clearly evinced exhaustion and anxiety. His tone of somber realism convinced many in the ExComm that Khrushchev was looking for a peaceful way out of the crisis."[14] Substantively, the letter contained a vague allusion to the possibility of resolving the crisis by trading the dismantling and removal of the missiles for a U.S. pledge not to invade Cuba, but the allusion was enough for Secretary of State Dean Rusk to remark that when the adversaries were "eyeball to eyeball, they blinked first."[15]

The next day, October 27, a second, much tougher letter from Khrushchev was broadcast by Radio Moscow before Kennedy could answer the first letter. In it Khrushchev demanded that the United States remove its missiles from Turkey in exchange for the removal of Soviet missiles from Cuba. This quick reversal surprised and confused some ExCom members. In part, the confusion stemmed from the fact that in the late stages of the crisis Kennedy took the matter out of the ExCom's hands and worked with a much smaller group of advisers, especially his brother Robert, the attorney general. During the revisit to the crisis several decades later by the surviving participants, it came out that late on the previous evening, October 26, Robert Kennedy had met secretly with Soviet Ambassador Anatoly Dobrynin, who raised the idea of a Turkish-Cuban trade. Robert Kennedy left the room and called the president, who indicated a readiness to discuss the idea further. Dobrynin informed his government at once, and shortly thereafter Khrushchev demanded the missile trade.

But for a while the crisis appeared to worsen on October 27 when a U.S. U-2 reconnaissance plane was downed by a surface-to-air (SAM) missile over Cuba. Since members of ExCom presumed that Khrushchev was too close to a conclusion of the crisis to risk its escalation by ordering the shoot-down, their reaction was more one of restraint than panic. It seems likely, however, that Khrushchev was shaken by the shoot-down since he presumed that it had been initiated by his own personnel in Cuba against his orders, thus indicating that he was losing control over the situation. And such a conclusion was justified inasmuch as it was later determined that the shoot-down resulted from an unauthorized order given by two Soviet generals.[16] Yet, at the time, the situation seemed very dire indeed. As one ExCom member re-called, "Our little group, seated around the cabinet table in continuous session that Saturday, felt nuclear war to be closer on that day than at any time in the nuclear age. If the Soviet ship continued coming, if the SAMs continued firing, if the missile crews continued working and if Khrushchev continued insisting on concessions with a gun at our head, then—we all believed—the Soviets must want a war and war would be unavoidable."[17]

In what is often viewed as a key to ending the crisis, on Saturday af-ternoon, October 28, President Kennedy ignored Khrushchev's second letter and instead answered the first letter with an offer to pledge that, in exchange for a withdrawal of the missiles from the island, the United States would not invade Cuba. Kennedy did not include an agreement to remove missiles from Turkey, at least partly out of con-cern for the domestic political consequences of publicly acknowledg-ing a missile trade; but several decades later those revisiting the crisis turned up evidence that the withdrawal of missiles from Turkey in the spring of 1963 was probably the result of a private deal struck along these lines. In any event, although the exact reasons why Khrushchev accepted Kennedy's public terms in a letter on October 28 remain ob-scure,[18] the acceptance brought the crisis to an end.

Protests in Tiananmen Square

For the Chinese people and innumerable foreign tourists alike, all roads converge on Tiananmen Square. Surrounded by historic build-ings and featuring many historic monuments, the square is located in the center of the 4,000-year-old nation's capital and spreads out across more than 100 acres. As the symbolic heart of China, not to mention the world's largest public quadrangle, the square in Beijing has been the scene of royal pageants, triumphant declarations of revolutionary success, popular upheavals, and military crackdowns. In the spring of 1989 it became the focus of a major crisis.

If the inception of a crisis is defined by the setting of a deadline, the one that culminated in Tiananmen Square began on May 20, when the top Chinese leadership announced that Beijing was to be placed under martial law: Journalists were forbidden from entering the zone of the city covered by the law, all public protests were banned, and troops were authorized to handle matters "forcefully." Operationally, the new law pertained especially to clearing Tiananmen Square of fasting stu-

dents and huge crowds of supporters from all segments of Chinese society. Two weeks later, during the night of June 3–4, the crisis came to
an end as the square was emptied by military forces that left behind
blood-splattered pavements, bullet-pocked buildings, burning vehicles, and the stench of human waste and death.

But if a crisis is bounded by the date when the opposing forces enter
onto a collision course, the one that reached a climax on June 4 began
much earlier. In retrospect, at least, the outlines of a collision were discernible on April 15 when the death of Hu Yaobang, the former general
secretary of the Chinese Communist Party, gave rise to spontaneous
outpourings of grief tinged with protests over continued repression by
the party. Some might even contend that the Chinese had already
started down the path to crisis at the time of the visits of two foreign
dignitaries—that of newly elected U.S. President George Bush in late
February 1989 and that of the recently elected president of the Soviet
Union, Mikhail Gorbachev, from May 15 to 18. The Bush visit can be
viewed as occurring during an early stage of the collision course: When
the president invited China's leading dissident, astrophysicist Fang
Lizhi, to a farewell banquet at the Great Wall Hotel in Beijing, the Chinese authorities prevented him from attending. As a result, he disap-
peared for several hours and then arrived at the Shangri-La Hotel
where, during the early hours of the morning, he was greeted by the
foreign press and held a news conference described as crossing

> a symbolic line in the coming-of-age of Chinese political dissidence. Outside
> lay the world of the party, with its secrecy, censorship, intimidation, and
> control. Inside lay a free-for-all of camera-wielding photographers, TV
> crews, anchormen, and reporters all clamoring to scoop the unexpurgated
> story of Fang's disappearance. It was the first time since the founding of the
> People's Republic that a Chinese political dissident in Beijing was being
> thrown together with so many foreign journalists for an uncensored press
> conference. It was, in short, the Chinese government's worst nightmare.[19]

But the nightmare grew worse in subsequent months and reached one
of its darkest moments when a long-scheduled visit of President
Gorbachev, anticipated by China's paramount leader as a significant
reconciliation, a watershed in Chinese diplomatic history, had to be re-
scheduled through backdoors to avoid the embarrassment of protesting publics.

Although Hu's death led to a worsening of the party's nightmare, for a while it precipitated a festive atmosphere in Beijing. And the more students and workers were able to use Hu's death as a basis for voicing their discontent over the repressiveness of Chinese politics without being curbed by the regime, the more they were emboldened to enlarge their demands and the more euphoric their seemingly uncontested protests became. On April 17, only two days after the announcement of Hu's death, thousands of students from different Beijing campuses gathered in the square to lay a funeral wreath at the base of the Monument to the Martyrs of the People, and the next day the number of people in the square swelled to more than 20,000. On the night of April 21, more than 100,000 gathered in the square before it was closed off for Hu's official funeral the next day. And each day the burgeoning crowds were accompanied by increasingly direct banners and wall posters that gave concrete expression to the complaints and aspirations of the still fledgling and inchoate movement.

A major reason these protests were not contested was that the Chinese leadership was divided between a hard faction that argued for harsh measures and a more lenient faction that, like Hu Yaobang before them, believed that China's future was best assured by opening a dialogue with the students. The hard-liners felt that it was possible to open up the Chinese economy to market forces without making comparable concessions in the political realm, whereas the more lenient faction argued on behalf of political freedoms commensurate with those that had been adopted in the economic realm. For several weeks this split in the leadership's ranks paralyzed its ability either to end or to accommodate the growing protests. Petitions submitted by the students calling for a dialogue and a redress of grievances went unanswered, and an April 26 editorial in the *People's Daily*, drawn almost verbatim from a speech by the paramount leader, Deng Xiaoping, attacked the students and threatened harsh measures to end their upheaval. In response to the editorial, the students began to evolve organizations of their own, which, the next day, gave rise to marches toward the square from several universities. The crowds numbered in the hundreds of thousands and were so large as to engulf the lines of unarmed police charged with stopping the marches.

In addition to facing sharp divisions within his own ranks, Deng was inhibited from taking harsher measures to quell the growing upheaval by two upcoming dates, May 4, the seventieth anniversary of the May

Fourth Movement initiated after a military crackdown on students in 1919, and May 15, the date Gorbachev was to arrive to normalize relations between the Soviet Union and China after decades of adversarial hostility. Thus it was that Deng allowed low-level contacts with the students on April 29 and 30 even as he also ordered the 38th Army Group into positions surrounding Beijing. And thus it was, too, that the head of the moderate faction of the leadership, Zhao Ziyang, made conciliatory speeches intended to garner support among the students. As a consequence, the division within the leadership hardened and the students interpreted Zhao's moderate gestures as a reason to hold firm for concrete forms of acquiescence to their demands.

By May 13 the protests had both expanded and contracted. Journalists and other professionals were observed participating in marches on May 4 and May 9, but at the same time things quieted down as a number of weary students became preoccupied with final exams and graduation. Fearful that the student movement might come apart, some of its leaders decided to sustain the momentum by calling for a hunger strike. Some 400 students signed up to participate in the fast, and on May 13 they bedded down in Tiananmen Square, surrounded themselves with banners proclaiming a readiness to die for democracy in China, and then held a press conference for hundreds of reporters, many of them from abroad.

Through word of mouth and hand-recorded accounts of BBC and Voice of America shortwave broadcasts, news of the hunger strike spread quickly throughout Beijing and, indeed, around the world. On May 15, the day of Gorbachev's arrival, ordinary citizens joined the students and professionals in the square and swelled the crowd to close to a million persons from every stratum of Chinese life. And these ranks were further enlarged by television anchors from the West and hundreds of other foreign journalists (along with their colleagues who operated the cameras and microphones) who arrived to cover the Gorbachev visit but who ended up more preoccupied with the hunger strike and the question of whether it would lead to deaths. As a result,

the fast soon became the best-covered and most eagerly watched political event in the history of the People's Republic. What made the presence of the augmented foreign press corps so catalytic was that this time TV producers were instantly able to beam images of students defying their Communist government around the world via satellite uplink dishes that the Chinese government had improvidently approved for the Sino-Soviet summit. And so just when the Party found itself most in need of controlling the foreign press, it was unable to staunch the hemorrhage of images that were being transmitted abroad and creating a groundswell of foreign support for the students.[20]

On May 17 the crowd grew even larger, reaching a point where it was called the "largest and most diverse urban protest demonstration in Chinese history."[21] A more elaborate account of the scale of the daily demonstrations was offered by a first-hand observer who described them as

> unlike anything I've ever seen before. No American student demonstration or mass civil-rights actions can begin to compare with [them]. From [Tiananmen Square] "People Power" ... has radiated out to control almost every Beijing intersection and, at last report, streets in forty other Chinese cities as well. This youth rebellion may not be able to hold out much longer, but ... without weapons, without communications other than *xiaodao xiaoxi*, or grapevine, without transportation other than bicycles, and trucks borrowed from farmers and work units, without even any agreement on what they were demonstrating for—except the right to demonstrate—the students and those protecting them are blocking a modern, well-equipped army. ... The sight of [Tiananmen Square] covered by more than a million young people, most of them not angry but, rather, good-naturedly eager to match their collective strength against the limits of state power ... is, quite simply, the most awesome thing I have ever seen.[22]

On May 18 Gorbachev left for home and the Chinese leadership, following a tumultuous Politburo meeting, decided to declare and impose martial law on Beijing. As troops stationed in the suburbs began to move toward the center of Beijing, so did more residents of the city from all walks of life move into the streets. It was estimated that by the morning of May 20 they numbered in excess of 2 million, many of whom erected street barriers out of anything they could find and other thousands of whom found their way to the square as a gesture of psychological support for the students.

The first columns of troops had not been equipped with live ammunition and, as a result, their progress was slow; eventually they came to a halt as they and their vehicles were engulfed by huge throngs of citizens. When the citizens began to realize that their huge numbers had successfully stopped the military advance, many of them began to talk sympathetically with the troops, offering them food and cigarettes.

The next ten days amounted to an uneasy calm before the storm as both sides rethought their strategy, appealed to the other to abandon the struggle or suffer the consequences, and otherwise prepared for a showdown. For the military this lull provided an opportunity to bring up reinforcements and infiltrate nonuniformed soldiers into the city's key crossroads. For the students this period was marked by factional arguments over whether to continue occupation of the square or to declare a victory and abandon it. Morale began to slip as increasing numbers of students returned to their campuses either out of fear or because they had exams. On May 30, however, the protest movement was rejuvenated by the arrival of a foam-and-plaster white monument that resembled the Statue of Liberty. It stood 37 feet high when assembled directly in front of Tiananmen Gate. This new symbol of the protest movement was televised around the world and seemed to many people everywhere to represent the triumph of democracy in China.

The uneasy calm gave way to heightened tensions as both sides used loudspeakers to rally their supporters, often suggesting they might have to give up their lives for their cause. During the night of June 3–4, armed columns of troops and tanks opened fire on those who stood in their path to Tiananmen Square. The night turned bloody, and scenes of defenseless civilians being run down and over by heavily armed soldiers were common. There are a variety of estimates of the number of dead and wounded, with the figures running from the hundreds to the thousands, but there are few disputes over the conclusion that for all practical purposes, after that night public protests in Tiananmen Square were over. From June 4, 1989, to the present, the party has maintained full control insofar as the rights of free speech and assembly are concerned. It has made token gestures by releasing and exiling some dissidents, but its resistance to world pressures to accompany economic liberalization with political freedom continues to be thoroughgoing.

The costs of this resistance for China have not been trivial. Quite aside from the consequences for public morale and cohesion within the country—and these are virtually impossible to estimate—the external repercussions of the crackdown in Tiananmen Square were considerable. The good feelings toward the Chinese that had cumulated abroad in the decade subsequent to Mao's death and with the opening up of the Chinese economy quickly collapsed. Tourism fell off. Foreign investors became wary. Human rights became ever more salient as a global issue. A picture of a lone Chinese man holding up a column of tanks in Beijing was widely reproduced and for many people became symbolic of the inequities and horror of the crisis in Tiananmen Square. The editors of a French journal, *Actuel,* were so upset by the massacre of students that they compiled a mock edition of the *People's Daily* with all the stories they were certain the Chinese regime would not want the people to read. They then faxed the mock edition to every fax machine in China.[23]

In short, the televised story of Tiananmen Square created, so to speak, a crisis for the multi-centric world and, indeed, for some of the states in the state-centric world. In the United States, for instance, the handling of relations with China became a major political issue that divided the Congress, the political parties, and the electorate. In a sense, therefore, as an international event the crisis in Tiananmen Square did not end with the crackdown on June 4, 1989, but continued for quite some time, and it still rankles many people in various parts of the world. Every subsequent June 4 the Chinese government has seen fit to take special precautions and, in effect, to close Tiananmen Square on that day.

Refugee Flights from Rwanda, Haiti, and Cuba

During the summer of 1994 three widely separated sequences of events—each with its own roots and yet in some important respects similar to the others—escalated into crisis proportions. In Rwanda, Haiti, and Cuba thousands upon thousands of citizens felt compelled to flee their homelands and seek refuge in safer havens. In all three cases the numbers of refugees were so extensive—in Rwanda the figure eventually exceeded 1 million—that crisis conditions evolved not only for those fleeing but also for the agencies and countries that sought to cope with the tragedies to which such instantaneous and massive migrations give rise. Given the complexity of world politics in the present era, it is perhaps not surprising that the three crises became, in curious and circuitous ways, inextricably linked to each other—for the world and the U.N., by the profound humanitarian questions they commonly posed; and, for the United States, by the proximity of its shores (and thus its politics) to both Haiti and Cuba.

The Cuban missile crisis and the Tiananmen Square massacre were marked by deadlines that locked the antagonists into a collision course. The same criterion cannot readily be used with respect to crises induced by spontaneous and massive migrations. Each of the three crises analyzed here was provoked by a specific stimulus—in the Rwandan case, by a major turn in a four-year-old civil war; in Haiti, by the expulsion of U.N. and OAS human rights observers; and in Cuba, by a decision of the country's leader, Fidel Castro, to let disgruntled citizens leave the island on rickety rafts—but none of these stimuli involved an immediate or obvious deadline. Rather, each triggered an enormous flow of humanity that precipitated a sense of urgency that virtually demanded innovative responses. In effect, deadlines were set by the sudden surge in the macro sum of myriad micro actions, by figures depicting huge movements of people that could not be ignored. The onset of such crises and their potential for powerful political repercussions can be readily inferred from the graphic presentation of one of the refugee flows shown in Figure 7.1.

In all crises, the specific triggering decision or event springs in itself from a series of prior developments that infuse a logic into the actions of those who precipitate and sustain the crisis. In the case of Rwanda, the outlines of a collision course became evident after a suspicious plane crash in April killed the country's president, a member of the majority Hutu tribe. This event led to a sharp escalation of a four-year-old civil war between his tribe and its longtime rivals, the minority Tutsi tribe. Hutu extremists in the government used the plane crash as an excuse to provoke and launch large-scale killings of Tutsis throughout the country. Subsequently, the Tutsi-led Rwandan Patriotic Front turned the tide in the civil war and routed the Rwandan army. As rebel offensives moved across the country, hundreds of thousands of Hutus, along with their government, fled out of fear that the Tutsis would seek revenge for the large numbers of Tutsis who had been massacred by Hutu mobs in what was widely called a genocidal campaign.

By July 15 the flight of the Hutus crossing the Rwandan border into Zaire had reached the rate of at least 2,000 persons per hour, with some estimates ranging to 10,000 an hour.[24] At that time the International Red Cross was the only organization in Zaire with food for refugees, and it had only enough for 150,000 people. The number of fleeing Hutus began to exceed 0.5 million, and in the several days that followed the figure surpassed 1.2 million as international relief agencies

TALLY

Fleeing Cuba

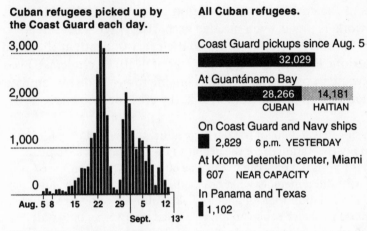

Cuban refugees picked up by the Coast Guard each day.

All Cuban refugees.

Coast Guard pickups since Aug. 5

32,029

At Guantánamo Bay

28,266   14,181
CUBAN   HAITIAN

On Coast Guard and Navy ships

2,829   6 p.m. YESTERDAY

At Krome detention center, Miami

607   NEAR CAPACITY

In Panama and Texas

1,102

*134 as of 6 p.m. Eastern time.

Sources: Immigration and Naturalization Service; United States Coast Guard.

FIGURE 7.1   Fleeing Cuban Refugees Picked Up by the U.S. Coast Guard, August 1–September 13, 1994

Source: Vernon Silver, "Some Cubans Are Released from Detention in Florida," *New York Times*, September 14, 1994, p. A6. Copyright © 1994 by The New York Times Company. Reprinted by permission.

pleaded with the Tutsi rebels to call a cease-fire in the hope that such an action would also halt the flood of refugees. Hoping to catch the government officials and militias who had conducted the genocidal campaign against their people, the rebel Patriotic Front did not announce a cease-fire until July 18. On July 19 the Tutsi-dominated victors installed a new government of reconciliation, named a moderate Hutu as president and prime minister, and pledged to protect all Rwandans except those that had participated in the earlier massacre of Tutsis.

In the meantime, the U.N. undertook to mobilize a global relief effort for the refugees. The United States began sending relief flights into Zaire carrying food, oil, and shelters. Yet, the crisis worsened. An estimated 2.4 million fled Rwanda by July 21, and the crowded, makeshift refugee camps in Zaire were soon overwhelmed by a cholera epidemic. Within two weeks refugees were dying at the rate of 1,800 a day. Bodies began piling up by roadsides as the death rate exceeded the capacity of relief officials to dig mass graves. Although it received permission to burn the corpses, the U.N. was reluctant to do so because such a procedure would violate Rwandan religious and cultural customs.

To end the crisis, the new coalition government, the U.N., and the relief workers urged, even pleaded with, the refugees in Zaire to return home. But many refused to move, their fear of death at the hands of the Patriotic Front exceeding their fear of death by cholera.[25] Even the new Rwandan prime minister was unable to persuade his family to return. From his point of view, in fact, the crisis had no end:

> I am sincerely fed up for not having a future for my children, for the people from my generation or for the people of the generations to come. ... A child who is 7 years old now can live maybe 60 years. When they are 67 years old, they will still remember what has happened in this country. Just imagine a whole generation that for about a half century is going to remember this. What do we do for people to forget? I think that we can only start by teaching children that we are one people.[26]

Although it is analytically confounding to conceive of a crisis lasting a half century, the exact point at which the Rwandan situation returned to "normal" is not easily fixed. Possibly August 31, 1994, is an appropriate date, since that is when the new Rwandan government was allowed to have its delegate take his seat at the United Nations even as the refugees began to straggle home; or perhaps September 6 might be considered the turning point, as that is when the man who led the rebel Patriotic Front to victory publicly vowed that Rwanda would become a multiparty democracy in which ethnic origins would be irrelevant, an announcement that appeared to one journalist to be consistent with a pattern in which "Rwanda does not have the feel of a military dictatorship."[27]

The developments that preceded the 1994 Haitian crisis can be traced back to the 1991 election of Father Jean-Bertrand Aristide as president of the country. Drawing on the support of the nation's poor (who make up 90 percent of the population and earn an average of about $120 a year), Aristide was the first person to break the small elite's stranglehold on Haitian politics by rising to the presidency. He received 67 percent of the vote in what was probably the country's first free and fair election. But the breakthrough was short-lived: Deeply loathed by the elite, seven months later, on September 30, 1991, Aristide was overthrown by a military coup and fled to the United States. He was replaced with a repressive military regime led by Lieutenant General Raoul Cedras that, for three years, refused to restore Aristide to power even as it killed off many of his supporters. In July 1993 Cedras signed a carefully negotiated agreement stipulating that he would step down by October 15, 1993, when Father Aristide would return to the presidency. But the so-called Governors Island agreement had no implementing clauses and, in effect, allowed Cedras to ignore its timetable and remain in power. When the United States then sent a warship to Haiti to enforce the agreement, the dock was crowded with threatening thugs who, in effect, scared the warship into steaming away. The incident lowered the White House's credibility to the point where it was widely believed that President Clinton would not move beyond economic punishment to the use of force. Encouraged by the weakness he perceived in Washington, Cedras subsequently refused to be cowed by U.S. threats. At the same time, however, his regime placated the outside world by admitting a ninety-two-member mission of U.N. observers to monitor human rights and arranging for a new civilian president, Emile Jonaissant, an eighty-one-year-old former judge and member of the conservative elite, to take office. Despite these formalities, however, the military retained control of Haiti through a brutal campaign of violence and murder that decimated Aristide's supporters (a U.N. report in June 1994 said that as many as fifty people were killed per month).

In the spring of 1994 the brutality of events in Haiti began to roil U.S. politics, with charges of racism leveled against President Clinton for his seeming indifference to trends on the island. A twenty-seven-day hunger strike by a black activitist, Randall Robinson, on behalf of Haiti contributed to a renewed involvement in Haitian issues by the Clinton administration. The U.N. was persuaded to impose a total trade and travel embargo on Haiti, and on June 15, 1994, the situation approached a crisis stage when Washington adopted a policy of offering refugees a chance to resettle permanently in the United States. In the next several weeks, more than 19,000 Haitians were plucked from flimsy boats by the U.S. Coast Guard, a number so large that the United States reversed its policy again and offered fleeing Haitians temporary refuge in other countries, taking them in the interim to the U.S. naval base at Guantánamo Bay in Cuba. At the same time, anxious to end the crisis and restore Father Aristide to the presidency, the United States located 2,000 Marines off Haiti's shores. On July 11, the army-backed Haitian government responded by ordering the immediate expulsion of the U.N. and OAS human rights monitors. This defiance of the international community intensified the crisis as the U.N. and several countries in the Western Hemisphere indicated a readiness to participate in multilateral efforts to topple the military regime.

As the crisis deepened during the summer of 1994, the Clinton administration became ever readier to implement its conviction that the Haitian election had been democratic, that the military had seized power illegally, and that nothing short of the withdrawal of General Cedras and other leaders and the return of Father Aristide was acceptable. Events moved quickly. The economic sanctions against Haiti were strengthened and leaks along Haiti's 165-mile border with the Dominican Republic were plugged. The U.N. authorized the United States to lead an invasion of Haiti if the end of the repressive regime could not otherwise be achieved. Officials talked openly of invading the island even as they avoided setting a specific deadline for Cedras and his regime to step down and allow Aristide to take over. Military exercises were held. Other countries in the Caribbean and South America were asked to join an invasion force, and thirteen agreed to do so.

Even as preparations for a military showdown continued to mount, however, the United States put off taking the final steps that would launch an invasion. The Clinton administration was reported to be split over whether to set a deadline for carrying out the invasion,[28] and on August 28, the administration announced that the Cuban refugee crisis necessitated postponing actions directed at Haiti. Since opposition to an invasion was considerable in the United States,[29] it seemed questionable whether an invasion would be undertaken before the November elections. In fact, however, on August 26 President Clinton approved an invasion plan that had been drawn up by the Pentagon. It called for an invasion around September 18, though the exact date was a closely held secret. White House Chief of Staff Leon E. Panetta was quoted simply as saying, "I can assure you that we are moving to increase the pressure,"[30] a statement that was reinforced with considerable publicity about the military build-up. Although the Cedras junta continued to doubt whether U.S. forces were headed toward the island, no one expressed such doubts in the United States. To the American public, an invasion seemed imminent, and members of Congress, the press, and opinion polls increasingly opposed such an action. Polls, in fact, showed that two-thirds of the public opposed an invasion. Ultimately, Congress scheduled a vote for September 19 that would require the administration to obtain its approval before an invasion could be launched. To head off criticism, President Clinton made a nationwide address at 9:00 P.M. September 16 in which he spoke of the need to restore democracy and human rights to Haiti as well as to curb the flow of refugees throughout the Americas; he referred to the members of the Haitian junta as "thugs" and told them, "Leave now, or we will force you from power."

Within minutes after delivering his speech, the president made a last ditch effort to get the junta to back down by calling upon former President Jimmy Carter, retired general Colin L. Powell, and Senator Sam Nunn to go to Haiti and try to make a deal without offering to stop or delay the invasion. The three distinguished emissaries took a U.S. Air Force jet to Haiti early on the morning of September 17 and for the next day and a half engaged in nonstop efforts to resolve the crisis. But the junta initially refused to step down, and as the bargaining moved into the early evening of September 18 President Clinton became agitated, knowing that the first planeloads of paratroopers would soon take off for Haiti and that his three emissaries might thus get caught up in a war. By phone Carter begged for more time, but Clinton would not give it, responding, "We've been friends for a long time, but I'm going to have to order you out of there in 30 more minutes. You've got to get out."[31]

With little time left, it was the mediation of President Jonaissant, who had been installed by the military but who at that moment insisted, "We'll have peace, not war," that led to a hastily drawn agreement in which the junta agreed to allow U.S. forces to enter Haiti as friendly occupiers. The military leaders also agreed to step down by October 15 and allow Aristide to resume his presidency. In return, the United States agreed to institute an amnesty for all those who had participated in human rights abuses, to end the economic sanctions, and not to insist that the junta leave Haiti after it stepped down. The next morning, twelve hours after the Carter team left Haiti, U.S. troops landed at the same airport and began the task of bringing stability and democracy to that troubled country. Difficulties immediately ensued, but for all practical purposes the crisis had reached, as a *New York Times* editorial put it, a "negotiated end—or intermission."[32]

As for the Cuban refugee crisis, it was rooted in long-standing ani-
mosities between Cuba and the United States that began with the revolution that brought Fidel Castro to power in 1959. The more immediate sources of the situation in the summer of 1994 can be traced to the
collapse of the Cold War and the Soviet Union several years earlier, developments that deprived Cuba of crucial economic aid on the scale of
$1 million a day, a subsidy it had received for decades. The end of the
Cold War thus precipitated a steep economic decline in Cuba to accompany the political repression that has long marked Cuban life. In
the middle of August 1994, Castro tapped into the unrest resulting
from these conditions by calling off the coastal patrols that had
guarded the shore to prevent Cubans from fleeing by sea—a decision
he later defended by saying, "There's no reason why the Cuban authorities should guard the border of the United States."[33] This policy
reversal brought on crisis conditions in the form of a sudden and substantial spurt of disgruntled Cubans fleeing on fragile rafts. As indicated in Figure 7.1, the number of refugees quickly exceeded more
than 3,000 a day (not counting several days of bad weather), and this
number only began to tail off as hasty diplomatic efforts reached a climax and indicated that the crisis would be resolved. The numbers in
Figure 7.1 represent those who were picked up by the U.S. Coast Guard
and do not include the many who never made it and drowned.

There may have been several calculations behind Castro's decision
to let his people flee. Perhaps he wanted to embarrass the United
States. Probably he was eager to facilitate the departure of Cuban dissidents (as he had done once before in 1980). And in all likelihood he
sought to force negotiations with the United States that might alter its
immigration policies and, most important, lift its thirty-year economic embargo of Cuba. Whatever the combination of reasons, however, the action was effective as the aggregation of micro decisions led
to a flood of refugees and, on August 21, to President Clinton reversing
a twenty-eight-year-old U.S. policy of granting political asylum to
nearly all Cuban refugees, a reversal that was seen by U.S. officials as
turning the tables on Castro even as it also pleased Floridians and Cu-
ban-Americans (whose votes were considered crucial in upcoming
elections). Rejecting a Castro proposal for negotiations, Clinton announced that henceforth refugees from Cuba would be held in detention until democratic reforms were adopted in Cuba. In addition, the

United States instituted punitive measures against Cuba that involved new restrictions on travel and cash transfers.

The reversal of U.S. policy was instantly controversial. Members of Congress warned that the plan would backfire, and the Cuban-American community in Miami mobilized to contest any negotiations that would alter the economic embargo. The flow of refugees continued, further clogging the Guantánamo base where they were taken to be detained along with rescued Haitians. Toward the end of August the refugee population on the base had grown to nearly 30,000 Cubans and Haitians who were housed in separate tent cities that the U.S. commandant of the refugee operation, Brigadier General Michael J. Williams, described as "a mess. ... You can't help feeling sorry for these people."[34]

In short, the crisis could not continue and, indeed, it was not long before an ending came into view. On August 29 the United States proposed negotiations with Cuba that would lower legal barriers to Cuban migrants in exchange for the reimposition of Cuban controls over illegal migration. At first Cuba insisted that a lifting of the embargo be included in the agreement, but the United States refused to discuss the matter and strengthened its hand by doubling Guantánamo's capacity to house refugees and by pressing nearby countries to accept up to 15,000 Cubans each. Embarrassed by the continuing flight of his people, Castro agreed on September 9 to cut off the flood of refugees in exchange for a U.S. promise to grant entry visas to at least 20,000 Cubans per year. Accordingly, crisis conditions ground to a halt, though it could hardly be said that the problems the United States and Cuba posed for each other had been permanently surmounted.

Interpreting Crises

It seems doubtful whether many observers would differ substantially with the foregoing outlines of the raw facts of the crises described. Presumably, both realists and postinternationalists would, despite their disparate interpretations of the events, agree that none of the situations were minor incidents. Realists may be dubious about classifying the Tiananmen Square and refugee episodes as "true" crises, but they would probably concede that these events were of sufficient importance to require efforts at theoretical explanation. In addition, proponents of both schools of thought would be likely to concur that the Cuban missile crisis, lasting as it did only thirteen days and ending with the dismantling of the missile sites, was the shortest and most clear-cut of the crises described and that it alerted the whole world to the dangers of a nuclear holocaust. Presumably, too, they would agree that the crisis—or what realists might call a "domestic upheaval"—in Tiananmen Square was the next shortest and next most clear-cut (since the protests were ended and order restored through decisive military action) even as it, too, had global repercussions in the sense that most of the world's governments were subsequently compelled to devote more attention to human rights issues. Similarly, the flight of Rwandan, Haitian, and Cuban refugees would likely be interpreted by both types of theorists as the longest and most murky of the crises—or domestic upheavals—with consequences that are not yet fully evident but that have clearly highlighted the problem of humanitarian interventions in the domestic affairs of sovereign states.

In all likelihood, moreover, there would not be much dispute over where the situations originated. Realists and postinternationalists would surely agree that the Cuban missile crisis had its origins in the world of states, that the Cuban refugee crisis began with a state decision made by Castro, and that the other upheavals were initiated by people in the nongovernmental sectors of their respective societies.

But these agreements on the raw facts do not tell us much. They are merely empirical summaries and not explanations of why the crises unfolded as they did. They do not account for what happens once analysis moves beyond mere description and confronts the theoretical tests posed by the crises: How is each case to be interpreted? What underlying dynamics of world politics do they reflect? In what respects, if any, do realists and postinternationalists differ as to the meanings they attach to the cases? And, whatever their explanations, can these cases be regarded as meeting the severe challenges that crises pose for theorists?

Our method for exploring these questions is to turn for guidance to Table 4.1 (see p. 58), which sets forth differences between realism and postinternationalism along several crucial dimensions, and then to extend the list of dimensions to those that are more specifically relevant to crisis conditions (see Table 7.1). The ensuing analysis highlights a number of ways in which realists and postinternationalists are likely to disagree sharply on the nature and meaning of each crisis.

TABLE 7.1 Comparison of Likely Realist and Postinternationalist Interpretations of Crises

	Realist Model	Postinternationalist Model
Essential nature of crises	Simple	Complex
Number of situations classified as crises	Few	Numerous
Identity of key actors	States	SFAs and SBAs
Locale of crises	High governmental decisionmaking bodies	Collective actions of citizens as well as governments
Onset of crises	When states set deadlines	Variable stimuli
Duration	Short, with crises having definitive endings	Possibly lengthy, sometimes with ambiguous endings
Nature of power employed	Military	Nonmilitary as well as military capabilities

Global Structures and the Exercise of Coercive Power

Perhaps the most obvious explanatory divergence derives from the conceptions of global structures held by realists and postinternationalists. The former are likely to question whether the protest and refugee situations were "true" crises, citing the fact that they did not involve direct confrontations between states. Given a conception of the world as organized around an anarchical interstate system, realists tend to regard as critical only those conflicts occurring between states. Sure, a realist might concede, the United States and other states reacted strongly to the massacre in Tiananmen Square and, yes, the United States subsequently sought to link trade and human rights issues in its relations with China; nevertheless, the core of the situation was essentially an internal Chinese matter, one in which the Chinese state did what states have always done—seek to take control of the situation and restore order even if violence may be necessary to accomplish this goal. Hence, realists conclude, the protests in China and their violent repression, however offensive they might be to Western sensibilities, did not amount to a true crisis. For similar reasons, they assert, the refugee situations cannot be regarded as crises. Tragic, yes; unspeakable horror, yes; but not crises because they did not involve an eyeball-to-eyeball confrontation of states; on the contrary, in many respects, their main actors were masses of people and international organizations. Then, eager to drive home the tightness of their logic, realists might well add a comparison to the Cuban missile crisis: That was a true crisis, not only because it pitted state against state, but also because it involved a confrontation in which the rawest form of power was used by both sides. The realist might well ask, How can one treat the Cuban missile crisis in the same breath with the others? "Surely, you are not going to argue that those thirteen days were a crisis for the multi-centric world! Why, the crisis ended before their actors could even begin to get involved!"

Not a problem, those committed to the turbulence model would be likely to respond. The bifurcated conception of global structures readily accommodates the different crises: The conflict over missiles occurred in the state-centric world; those involving the flight of refugees emanated from the multi-centric world; and the protests in China entangled actors in both worlds. In other words, postinternationalists do not deny that interstate crises exist or that they are important. Quite to the contrary, their analytic antennae are tuned into such developments and the exercise of violent power they may involve. But at the same time, their notion of a bifurcation that allows for serious and meaningful conflicts to occur among sovereignty-free actors or between them and states makes it possible for proponents of postinternationalism to treat the Chinese and refugee situations as no less "true" crises than the conflict over missiles in Cuba. Realist theory can envision wholly state-centric crises but tends to downplay crises that arise wholly in the multi-centric world or in interactions between the state- and multi-centric worlds. It may acknowledge the occurrence of the other two types of situations, but it will view them as events with little lasting importance.

As indicated in both Tables 4.1 and 7.1, since realists are preoccupied with power in military confrontations and postinternationalists are concerned with its operation in diverse circumstances, it is hardly surprising that the two are likely to differ in the kinds of situations that provoke them to attach the descriptor "crisis." For realists, crises refer primarily to time-compressed situations where vital national interests are at stake or where there is a significant prospect of war.[35] Thus they would be unlikely to characterize intense conflicts over trade, money, environmental, or human rights problems as crises. Not so for postinternationalists. Viewing power as generated by multiple sources, they are prepared to view a variety of situations as giving rise to intense, deadline-pervaded crises. Thus they might well characterize

President Nixon's sudden decision to take the United States off the gold standard on August 15, 1971, as a true crisis in the same way they are likely to discern the presence of crisis in a cholera epidemic among Rwandan refugees who fled to Zaire. Indeed, the range of situations postinternationalists deem as crises might be wide enough to include the initial rejection of the European Union's Maastricht Treaty by Danish citizens, the protests in the heart of Berlin, Prague, Budapest, and other European cities that brought an end to the Soviet empire, the near collapse of Security Council operations in the face of the Bosnian situation, and perhaps even the final days of the Antarctic negotiations on the mining moratorium.

Boundaries, Sovereignty, and the Identity of Actors

A number of the differences between the two theories revolve around the boundary between foreign and domestic affairs and the identity of the key actors in world politics. As indicated in Table 4.1, the nature of sovereignty provides the crucial lever in this set of theory characteristics. Since realists are inclined to view the sovereignty of states as undiminished, they can also assume that states are unitary actors, that citizens are not relevant to foreign affairs, and that the line between domestic and foreign affairs is quite clear and solid. These interconnected propositions have important implications for how realists are likely to interpret the dynamics of crises. For them, states make decisions and take actions. Individuals matter only in the sense that as officials they speak for the state and can act on behalf of its interests. Concrete and identifiable persons "stand in" for the country, but ordinary citizens are of no consequence except as tokens of a state's power—as soldiers or as productive workers who can advance their country's economic power. When the leadership of a country announces that forces will be sent somewhere, realists presume that the forces will be sent. Thus it was that in the Cuban missile crisis "politics stopped at the water's edge" (to quote an oft-used slogan) as the Navy set out to inspect and halt ships from the Soviet bloc carrying materials for the missile sites. For realists, in other words, crises are occasions when the participation of citizens is likely to be minimal. Because the time horizon narrows so sharply, publics and transnational groups, which are generally deemed irrelevant by realism in any event, are truly left as mere bystanders. All the key decisions get made at the highest level—state to state—as the military and diplomatic arms of governments swing into action, while domestic agencies, whose voices are unlikely to penetrate the crisis deliberations, stay out of the picture.

Inasmuch as authority is most effectively backed up by the threat or use of force, realists tend to presume that military maneuvers are indicative of the buildup of crises. If a currency collapses and finance ministers quickly gather in a cooperative effort to stem the changing monetary values, realists would be hard pressed to describe such a situation as a crisis. A problem, yes; an imbalance, yes; but not a crisis in the sense that states are on a collision course. Viewed in this way, realists might even concede that the last few days of the Haitian situation approached a true crisis inasmuch as U.S. forces were bearing down on the island in a test of wills between two states. The fact that the collision course flowed from a repressive regime and fleeing refugees would likely be viewed by realists as a peripheral and not an essential feature of the crisis.

Since those who employ the turbulence model are inclined to conceive of the sovereignty of states as undergoing erosion and the foreign-domestic boundary as thus porous and endlessly in flux, they are unlikely to treat states as unitary actors. To be sure, the decisions that get made in the state-centric world are those of leaders who act on behalf of their countries, but postinternationalists are too sensitive to the operation of societal variables to ignore evidence that governmental decisionmaking processes consist of bureaucratic and top-level conflicts fueled by groups within the society. In instances such as the Cuban missile crisis, they would concede, these groups are mere bystanders; they are unable to exert direct influence, either because of a shortage of time or because the crisis deliberations are conducted in secret. Even under these circumstances, however, postinternationalists might contend that the leaders are not unmindful of the political and societal implications of their decisions. In the Cuban missile crisis, for instance, Kennedy could not publicly appear to be exchanging the removal of missiles in Turkey for a comparable action in Cuba precisely because such a trade was prohibited by the givens of American domestic opinion. Even in dire diplomatic and military crises, postinternationalists might thus argue, the policies adopted are not entirely those of a unitary actor.

This is not to imply, however, that postinternationalist theory is oblivious to territorial boundaries. Its adherents do not posit a borderless world so much as they conceive of its boundaries as fluctuating from issue to issue and as being crossed readily by a host of actors on both sides of the legally established lines that separate states.

Citizens, Publics, and Societal Institutions

It is not difficult to deduce from the foregoing why realists focus on decisionmaking processes in their interpretations of crises. Since they view crises as occurring exclusively between states as unitary actors, they need not be concerned about publics or societal institutions and can concentrate on how and why officials converged around a plan for action as the collision course neared a climax. In contrast, it is precisely because postinternationalists attach importance to the orientations and collective actions of public and societal institutions that they are not especially preoccupied with decisional processes. In focusing on the protests in Tiananmen Square, for example, analysts of this school would probably not investigate who, in the inchoate movement that converged on China's main square, first decided to resist the government's overtures to call off the rallies, how the decision was made, or what form the decisionmaking process took. Rather, their analyses are likely to stress the dynamics of aggregation that resulted in the protests. Far from being bystanders, publics and transnational actors such as television reporters are seen as occupying the center of the world stage and initiating events that compel responses by state officials. Likewise, although predisposed to attach the crisis label to sudden and massive movements of people across national boundaries, postinternationalists are unlikely to probe for any collective decisions that may have led to flight on the part of the thousands of Cuban and Haitian refugees and hundreds of thousands of Rwandans. What counts is not the decisionmaking process of discrete individuals but the convergence and aggregation of innumerable individuals around the same choices.

Thus, for those who employ the turbulence model, the crises generated by mass migrations highlight the underlying tensions at work in national and international systems. These tensions affirm their premise that the skills of individuals have undergone transformation to the point where individuals are prepared to respond to authority by acting decisively in their own interests. To flee a tyranny or a stagnant economy is to engage in deep and serious calculations—estimates that require a readiness to pull up roots and leave all that has meant home and tradition—and to reach conclusions that are painful and profoundly unsettling. The turbulence model allows for actions reflecting these calculations and posits their aggregation as part of the pervasive authority crises that mark world politics in this era. Similarly, the aggregation of individual decisions that lead to a run on a country's currency and subsequently to a hasty meeting of finance ministers is likely to affirm the postinternationalist perspective that crises need not evolve in a military context. Indeed, for adherents of this theory the recurrence of currency situations that they regard as crises is not surprising; such imbalances merely reflect the erosion of sovereignty and the inability of states to control sharp fluctuations in their economic institutions.

Realists might counter that, even if one was to stretch the word "crisis" to cover the Chinese and refugee situations, it makes sense to do so only because, at the crucial stage, states were obliged to step in. After all, they would reiterate, the refugee situation in Haiti culminated with the U.S. state launching an invasion against the Haitian state, and in the same manner the Cuban refugee situation did not come to an end until the heads of the U.S. and Cuban states negotiated a settlement. And in the case of Rwanda, the situation did not ameliorate until the United States and the U.N. undertook efforts to end the cholera epidemic, recognize the new coalition government, and otherwise restore order to that troubled and deeply divided country. Only by severely distorting the dynamics of these situations, realists might conclude, can refugee situations be interpreted as unfolding outside the context of interacting states. Not at all, retort postinternationalists; the underlying dynamics involved restless masses of people engaging in collective actions that were widely reported by the television media. Only as the situations entered their final phases did states and their international organizations become involved. Indeed, they had no choice: The dynamism of the skill revolution and the global authority crisis forced their hand and left them to take mopping-up roles that were essentially peripheral to the central problems posed by the flight of huge numbers of people.

Sensitivity to Change

Underlying the different responses of the two theories to crisis conditions is a huge gap in their understanding of the dynamics of change. Being inclined to presume that the course of events springs from the constancy of national goals and power distributions, realists are much less ready to discern change factors at work in world politics than are those who subscribe to the turbulence model. Realist theory anticipates little change, and thus its practitioners notice little change. To the extent that policymakers view the world through realist lenses, this tendency to perceive constancy has the paradoxical consequence of heightening the probability of crises in the state-centric world. Why? Because they may ignore underlying indicators of pending conflict and then be surprised and threatened when deeply embedded tensions surface into full-blown and unmanageable discord.

In contrast, postinternationalist theory rests on the presumption the world is undergoing vast transformations. Constancy is acknowledged, but it tends to be treated less as a central tendency and more as a set of restraints that channel, hinder, and delay the playing out of the transformations. Consequently, being readier to probe the underpinnings of surface tranquility than their realist counterparts, postinternationalists discern the onset of crises earlier and thus tend not to be surprised as the likelihood of a collision increases. Indeed, given their perspective that change is a worldwide phenomenon and that global repercussions can flow from localized conflicts, postinternationalists are likely not only to anticipate many more crises than realists but also to look for them as emanating from a wider variety of sources—from newly empowered citizens, from financially paralyzed international organizations unable to act decisively, from governmental agencies in the domestic arena pursuing goals that take them across fluid foreign-domestic boundaries, from the worldwide and intense coverage of news media that brings distant events close to home, and from the many other SFAs that an increasingly fragmented and turbulent world has accorded roles on the global stage. Thus it is, to cite concrete illustrations, that the U.S. Department of Commerce provoked a trade crisis over construction contract rules in Japan and that humanitarian organizations were drawn into crisis by the huge flow of Rwandan refugees; it was as a result of these events that the organizations pressed their crises onto the agenda of the state-centric world. No less important, the turbulence model encourages its adherents to look to the role played by the mass media of communications in hastening the pace of movement along the collision course of crises. It is not coincidental that television coverage of Tiananmen Square and the tragic circumstances of fleeing refugees are viewed by postinternationalists as part and parcel of the cascades that sustained those crises.

Given the orientation of realist theory toward constancy and that of turbulence theory toward change, it is not surprising that the two perspectives differ in the degree to which they see complexity as relevant to the onset and unfolding of crises. For example, whereas realists tend to view a crisis as an event that comes to some particular end (and that's that), postinternationalists are likely to discern the makings of a crisis as arising out of complex streams of action—out of cascades rather than events—that may not have clear-cut terminations. They are inclined to see crises as occurring at those points where multiple cascades coalesce, clash, and then resume until such time as they converge again. For postinternationalists, in other words, deadlines precipitate crises but do not necessarily bring them to climactic endings. Thus, the crisis over protests in Tiananmen Square did not finally wind down until 1994, when the Clinton administration decided not to make trade with China conditional upon an improvement of human rights in that country. Nor are postinternationalists deterred from viewing the movement of vast numbers of refugees as crises even though neither the plight of those who fled nor that of those who remained may show any sign of abating. Again, in other words, postinternationalists are disposed to measure crises by the persistence of specifiable conditions and not by specifiable decisions that lead to specifiable actions and interactions.

The turbulence model, in short, inclines its adherents to regard crises as having multiple origins and unfolding in multiple locales. Just as they perceive the Rwandan situation as a crisis for humanitarian organizations as well as states, so are they likely to regard, say, the strife in the former Yugoslavia as a crisis for both Bosnia and the United Nations. Wherever circumstances turn sharply for the worse—whether it be in the areas of human rights, trade, money, or simply the dignity and well-being of people—postinternationalists are likely to speak of the onset of crises.

Staunch realists would interpret these events as merely the normal problems that mark the day-to-day routines and conflicts of world politics. For them, mass protests and subsequent governmental involvement are essentially peripheral developments in world politics, a presumption that those less wedded to the realist model tend to find questionable even as they concede that the Chinese state did in the end get its way without compromising its position on human rights. For those who subscribe to the turbulence model, it does not seem logi-

cal to treat mass protests in front of a global television audience as routine. For them, the crisis in Tiananmen Square was an obvious instance
of micro and micro-macro parameters playing a central role in the
course of events.

Conclusion

Clearly, both the realist and turbulence models are capable of meeting
the tests that crises pose. Neither realists nor postinternationalists
need lose any sleep over how to interpret those moments in world politics that explode into crises. Both have conceptual tools that enable
them to offer explanations that are meaningful and that preserve the
integrity of their perspectives.

To be sure, the reader may find fault with how one or the other theory classifies and analyzes crises, but such conclusions are indicative of
the reader's theoretical orientations and not of fatal flaws in either
model. Indeed, if crises serve to provoke theoretical impulses on the
part of readers, they are likely to value the next chapter and its effort to
suggest how analysts might perfect their skills at thinking theory more
thoroughly.

8
Toward Thinking Theory Thoroughly

There are surely many urgent problems on the global agenda that could usefully be probed in case analyses such as those presented in the previous three chapters. These include severe environmental challenges, the pathos of a crumbling Yugoslavia, the startling successes of economic development in parts of Asia, the fundamentalist upheavals in Egypt and Algeria, the end of apartheid in South Africa, the twists and turns of U.S.-Japanese relations, and so on through a seemingly endless list of situations. But for two reasons we have chosen neither to proliferate our case analyses nor even to offer a representative sample of present-day crises. One reason is the conviction that political situations rapidly become obsolete and that thus the cases would quickly become exercises in historical documentation. The other, more important reason for stopping here is that our purpose has not been to provide an overview of world politics today. Rather, we have sought to elaborate one main point: that whatever may be the problem of concern, and whenever it may have emerged on the global agenda, it cannot be adequately grasped unless one is self-conscious about the theory one employs to perceive, describe, and assess it.

We have sought to demonstrate this main point by outlining two theoretical perspectives (in Chapters 2 and 3) and then comparing them (Chapter 4) before applying them to empirical cases (in Chapters 5, 6, and 7). So far so good, the reader might conclude, but how I do use this form of inquiry? You have persuaded me that I ought to be self-conscious about the theories I employ, but you have provided no clues whatever about how I might be my own theorist. Can you suggest some guidelines I might follow now that you've got me hooked on the virtues of theory?

The question is a fair one. We are delighted that our main point may seem reasonable and worthy of pursuit. So we accept the obligation to enumerate some simple—yet powerful—rules of thumb for proceeding from a passive observer of world politics to that of an active theorist.

But first it should be noted that to some extent the inclination to perceive and assess the course of events as expressive of larger forces may not be a talent that is easily learned: It may also be a cast of mind, a personality trait, or a philosophical perspective that some acquire early in life. To the degree that this is so, of course, our rules of thumb are not likely to be of much help. One can be introduced to the nature of theories, taught the various purposes theories can serve, exposed to the controversies over the relative worth of different theories, and instructed on the steps required for the construction of viable theories. And, to solidify these lessons, one can then be given the task of formulating concrete hypotheses and tying them together into a theoretical framework. Learning the skills underlying the design of theories is not, however, the equivalent of learning how to think theoretically. To move beyond the dos and don'ts of theoretical design, one has to acquire not a set of skills but rather a set of predispositions, a cluster of habits, a way of thinking, a mental lifestyle—or whatever may be the appropriate label for that level of intellectual existence that governs the use of skills and the application of values. It is this more fundamental dimension of the life of the mind that may not be readily teachable or learnable, a caveat that needs emphasis at the outset because the ensuing nine rules of thumb amount to nothing less than a pronouncement on how to think theoretically.

Nine Preconditions for Creative Theorizing

The task of disciplining ourselves to think theoretically consists, first, of identifying the cognitive inclinations and perceptual impulses from which creative theory springs and, second, of forming intellectual habits that assure the prevalence of these inclinations and impulses whenever we turn to theory-building endeavors. The central question examined here is as follows: What are the mental qualities that best enable one to "think theory," and how can their acquisition be best assured? Nine such qualities seem especially conducive to the development of good theorists. Each of the nine seems equally important and there is some overlap among them. Accordingly, the sequence of their elaboration here should not be interpreted as implying a rank order-ing.

Rule 1: To think theoretically one has to avoid treating the task as that of formulating an appropriate definition of theory.

Let us start with the proposition that the task of thinking theoretically is not one of developing a clear-cut definition. On balance, it is proba-bly preferable to have a precise conception of the nature of theory rather than a vague one, but definitional exactness is not the only cri-terion of thinking theoretically and it may not even be a necessary re-quirement for such thought. It is easy to imagine a young student thinking theoretically about international phenomena well before his or her first course on the subject turns to the question of what consti-tutes theory and the various uses to which it can be put. Indeed, we have had the good fortune of encountering a few students who were, so to speak, born theoreticians. From their very first comments in class as freshmen, it was clear that they thought theoretically even though they had never had any methodological training or exposure to the history of international relations.

Most of us are not so lucky. We have to be trained to think theoreti-cally and then have to engage in the activity continuously in order to achieve and sustain a genuinely theoretical perspective. Hence, the fact that a few among us can maintain such a perspective without training and practice is a useful reminder that definitional clarity is not a prerequisite to creative theorizing.

The reminder is important because many of us tend to exaggerate the importance of exact definitions. To be clear about the nature of theory is not to guarantee the formulation of meaningful theory. Such clarity can be misleading. It can provide a false sense of security, a mis-guided confidence that, once one is equipped with a clear-cut defini-tion, one needs only to organize one's empirical materials in the proper way. It is our impression that much of the writing in the field derives from this premise that good definitions automatically yield good theories, as if the definitions somehow relieve the observer of the need to apply imagination and maintain philosophical discipline.

To be sure, much of the writing in the field also suffers from loose and ambiguous conceptions of theory, from a confusion between the-ory and method. Such research would, obviously, be more valuable if it

proceeded from a tighter and clearer notion of what the theoretical enterprise entails. So, to repeat, we are not arguing against definitional
clarity. On the contrary, we believe it is highly appropriate to help students achieve such clarity by introducing them to the vast array of articles and books now available on the dynamics, boundaries, uses, and
abuses of theory in the international relations field. But we are arguing
for more than definitional clarity. In digesting the literature on theory
and building a more elaborate conception of what it involves, one has
to avoid leaning too heavily on definitions for guidance. Also needed
is a cast of mind, a mental set that builds on definitions and encourages creative theorizing.

Rule 2: To think theoretically one has to be clear as to whether one aspires to empirical theory or value theory.

Progress in the study of international affairs depends on advances in
both empirical and value theory. But the two are not the same. They
may overlap; they can focus on the same problem; and values always
underlie the selection of the problems to which empirical theories are
addressed. Yet they differ in one overriding way: Empirical theory
deals essentially with the "is" of international phenomena, with
things as they are if and when they are subjected to observation,
whereas value theory deals essentially with the "ought" of international phenomena, with things as they should be if and when they
could be subjected to manipulation. This distinction underlies, in
turn, entirely different modes of reasoning, a different rhetoric, and
different types of evidence.

The habit of making the necessary analytic, rhetorical, and eviden-
tial distinctions between empirical and value theory can be difficult to
develop. Indeed, such a habit can be weak and elusive for any of us
who have strong value commitments and a deep concern for certain
moral questions. The more intense are our values, the more are we
tempted to allow our empirical inquiries to be guided by our beliefs
rather than by our concern for observation. For this reason, becoming
habituated to the is-ought distinction is extremely difficult. One can
understand the distinction intellectually and even explain and defend
it when pressed, but practicing it is another matter. Empirical analysis
can easily slip into moral judgment without one being aware of it, as if
one somehow fears that one's values and goals will be undermined if
one allows oneself to focus on observable phenomena. Such a result, of

course, need not be the case. On the contrary, moral values and policy goals can be well served, even best served, by putting them aside and proceeding detachedly long enough to enlarge empirical understanding of the obstacles that hinder realization of the values and progress toward the goals.

This is the one line of reasoning on behalf of thinking theoretically that the most value-committed citizens find persuasive. If empirical theory is posited as a tool of moral theory, fledgling theorists can approach it instrumentally and see virtue in habituating themselves to distinguishing between the two. It takes a while, however, before the perceived virtues of habituation are translated into actual habits, and, in fact, some people never manage to make the transition, hard as they may try. Impatient with the need for change, convinced that time is too scarce to afford the slow pace of empirical inquiry, many simply give up and dismiss the is-ought distinction as one of those picayune obsessions to which some academics fall prey.

It is our impression that impatience with empirical theorizing is likely to be especially intense among students of international relations from developing countries. An intense consciousness of the long-standing injustices built into developed–developing country relationships, the lure of dependency theory, and perhaps a frustration over the premises of social science in developed countries have encouraged resistance to detached empirical theorizing on the part of theorists in developing countries. Their resistance gives analysts in developed countries pause: Is the insistence on habituating oneself to the is-ought distinction yet another instance of false superiority, of projection onto the developing world practices that have worked in industrial societies? It could be. We are keenly aware of the biases that may underlie our intellectual endeavors and thus we are not prepared to brush aside the idea that the is-ought distinction may be inappropriate to theorizing in much of the world. Still, the habit remains and resists being broken. The relevance of the distinction strikes us as global, as independent of any national biases, as necessary to thinking theoretically wherever and whenever enlarged comprehension is sought. Empirical theory is not superior to moral theory; it is simply preferable for certain purposes, and one of these is the end of deepening our grasp of why international processes unfold as they do.

Aware that our own expertise, such as it may be, lies in the realm of empirical theory, the ensuing discussion makes no pretense of being relevant to thinking theoretically in a moral context. All the precepts that follow are concerned only with those mental qualities that may render us more thoroughgoing in our empirical theorizing.

Rule 3: To think theoretically one must be able to assume that human affairs are founded on an underlying order.

A prime task of empirical theory is to explain why international phenomena are structured as they are and/or behave as they do. To perform this task one must assume that each and every international phenomenon is theoretically explicable, that deeper understanding of its dynamics could be achieved if appropriate instruments for measuring it were available. To assume that everything is potentially explicable is to presume that nothing happens by chance, capriciously, at random—that for every effect there must be a cause. That is, there must be an underlying order out of which international relations springs. If this were not the case, if events could occur for no reason, there would be little point in theorizing. If some events are inherently inexplicable, efforts to build creative theory are bound to fall short to the extent that they embrace phenomena that may occur at random. Indeed, in the absence of the assumption of an underlying order, attempts to fashion theory are futile, pointless exercises, a waste of time that could be better spent writing poetry, playing tennis, or tending the garden.

This is not to say that thought only acquires the status of theory when it purports to account for every event. As indicated below, theory is also founded on the laws of probability; hence, it only purports to account for central tendencies. But this claim is unwarranted if an assumption of underlying order is not made—that is, to think theoretically one must presume that there is a cause for every effect even though one does not seek to explain every effect.

Some people have a difficult time becoming habituated to the assumption of an underlying order. They see this premise as a denial of their own freedom. To presume there is a cause for everything, they reason, is to deprive people of free will, perhaps even to relieve them of responsibility for their actions. The assumption of an underlying order does not necessarily have such implications, however. One's freedom of choice is not lessened by the fact that the choices made are not random and instead derive from some source. Yet, fearful about compromising their own integrity, many people cannot accept this subtlety and insist on the premise that people have the capacity to cut themselves off from all prior experience and to act as they please for no rea-

'o support their resistance to the assumption of an
they will often cite instances of international history
:ted occurred or when a highly deviant, impetuous,
on was undertaken, as if somehow irrationality and
impetuosity are capricious and do not stem from any sources.

Besides patiently reassuring those who may be dubious that there
are no insidious threats in the assumption of an underlying order, one
can lessen, even perhaps break, someone's resistance to the idea by
pointing out how the assumption offers hope for greater understanding and deeper comprehension. To presume that there is a cause for every effect is to assume that everything is potentially knowable, that inquiry can pay off, that one is not necessarily destined to go down an
intellectual path that dead ends, leads nowhere. The assumption of an
underlying order, in other words, is pervaded with hope. We do not
make the assumption just so we can be hopeful, but making it does
have that consequence. Assuming that the affairs of people are patterned and that the patterns are susceptible to being uncovered enables us to view ourselves as fully in charge of our own investigations,
limited only by our imaginations and the resources at our disposal. It
allows us to approach the chaos we perceive in the world around us as
a challenge, as an orderliness that has yet to be identified and traced,
and permits us to dare to think theory thoroughly.

Rule 4: To think theoretically one must be predisposed to ask about every event, every situation, or every observed phenomenon, "Of what is it an instance?"

Of all the habits one must develop to think theoretically, perhaps none
is more central than the inclination to ask this question at every opportunity. It must be a constant refrain, a melody that haunts every
lurch forward in the process of moving from observations to conclusions. For to see every event as an instance of a more encompassing
class of phenomena is to sustain the search for patterns and to avoid
treating any phenomenon as inherently unique. To think theoretically
is to be at home with abstractions, to generalize, to discern the underlying order that links otherwise discrete incidents, and such a mode of
thinking cannot be achieved and maintained unless every observed
phenomenon is approached as merely one instance of a recurring sequence.

Again, many may have a hard time building up this habit. They may be inclined to probe for the special meaning of an event, to explore it for what sets it apart from all other events, rather than to treat it as an instance of a larger pattern. They may, for example, want to understand the collapse of the Soviet Union, rather than collapsing systems as a social process, and to the extent that this is their preference, to that extent they resist building up the impulse to always reach for more general theoretical insights. Indeed, all too many people simply do not know where to begin when asked to indicate of what pattern some event they regard as important is an instance. Their faces turn blank and their tongues turn silent. They are paralyzed. They do not know what it means to treat the event as merely an instance of something, as just part of a larger category. And so they stumble, mumble, or otherwise resist thinking in those elementary terms out of which theorizing springs.

Our response here is twofold. First, we stress the pleasure, the sheer joy, to be had from taking steps up the ladder of abstraction. Fitting pieces into larger wholes offers, we believe, a special sense of satisfaction, a feeling of accomplishment not unlike that which accompanies solving a puzzle or a mystery. Indeed, theory building can readily be viewed as puzzle solving, as uncovering the dynamics embedded deep in the interstices of human relationships, and there are few among us who are not intrigued by the challenge of solving puzzles.

If one's curiosity does not succeed in getting one to ask habitually, "Of what is this an instance?" (and often it is not a sufficient incentive), one can revert to a second line of reasoning. The implications of stumbling and mumbling are unmistakable: To be paralyzed by the question "Of what is this an instance?" is to not know what one is interested in, to be lacking questions that generate and guide one's inquiry, to be confused by the phenomenon one claims to be worthy of investigation. If there is an underlying order, no phenomenon exists in isolation, unique only unto itself, and thus there is always an answer to the of-what-is-this-an-instance question, whether we know it or not. Accordingly, the task is not one of figuring out an answer presently unknown to us; it is rather that of explicating an answer that we have already acquired but that has yet to surface.

We are arguing, in other words, that one does not get interested in an international phenomenon for no reason, that the interest stems from a concern about a more encompassing set of phenomena, and that there is therefore no need to be paralyzed by the question if one presses oneself to move up the ladder of abstraction. Once shamed into acknowledging that their concerns are not confined to the lowest rung on the ladder, most people are willing to begin to venture forth and approach the phenomena they observe as mere instances of something else.

Rule 5: To think theoretically one must be ready to appreciate and accept the need to sacrifice detailed descriptions for broad observations.

One cannot begin to mount the rungs of the ladder of abstraction if one is unable to forgo the detailed account, the elaborated event, the specific minutiae. As indicated, the theoretical enterprise is committed to the teasing out of central tendencies, to encompassing ever greater numbers of phenomena, to moving up the ladder of abstraction as parsimoniously as possible. Thus, theory involves generalizing rather than particularizing and requires relinquishing, subordinating, and/or not demonstrating much of one's impulse to expound everything one knows. It means, in effect, that one must discipline oneself to accept simple explanations over complex ones.

These are not easy tasks. Most of us find comfort in detail. The more details we know, the more we are likely to feel we have mastered our subject. To forgo much of the detail is to opt for uncertainties, to expose ourselves to the criticisms of those who would pick away at our generalizations with exceptions. The temptations to fall back on details are thus considerable and much concentration on the upper rungs of the ladder of abstraction is required if the temptations are to be resisted.

Happily, this step is less of a problem for beginners than it is for more mature theorists who are introduced late to the theoretical enterprise. The former have yet to acquire extensive familiarity with details and are therefore not likely to feel threatened by the loss of their knowledge base. They want to focus on the unique, to be sure, but at least it is possible to expose them to the case of theorizing before they find security in endless minutiae. Exactly how more mature analysts accustomed to the comforts of detail can be persuaded to be theoretically venturesome is, we confess, a problem for which we have yet to find anything resembling a solution.

Rule 6: To think theoretically one must be tolerant of ambiguity, concerned about probabilities, and distrustful of absolutes.

To be concerned about central tendencies, one needs to be accepting of exceptions, deviations, anomalies, and other phenomena that, taken by themselves, run counter to the anticipated or prevailing pattern. Anomalies ought not be ignored, and often explorations of them can lead to valuable, path-breaking insights, but neither can anomalies be allowed to undermine one's focus on central tendencies. Empirical theories deal only with probabilities and not with absolutes, with how most phenomena are likely to respond to a stimulus and not with how each and every phenomenon responds. Theorists simply do not aspire to account for every phenomenon. They know there will be anomalies and exceptions; indeed, they are suspicious on those unlikely occasions when no exceptions are manifest. Their goal, however, is to build theories in which the central tendencies encompass the highest possible degree of probability, with certainties and absolutes being left for ideologues and zealots to expound.

Although they engage in such thinking continuously in their daily lives, some people tend to be resistant to the necessity of thinking probabilistically when they turn to theorizing. More accurately, they tend to be reluctant to ignore ambiguity, to be restless with anything less than perfect certainty, as if any exception to anticipated central tendencies constitutes a negation of their reasoning. This low tolerance of ambiguity is difficult to contest. Some people, fearful of uncertainty, can get fixated on the exception, and it is very hard at that point to recapture an interest in central tendencies. The very rhetoric of their everyday language—that things are "completely" the case or that an observation is "absolutely" accurate—reinforces their intolerance of ambiguity. In this mood only the "whole truth" seems valid, and central tendencies appear as partial rather than legitimate forms of knowledge.

We confess to perplexity over how to handle this obstacle to theorizing. In the past we have tried elaborating on the many ways in which probabilistic thinking underlies daily life. We have tried drawing analogies between the physicist and the political scientist, pointing out that the former does not aspire to account for the behavior of every atom any more than the latter aspires to account for every voter. We have tried stressing the noxious values that derive from a concern with

absolutes. Neither alone nor in combination, however, do such tech-
niques seem to have any effect. Whatever its sources, for some people
intolerance of ambiguity is apparently too deep-seated to yield to reasoning or persuasion. So, reluctantly, we have concluded that those
with a low tolerance of ambiguity and a high need for certainty are unlikely to ever think theory thoroughly.

Rule 7: To think theoretically one must be playful about international phenomena.

At the core of the theorizing process is a creative imagination. The underlying order of world affairs is too obscure and too complex to yield
to pedestrian, constricted, or conventional minds. Only deep penetra-
tion into a problem, discerning relationships that are not self-evident
and might even be the opposite of what seems readily apparent, can
produce incisive and creative theory. Thus, to think theoretically one
must allow one's mind to run freely, to be playful, to toy around with
what might seem absurd, to posit seemingly unrealistic circumstances
and speculate about what would follow if they were ever to come to
pass. Stated differently, one must develop the habit of playing and en-
joying the game of "as if"—that is, specifying unlikely conditions and
analyzing them as if they prevailed.

Put in still another way, good theory ought never be embarrassed by
surprises, by unanticipated events that have major consequences for
the system on which the theory focuses. A Hitler-Stalin pact, a Nixon
resignation, a Sadat peace initiative, or a Cold War's end should not
catch the creative theorist unawares, because part of his or her creativity involves imagining the unimaginable. One imagines the unimaginable by allowing one's variables to vary across the entire range of a continuum even if some of its extreme points seem so unlikely as to be
absurd. To push one's thinking beyond the previously imagined ex-
tremes of a continuum is to play the game of "as if," and it involves a
playfulness of mind that mitigates against surprises as well as facilitates incisive theorizing.

How one develops playfulness is, of course, another matter. In some
important sense it is an intellectual quality that cannot simply be
adopted. One acquires—or perhaps inherits—creativity early in life
and no amount of subsequent training can greatly enhance the imagi-
native powers of those with tunnel vision and inhibited mentalities.

And yet, encouraging playfulness can bring out previously untapped talents in some people. Many have become so used to letting others do their thinking for them that their creative impulses have never been legitimated and, accordingly, they have never even heard of the "as if" game. So no harm can be done by pressing others (not to mention ourselves) to be playful and flexible in their thinking, and just conceivably such an emphasis may produce some unexpected results.

Rule 8: To think theoretically one must be genuinely puzzled by international phenomena.

Creative use of the imagination requires humility toward international phenomena. One must be as concerned about asking the right questions about the order underlying world affairs as one is about finding the right answers. To focus only on answers is to be sure about the questions one wants to probe, and this certainty imposes unnecessary limits on one's capacity to discern and integrate the deeper structures of global politics. If, however, one is genuinely puzzled by why events unfold as they do, one is committed to always asking why they occur in one way rather than another and, in so doing, pressing one's theoretical impulses as far as possible.

Genuine puzzles are not simply open-ended questions; they involve, rather, perplexity over specific and patterned outcomes. To be genuinely puzzled about the declining capacity of governments to govern effectively, for example, one does not ask, "Why do governments do what they do?" Rather, one asks, say, "Why are most governments unable to control inflation?" or "Why do they alter their alliance commitments under specified conditions?" Genuine puzzles, in other words, are not idle, ill-framed, or impetuous speculations. They encompass specified dependent variables for which adequate explanations are lacking. We do not see how one can begin to think theoretically if one does not discern recurrent outcomes that evoke one's curiosity and puzzlement. Some analysts may believe they are starting down the road to theory when they start asking what the outcomes are, but such a line of inquiry leads only to dead ends, or worse, to endless mazes, because one never knows when one has come upon a relevant outcome. Genuine puzzles can lead us down creative paths, however, because they discipline us to focus on particular patterns.

One cannot instruct others in how to be puzzled. The ability is very much a matter of whether curiosity has been repressed or allowed to flourish at an early age. It is possible, however, to persist with the simple question, "What genuinely puzzles you about international affairs?" Repetition of the question may prove to be sufficiently challenging to facilitate a maximum expression of curiosity, whatever potential along these lines a person may possess.

Rule 9: To think theoretically one must be constantly ready to be proven wrong.

Perhaps nothing inhibits the ability to be intellectually puzzled and playful more than the fear of being embarrassed by the inaccuracies of one's theorizing. Many of us have fragile egos that are so sensitive to error as to lead us to a preference for sticking close to conventional wisdom rather than risking speculation that may be erroneous. It is as if our stature as thoughtful persons depends upon the soundness of our observations.

Fragile egos are not readily bolstered, and some may never be capable of venturing forth. However, there is one line of reasoning that some may find sufficiently persuasive to lessen their fears of appearing ridiculous. It involves the notion that comprehension of international phenomena can be substantially advanced even if theories about them prove to be woefully wrong. Such progress can occur in two ways. First, falsified theory has the virtue of indicating avenues of inquiry that no longer need be traversed. Doubtless, egos are best served by theoretical breakthroughs, but if one presumes that knowledge is at least partly developed through a process of elimination, there is satisfaction to be gained from having narrowed the range of inquiry through theory that subsequently proves fallacious.

Second, unsound theory can facilitate progress by provoking others into demonstrating its falsity and attempting to show how and why it went astray. Indeed, if we assume that the erroneous theory focuses on significant matters, we may conclude that, often, the more outrageous the theory is, the more it is likely to provoke further investigation. Thus, even if one cannot negotiate a theoretical breakthrough on one's own, one can serve one's ego by the possibility that one's errors may sustain the knowledge-building process. This idea is surely what one astute analyst had in mind when he observed, "It is important to err importantly."[1]

Conclusion: Bringing It All Together

Plainly, there is no easy way to evolve the habit of thinking theoretically. Indeed, if the foregoing nine precepts are well founded, it can be readily argued that theorizing is the hardest of intellectual tasks. Clearing away the confusion of day-to-day events and teasing out their underlying patterns is not merely a matter of applying one's mental skills. Sustained, disciplined, and uninhibited work is required, and even then theory can be elusive, puzzles difficult to identify, details hard to ignore, and probabilities tough to estimate. And the lures and practices of nontheoretical thinking are always present, tempting us to forgo the insecurities and ambiguities of high levels of abstraction in favor of the comfortable precision available at low levels.

Yet the payoffs for not yielding to the temptations and persisting to think theoretically are considerable. There is an exhilaration, an exquisiteness, to be enjoyed in the theoretical enterprise that virtually defies description. Stimulated by the rarefied atmosphere, energized by the freedom to roam uninhibitedly across diverse realms of human experience, one gets giddy at high levels of abstraction. It is that special kind of giddiness that comes from the feeling that one is employing all the resources and talents at one's command, moving beyond anything one has done before. And if one should be so fortunate as actually to achieve a theoretical breakthrough, then the exhilaration, the excitement, and the sense of accomplishment can approach the thrill of discovery that Darwin, Einstein, Freud, and the other great explorers of underlying order must have experienced at their moments of breakthrough.

For all the difficulties it entails, then, thinking theoretically is, on balance, worth the effort. And so, therefore, is the effort to do so thoroughly. The habits of theoretical thinking are not easy to develop, but we can testify to the enormous pleasures that come with success in this regard. And in encouraging others to think theoretically, we hope that we, too, will refine and enlarge our own capacities for comprehending the underlying order that sustains and alters the human condition.

Notes

Chapter 1

1. Although philosophers of science often draw technical distinctions among theories, paradigms, and models, in subsequent chapters we shall use the terms interchangeably.

Chapter 2

1. Thucydides, *The Peloponnesian War,* trans. Rex Warner (New York: Penguin, 1978), p. 402.

2. Ibid., p. 49.

3. Robert Connor, *Thucydides* (Princeton: Princeton University Press, 1984), p. 3.

4. Hans Morgenthau, *Power Among Nations,* 3rd ed. (New York: Knopf, 1964), p. 4.

5. Ibid.

6. E. H. Carr, *The Twenty Years Crisis* (London: Macmillan, 1946).

7. Some scholars claim neorealism and structural realism are distinct enough to be treated as separate variants. See Barry Buzan, Charles Jones, and Richard Little, eds., *The Logic of Anarchy: Neorealism to Structural Realism* (New York: Columbia University Press, 1993), p. 9.

8. Kenneth N. Waltz, *Theory of International Politics* (Reading, Mass.: Addison-Wesley, 1979), p. 73.

9. Joseph M. Grieco, "Anarchy and the Limits of Cooperation: A Realist Critique of the Newest Liberal Institutionalism," *International Organization,* Vol. 42, No. 3 (Summer 1988), pp. 485–507, reprinted in David A. Baldwin, ed., *Neorealism and Neoliberalism: The Contemporary Debate* (New York: Columbia University Press, 1993), p. 127.

10. Robert O. Keohane, *After Hegemony* (Princeton: Princeton University Press, 1984), especially pp. 27–29.

11. Joseph M. Grieco argues that the international environment penalizes states that don't protect themselves. See Grieco, "Anarchy and the Limits of Cooperation," p. 488.

12. Graham Allison, *The Essence of Decision: Explaining the Cuban Missile Crisis* (Boston: Little, Brown, 1971), p. 28. The literature on rational choice as applied to the behavior of states is quite large. To get a taste of the variety, see Robert Axelrod, *The Evolution of Cooperation* (New York: Basic Books, 1984); Robert Gilpin, *War and Change in World Politics* (New York: Cambridge Univer-

sity Press, 1981); Baldwin, *Neorealism and Neoliberalism*; Duncan Snidal, "Relative Gains and the Pattern of International Cooperation," *American Political Science Review*, Vol. 85 (September 1991), pp. 701–726. The Snidal article offers evidence against the neorealist notion that states pay the most attention to relative gains by noting that relative gains are situational rather than constant.

13. George Tsebelis, *Nested Games* (Berkeley: University of California Press, 1990), p. 18.

14. Robert O. Keohane, ed., *Neorealism and Its Critics* (New York: Columbia University Press, 1986), p. 7.

15. Ibid., p. 11.

16. Tsebelis offers a more formal discussion of rationality rules in *Nested Games*, pp. 18–28.

17. Keohane, *After Hegemony*, p. 66; Arnold Horelick and Myron Rush, *Strategic Power and Soviet Foreign Policy* (Chicago: University of Chicago Press, 1965).

18. See Alan James, *Sovereign Statehood* (London: Allen Unwin, 1986), for a discussion of the various meanings of sovereignty.

19. Ibid., p. 39.

20. Oran Young, "Anarchy and Social Choice: Reflections on the International Polity," *World Politics*, Vol. 30 (January 1978), pp. 241–263. However, Young is not a realist; he believes the "international political system exhibits a high degree of heterogeneity with respect to the basic principles of organization of its members" (p. 243).

21. Robert Jervis, "Cooperation Under the Security Dilemma," *World Politics*, Vol. 30 (January 1978), pp. 167–214. Jervis explains how the anarchical structure of the system causes problems for cooperation: "Because there are no institutions or authorities that can make and enforce international laws, the policies of cooperation that will bring mutual rewards if others cooperate may bring disaster if they do not" (p. 167).

22. Stephen M. Meyer, "Verification and Risk in Arms Control," *International Security*, Vol. 8 (Spring 1984), pp. 111–126.

23. See especially Hedley Bull, *The Anarchical Society* (London: Macmillan, 1977).

24. Ibid., p. 16.

25. Ibid., p. 17.

26. Ibid., p. 18.

27. Ibid., p. 19.

28. There are many other approaches to the study of power. See, for instance, David A. Baldwin, *Paradoxes of Power* (London: Basil Blackwell, 1989); Zeev Maoz, "Power, Capabilities, and Paradoxical Outcomes," *World Politics*, Vol. 41 (January 1989), pp. 239–266; Jeffrey Hart, "Three Approaches to the Measurement of Power in International Relations," *International Organization*, Vol. 30 (April 1976), pp. 299–305.

29. For more on the impact of great powers, see Jack S. Levy, "Theories of General War," *World Politics*, Vol. 37 (April 1985), pp. 344–374, especially pp. 366–368.

30. Waltz, *Theory of International Politics*, p. 131.

31. To understand more fully the logic of land versus sea power, see Paul Kennedy, "Mahan versus Mackinder: Two Interpretations of British Sea Power," in his book, *Strategy and Diplomacy, 1870–1945* (London: Fontana, 1984).

32. Waltz, *Theory of International Politics,* p. 126.

33. Paul Kennedy, *The Rise and Fall of the Great Powers* (New York: Random House, 1987), especially pp. 432, 533–534.

34. Susan Strange, "The Persistent Myth of Lost Hegemony," *International Organization,* Vol. 41 (Autumn 1987), pp. 551–574.

35. Kenneth N. Waltz, "A Response to My Critics," in Keohane, ed., *Neorealism and Its Critics,* p. 342.

36. Charles Krauthammer, "The Unipolar Moment," *Foreign Affairs,* Vol. 70, No. 1 (1990–1991), pp. 23–33.

37. Kennedy, *The Rise and Fall of the Great Powers,* p. 535.

38. Some believe that the concept is an "obscurity enshrined" that should be laid to rest because, although everyone uses the term, it has many meanings and therefore is useless as an analytical concept. See Ernst B. Haas, "The Balance of Power: Prescription, Concept or Propaganda?" *World Politics,* Vol. 5 (July 1953), pp. 442–477.

39. Bull, *Anarchical Society,* pp. 106–107.

40. Ibid., p. 11.

41. Ibid., pp. 10–11. For more distinctions between traditional realism and neorealism, see James E. Dougherty and Robert L. Pfaltzgraff, *Contending Theories of International Relations,* 3rd ed. (New York: Harper & Row, 1990), pp. 30–35.

42. As quoted in F. H. Hinsely, *Power and the Pursuit of Peace* (Cambridge: Cambridge University Press, 1963), p. 64.

43. Stephen Walt, "Alliance Formation and the Balance of Power," *International Security,* Vol. 9 (Spring 1985), pp. 3–43.

44. These categories were derived from Edward Vose Gulick, *Europe's Classical Balance of Power* (Ithaca, N.Y.: Cornell University Press, 1955), Chap. 3.

45. Connor, *Thucydides,* p. 123.

46. Tsebelis, *Nested Games,* p. 69. See also Axelrod, *The Evolution of Cooperation,* pp. 10–11, 20.

47. Connor, *Thucydides,* pp. 124–125.

48. Bull, *Anarchical Society,* p. 106.

49. Morgenthau, *Power Among Nations,* p. 163.

50. Keohane, *After Hegemony,* p. 46.

51. Walt, "Alliance Formation and the Balance of Power," pp. 18–24. For his extended treatment of the subject, see Stephen Walt, *The Origins of Alliances* (Ithaca, N.Y.: Cornell University Press, 1987).

52. David Forsythe, *The Internationalization of Human Rights* (Lexington, Mass: Lexington Books, 1991), p. 92.

53. Stephen Krasner, ed., "Structural Causes and Regime Consequences: Regimes as Intervening Variables," *International Regimes* (Ithaca, N.Y.: Cornell University Press, 1983), p. 1.

54. Levy, "Theories of General War," p. 345.

55. John Gerard Ruggie, "Continuity and Transformation in the World Polity: Toward a Neorealist Synthesis," in Keohane, ed., *Neorealism and Its Critics*, pp. 131–157.

56. Ruggie, "Continuity and Transformation," p. 141.

57. Christopher Layne, "Kant or Cant: The Myth of the Democratic Peace," *International Security*, Vol. 19 (Fall 1994), pp. 10–11.

Chapter 3

1. An extensive presentation of this paradigm can be found in James N. Rosenau, *Turbulence in World Politics: A Theory of Change and Continuity* (Princeton: Princeton University Press, 1990).

2. For a discussion of the role anomalies played in the construction of the postinternational model, see ibid., pp. 92–98.

3. John Lukacs, "The Short Century—It's Over," *New York Times*, February 17, 1991, Sec. IV, p. 13.

4. For the historical analysis that underlies this conclusion, see Rosenau, *Turbulence in World Politics*, Chap. 5.

5. For an extended effort to demonstrate and explain this expanding skill, see James N. Rosenau, "The Relocation of Authority in a Shrinking World: From Tiananmen Square in Beijing to the Soccer Stadium in Soweto via Parliament Square in Budapest and Wencelas Square in Prague," *Comparative Politics*, Vol. 24 (April 1992), pp. 253–272.

6. It is worth noting that the sovereignty principle began to be undermined when it was redefined during the decolonizing processes of the former European empires after World War II. In using self-determination as the sole criterion for statehood, irrespective of whether a former colony had the consensual foundations and resources to govern, a number of sovereign states were created, recognized, and admitted to the U.N. even though they were unable to develop their economies and manage their internal affairs without external assistance. As a result of these weaknesses, the value of sovereignty seemed less compelling once the struggle for independence was won and the tasks of governance taken on. Rather than being an obvious source of strength, sovereignty thus often seemed to be less a source of independence than an invitation to interdependence. For an extensive discussion of how the sovereignty principle got redefined—how "decolonization amounted to nothing less than an international revolution ... in which traditional assumptions about the right to sovereign statehood were turned upside down"—in the processes of decolonialization, see Robert H. Jackson, *Quasi-states: Sovereignty, International Relations and the Third World* (Cambridge: Cambridge University Press, 1990), Chap. 4 (the quotation is from p. 85).

7. For an explanation of why the terms "sovereignty-bound" and "sovereignty-free" seem appropriate as labels to differentiate between state and nonstate actors, see Rosenau, *Turbulence in World Politics*, p. 36.

8. For a cogent discussion of one major aspect of the organizational explosion, see Lester M. Salamon, "The Rise of the Nonprofit Sector," *Foreign Affairs,* Vol. 73 (July/August 1994), pp. 109–122.

9. The pace of technological advance shows no sign of slowing down. It is estimated that by the end of the century new generations of supercomputers will be capable of calculating more than a trillion operations each second. See "Transforming the Decade: 10 Critical Technologies," *New York Times,* December 1, 1991, p. 18.

10. On the first night of the Gulf War, CNN's prime time viewership went from its normal 560,000 to 11.4 million. See Thomas B. Rosenstiel, "CNN: The Channel to the World," *Los Angeles Times,* January 23, 1991, p. A12.

11. An account of *Actuel's* efforts can be found in *Europe: Magazine of the European Community* (April 1990), pp. 40–41.

12. For an extensive elaboration of the diverse ways in which the microelectronic revolution has influenced the conduct of public affairs, see Rosenau, *Turbulence in World Politics,* Chap. 13.

13. For discussions along these lines, see James N. Rosenau, "The State in an Era of Cascading Politics: Wavering Concept, Widening Competence, Withering Colossus, or Weathering Change?" in J. A. Caporaso, ed., *The Elusive State* (Newbury Park: Sage Publications, 1989), pp. 17–48; and Giulio M. Gallarotti, "Legitimacy as a Capital Asset of the State," *Public Choice,* Vol. 63 (1989), pp. 43–61.

14. There is considerable evidence, for example, that the collapse of authority in East Germany in fall 1989 was stimulated by the televised scenes of authority being challenged in Tiananmen Square several months earlier. See Tara Sonenshine, "The Revolution Has Been Televised," *Washington Post National Weekly Edition,* October 8–14, 1990, p. 29.

15. An account of the loyalty and membership problems faced by Norway can be found in William E. Schmidt, "Norway Again Debates European Membership, Rekindling Old Hostilities," *New York Times,* May 6, 1991, p. A3.

16. John Darnton, "Vote in Norway Blocks Joining Europe's Union," *New York Times,* November 29, 1994, p. 1.

17. The quotes are taken from Alan Riding, "France Questions Its Identity as It Sinks Into 'Le Malaise,'" *New York Times,* December 23, 1990, pp. 1, 7.

18. The conception of developing countries as quasi-states can be found in Jackson, *Quasi-states,* Chaps. 1 and 7.

19. For a useful delineation between positive and negative sovereignty, see Jackson, *Quasi-states,* pp. 26–31.

20. For an extended analysis of the future scenarios inherent in the turbulence model, see Rosenau, *Turbulence in World Politics,* Chap. 16.

Chapter 4

1. *Casenote Legal Brief—International Law* (Beverly Hills: Casenote Publishing Co., 1988), p. 25.

2. Michael Akehurst, *A Modern Introduction to International Law,* 6th ed. (London: George Allen and Unwin, 1984), p. 14.

3. Kenneth N. Waltz, *Theory of International Politics* (Reading, Mass: Addison-Wesley, 1979), p. 94.

Chapter 5

1. Wei-chin Lee, "China and Antarctica: So Far and Yet So Near," *Asian Survey,* Vol. 30 (June 1990), pp. 576–586.

2. Matthew Howard, "The Convention on the Conservation of Antarctic Marine Living Resources: A Five-Year Review," *International and Comparative Law Quarterly,* Vol. 38 (January 1989), pp. 104–149.

3. P. W. Quigg, *A Pole Apart: The Emerging Issue of Antarctica* (New York: New Press, 1983), p. 18.

4. For additional information on how states acquire territory, see Michael Akehurst, *A Modern Introduction to International Law,* 6th ed. (London: George Allen and Unwin, 1984), Chap. 11; and Gerhard von Glahn, *Law Among Nations,* 5th ed. (New York: MacMillan, 1986), Chap. 15. For a summary of the application of this law to the Antarctic, see Steven J. Burton, "New Stresses on the Antarctic Treaty: Toward International Legal Institutions Governing Antarctic Resources," *Virginia Law Review,* Vol. 65 (1979), especially pp. 458–470.

5. Jack Child, *Antarctica and South American Geopolitics: Frozen Lebensraum* (New York: Praeger, 1988), offers a detailed survey of how South American states, notably Chile and Argentina, view Antarctica.

6. Peter J. Beck, *The International Politics of Antarctica* (New York: St. Martin's, 1986), p. 37. In a more recent publication, Beck assesses whether security still matters in Antarctic politics. See Peter J. Beck, "Antarctica as a Zone of Peace: A Strategic Irrelevance? A Historical and Contemporary Survey," in R. A. Herr, H. R. Hall, and M. G. Howard, eds., *Antarctica's Future: Continuity or Change?* (Hobart, Tasmania, Australia: Tasmanian Government Printing Office, 1990), pp. 192–224.

7. Beck, *The International Politics of Antarctica,* p. 41.

8. Quoted in ibid., p. 52.

9. James E. Mielke, "Antarctic Mineral Resource Activities: Regulate or Prohibit?" *CRS Review* (November/December 1990), pp. 22–23.

10. Christopher Beeby, "The Antarctic Treaty System as a Resource Management Mechanism—Nonliving Resources," in Polar Research Board, *Antarctic Treaty System,* proceedings of a workshop held at Beardmore South Field Camp, Antarctica, January 7–13, 1985 (Washington, D.C.: National Academy Press, 1986), p. 271.

11. William Westermeyer and Christopher Joyner, *Negotiating a Minerals Regime for Antarctica,* Pew Case Study #134 (Washington, D.C.: Institute for the Study of Diplomacy, Georgetown University, 1988), p. 6.

12. Howard, "The Convention on the Conservation of Antarctic Marine Living Resources," p. 111. For a number of perspectives on the living resources

question, see Francisco Orrego Vicuna, ed., *Antarctic Resources Policy* (Cambridge: Cambridge University Press, 1983).

13. For a discussion of the complex relationship between the Antarctic Treaty and the Law of the Sea, see Christopher Joyner, *Antarctica and the Law of the Sea* (Dordrecht, The Netherlands: Nijhoff, 1992).

14. Beeby, *Antarctic Treaty System,* p. 277.

15. For an overview of the institutional choices, see Beeby, "The Antarctic Treaty System as a Resource Management Mechanism," or Westermeyer and Joyner, *Negotiating a Minerals Regime.*

16. Barry Buzan, "Negotiating by Consensus: Developments in Technique at the United Nations Conference on the Law of the Sea," *American Journal of International Law,* Vol. 75 (1981), pp. 324–348.

17. See James N. Rosenau, "Before Cooperation: Hegemons, Regimes, and Habit-Driven Actors in World Politics," *International Organization,* Vol. 40 (Autumn 1986), pp. 849–894.

18. For a history of the IGY, see Sydney Chapman, *IGY: Year of Discovery* (Ann Arbor: University of Michigan Press, 1959). A discussion of plans for Antarctic science in the IGY can be found in American Geophysical Union, *Antarctica in the International Geophysical Year* (Washington, D.C.: National Academy of Sciences, 1956).

19. The National Academy of Sciences, although not a government agency, was chartered by Congress. See Philip M. Boffey, *The Brain Trust of America: An Inquiry into the Politics of Science* (New York: McGraw Hill, 1975); or Rexmond C. Cochrane, *The National Academy of Science: The First Hundred Years* (Washington, D.C.: National Academy Press, 1978).

20. For a detailed discussion of SCAR, see James H. Zumberge, "The Antarctic Treaty as a Scientific Mechanism—The Scientific Committee on Antarctic Research and the Antarctic Treaty System," in Polar Research Board, *Antarctic Treaty System,* pp. 153–168.

21. Walter Sullivan, "Poland Requests Role in Antarctica," *New York Times,* April 4, 1959, p. 16.

22. Walter Sullivan, "Academic Talent Sought at Poles," *New York Times,* September 24, 1959, p. 11.

23. Patrick G. Quilty, "Antarctica as a Continent for Science," in Herr et al., eds., *Antarctica's Future,* p. 29.

24. James N. Rosenau, *Turbulence in World Politics: A Theory of Change and Continuity* (Princeton: Princeton University Press, 1990), p. 306.

25. Ibid., p. 308.

26. W. K. Chagula, B. T. Feld, and A. Parthasarathi, eds., *Pugwash on Self-Reliance* (Dar es Salaam, Tanzania: Anakar Publishing House, 1977), p. 2.

27. The scientists' movement is explored in Alice Kimball Smith, *A Peril and a Hope* (Cambridge: MIT Press, 1970). The December 1985 edition (Vol. 41, No. 11) of the *Bulletin of the Atomic Scientists* is devoted to the relationship between the scientists' movement and the *Bulletin.*

28. Isaac Asimov, *The Ends of the Earth* (New York: Weybright and Talley, 1975), p. 341.

29. Bernard P. Herber, "Mining or World Park? A Politico-Economic Analysis of Alternative Land Use Regimes in Antarctica," *Natural Resources Journal,* Vol. 31 (1991), pp. 839–859.

30. Ibid., p. 841.

31. Polar Research Board, *Antarctic Treaty System,* p. 276.

32. In 1947, a "proposal was made in the Trusteeship Council that the polar regions ... should be placed under the aegis of the UN." This might well have happened had the Arctic not been included with Antarctica. From Philip Quigg, *Antarctica: The Continuing Experiment* (New York: Foreign Policy Association, March/April 1985), p. 37.

33. Ibid., pp. 37–38.

34. This concept is discussed by Bernard P. Herber, "The Common Heritage Principle: Antarctica and the Developing Nations," *The American Journal of Economics and Sociology,* Vol. 50 (October 1991), pp. 391–406.

35. Moritaka Hayashi, "The Antarctica Question in the United Nations," *Cornell International Law Journal,* Vol. 19 (1985), p. 288.

36. For a general discussion of the aims of nongovernmental organizations in Antarctic matters, see Anthony Parsons, *Antarctica: The Next Decade* (Cambridge: Cambridge University Press, 1987), Chap. 3.

37. Christoper C. Joyner, *The Role of Domestic Politics in Making United States Antarctic Policy* (Lysaker, Norway: Fridtjof Nansens Institutt, IARP Publication Series, No. 2, 1992).

38. Malcolm Browne, "France and Australia Kill Pact on Limited Antarctic Mining and Oil Drilling," *New York Times,* September 25, 1989, p. A10.

39. Paul Bogart, "On Thin Ice," *Greenpeace,* Vol. 13, No. 5 (September–October 1988), pp. 7–11.

40. Malcolm Browne, "Pact Would Ban Antarctic Mining," *New York Times,* September 25, 1989, p. A10.

41. Westermeyer and Joyner, *Negotiating a Minerals Regime for Antarctica,* p. 14.

42. Ibid.

43. Ibid. See also Christopher C. Joyner, "The Antarctic Minerals Negotiating Process," *American Journal of International Law,* Vol. 81, No. 4 (October 1987), especially pp. 895–897.

44. This issue is explored in depth in O. Rothwell, *A World Park for Antarctica* (Hobart, Tasmania, Australia: Institute of Antarctic and Southern Ocean Studies, University of Tasmania, 1990).

45. Mielke, "Antarctic Mineral Resources Activities," p. 24.

46. S.K.N. Blay, "New Trends in the Protection of the Antarctic Environment: The 1991 Madrid Protocol," *American Journal of International Law,* Vol. 86 (April 1992), pp. 377–399.

47. "Pact Would Ban Antarctic Mining," *New York Times,* May 1, 1991, p. A9.

48. Malcolm W. Browne, "U.S. Agrees to Protect Minerals in Antarctic," *New York Times,* July 6, 1991, p. 1.

49. Gillian Triggs, "A Comprehensive Environmental Regime for Antarctica: A New Way Forward," in Herr et al., *Antarctica's Future,* pp. 103–118.

50. There need not be a break between economic development and environment. Pollution prevention policies can produce jobs even as they reduce negative impacts on the environment. But this formulation, at least so far, applies in areas already "developed." The concept of sustainable development is not appropriate in the unique circumstances of Antarctica proper, although it may well come to govern fisheries in the Southern Ocean. The environmental rule for Antarctica seems increasingly to boil down to the following: no development, no pollution.

51. There is an exception to this rule. Some countries, like Costa Rica, say that rich northern countries should pay for any samples of flora and fauna, on the grounds that the raw genetic information has monetary value. The effect of such a rule would both preserve the environment and redistribute the wealth (and probably scientific knowledge as well). This practice would also be a remarkable use of sovereignty. For more on biodiversity in Costa Rica, see John Hamilton, "Cathedrals of the 21st Century," in his *Entangling Alliances* (Cabin John, Md.: Seven Locks Press, 1990). Edward O. Wilson's *The Diversity of Life* (New York: Norton, 1992) provides a sound grounding in the whole subject of biodiversity.

52. Although we have treated the scientific community as though it were a single entity with standards of virtue and reason beyond the reach of most individuals, this is, of course, not the case. Deeper analysis would have to ask when and where controversies within this community are likely to emerge and to what effect. It is quite likely that the still small Antarctic scientific community might well enter into conflict with the larger "atmosphere" or "oceans" communities. Or that the chemical, physical, and biological components within each of these areas might argue over what to do and how to spend available funds. The potential for conflict as different scientific organizations sought to maintain autonomy would, presumably, be quite high. Outside of places like Antarctica, this conflict could prove disastrous for the actual management of environmental problems: Rome could burn while the scientists fiddled. That would provoke lack of compliance by activist environmental groups, who then might provoke action by states.

Chapter 6

1. For a cogent discussion of the U.N. as part of the processes of international institutionalization, see Margaret P. Karns, "The Changing Architecture of World Politics: Multilateralism, Cooperation, and Global Governance," in Kenneth W. Thompson, ed., *Community, Diversity and a New World Order: Essays in Honor of Inis L. Claude, Jr.* (Lanham, Md.: University Press of America, 1994), pp. 267–284.

2. A full diagram of the vast array of specialized agencies, programs, regional commissions, functional commissions, special funds, ad hoc bodies, and offices that make up the U.N. system would include more than fifty distinct units, some thirty of which have executive heads that are subject to periodic

election or appointment. For one effort to pull together diagrammatically all the units of the U.N. system, see Brian Urquhart and Erskine Childers, *A World in Need of Leadership: Tomorrow's United Nations* (Uppsala, Sweden: Dag Hammarskjöld Foundation, 1990), pp. 90–91.

3. Quoted in Brian Hall, "Blue Helmets, Empty Guns," *New York Times Magazine,* January 2, 1994, p. 22.

4. Ibid., p. 23.

5. For another explanation that supplements rather than contradicts this interpretation of the U.N.'s success in these situations, see James N. Rosenau, "Interdependence and the Simultaneity Puzzle: Notes on the Outbreak of Peace," in C. W. Kegley, Jr., ed., *The Long Postwar Peace: Contending Explanations and Projections* (New York: HarperCollins Publishers, 1991), pp. 307–328.

6. Hall, "Blue Helmets, Empty Guns," p. 23.

7. Quoted in Paul Lewis, "Reluctant Warriors: U.N. Member States Retreat from Peacekeeping Roles," *New York Times,* December 12, 1993, p. 22.

8. For instances of this argument being advanced in the United States, see Brian Urquhart, "Sovereignty vs. Suffering," *New York Times,* April 17, 1991, p. A15; Jonathan Mann, "No Sovereignty for Suffering," *New York Times,* April 12, 1991, Sec. 4, p. 17; and editorial, "The U.N. Must Deal with Kurds' Plight," *Los Angeles Times,* April 30, 1991, p. B6.

9. See, for example, B. Drummond Ayres, Jr., "A Common Cry Across the U.S.: 'It's Time to Exit,'" *New York Times,* October 9, 1993, p. 1; Elaine Sciolino, "The U.N.'s Glow Is Gone," *New York Times,* October 9, 1993, p. 1; R. W. Apple, Jr., "Policing a Global Village," *New York Times,* October 13, 1993, p. 1; and Lewis, "Reluctant Warriors," p. 22.

10. Randolph Ryan, "Can the UN Keep Peace?" *Boston Globe,* June 19, 1993.

11. Brian Urquhart, "The UN and International Security After the Cold War," in Adam Roberts and Benedict Kingsbury, eds., *United Nations, Divided World: The UN's Role in International Relations* (Oxford: Clarendon Press, 1993), pp. 81–103.

12. Quoted in Lewis, "Reluctant Warriors," p. 22. Perhaps a good measure of the extent to which the secretary general is torn in opposing directions by the bifurcated world is to be found in the fact that, just as here he perceives "a new reality" in the resistance of member states to peacekeeping operations, so did he discern a few months earlier "a new reality ... that a growing number of member states are concluding that some problems can be addressed most effectively by U.N. efforts." Boutros Boutros-Ghali, "Don't Make the U.N.'s Job Harder," *New York Times,* August 20, 1993, p. A29.

13. Quoted in Sciolino, "The U.N.'s Glow Is Gone," p. 7.

14. Boutros-Ghali, "Don't Make the U.N.'s Job Harder," p. A29.

15. See, for example, John Gerard Ruggie, ed., *Multilateralism Matters: The Theory and Praxis of an Institutional Form* (New York: Columbia University Press, 1993).

16. Boutros-Ghali, "Don't Make the U.N.'s Job Harder," p. A29.

17. For instance, see Donatella Lorch, "In Another Part of Somalia, Resentment of the U.N.," *New York Times,* September 30, 1993, p. A3.

18. Interestingly, after the enmity of General Aidid led him to refuse a U.N. offer of transportation to peace talks in Ethiopia designed to bring order to Somalia, he was ferried to the talks on a U.S. Army jet on the grounds that his participation in the meeting was crucial to its success. Upon arrival in Ethiopia, moreover, Aidid was escorted to the talks by U.S. military bodyguards. The fact this event transpired just two months after the killing of eighteen U.S. soldiers in a battle with Aidid's forces evoked considerable criticism in Washington, but the United States insisted it had little choice in the situation if the talks were to proceed. These circumstances suggest, on the one hand, that Aidid is well-ensconced in the realist world (he is interested in who has power), but, on the other hand, that the United States is more likely to engage in cooperative behavior when the U.N. is involved. In effect, the United States was unwilling to use the power that Aidid ascribed to it. See Douglas Jehl, "Clinton Defends Use of U.S. Plane to Take Fugitive Somali to Talks," *New York Times,* December 7, 1993, p. A5.

19. R. W. Apple, Jr., "U.N. and the Pentagon," *New York Times,* February 14, 1993, p. 18.

20. Steven A. Holmes, "Clinton May Let U.S. Troops Serve Under U.N. Chiefs," *New York Times,* August 18, 1993, p. 1.

21. Barton Gellman, "U.S. Reconsiders Putting GIs Under U.N.," *Washington Post,* September 22, 1993, p. 1.

22. Douglas Jehl, "New U.S. Troops in Somalia Are Still Tied to U.N. Operation," *New York Times,* November 15, 1993, p. A11.

23. For an elaboration of the role of transnational organizations and other private actors in the emergent pattern of externally monitored elections, see James N. Rosenau and Michael Fagen, "Domestic Elections as International Events," in Carl Kaysen, Robert A. Pastor, and Laura W. Reed, eds., *Collective Responses to Regional Problems: The Case of Latin America and the Caribbean* (Cambridge, Mass.: American Academy of Arts and Sciences, 1994), pp. 29–68.

24. For a discussion of the self-imposed standards used by the U.N., see David Stoelting, "The Challenge of U.N. Monitored Elections in Independent Nations," *Stanford Journal of International Law,* Vol. 28 (Spring 1992), passim.

25. The turbulence model locates the 1950s as the onset of parametric transformations in world politics. See Rosenau, *Turbulence in World Politics: A Theory of Change and Continuity* (Princeton: Princeton University Press, 1990), pp. 107–112.

26. Stoelting, "The Challenge of U.N. Monitored Elections in Independent Nations," p. 377.

27. Ibid., p. 378.

28. Ibid., p. 378.

29. Samuel P. Huntington, *The Third Wave: Democratization in the Late Twentieth Century* (Norman: University of Oklahoma Press, 1991), pp. 183–185.

30. Stoelting, "The Challenge of U.N. Monitored Elections in Independent Nations," p. 374.

31. Thomas M. Franck, "The Emerging Rights to Democratic Governance," *American Journal of International Law,* Vol. 86 (January 1992), pp. 72–73.

32. Boutros Boutros-Ghali, *Report on the Work of the Organization from the Forty-sixth to the Forty-seventh Session of the General Assembly* (New York: United Nations, 1992), p. 36.

33. Stoelting, "The Challenge of U.N. Monitored Elections in Independent Nations," p. 372.

34. Paul Lewis, "The U.N. Is Showing Promise as Poll Watcher for the World," *New York Times,* May 30, 1993, Sec. 4, p. 5.

35. Paul Lewis, "U.N. Rebukes Myanmar Leaders on Human Rights and Democracy," *New York Times,* December 7, 1993, p. A10.

36. Alan Riding, "Rights Forum Ends in Call for a Greater Role by U.N.," *New York Times,* June 26, 1993, p. 2.

37. Paul Lewis, "U.N. Agrees to Create Human Rights Commissioner," *New York Times,* December 14, 1993, p. A14.

38. Paul Lewis, "U.N. Chief Bars Chinese Dissident's News Briefing," *New York Times,* May 26, 1993, p. A10.

39. For a vigorous complaint that the secretary general "has sought to assume unprecedented powers and functions that the United Nations Charter vests in the Security Council," see Jeane Kirkpatrick, "Boutros-Ghali's Power Grab," *Washington Post,* February 1, 1993, p. A19. On the same point, also see Richard L. Armitage, "Bend the U.N. to Our Will," *New York Times,* February 15, 1994, p. Al9.

40. Boutros Boutros-Ghali, *An Agenda for Peace* (New York: United Nations, 1992), p. 9.

41. For an extensive elaboration of this point, see James N. Rosenau, "Sovereignty in a Turbulent World," in Michael Mastanduno and Gene Lyons, eds., *Beyond Westphalia: National Sovereignty and International Intervention* (Baltimore: Johns Hopkins University Press, 1995).

42. See, for example, Boutros-Ghali, *Report on the Work of the Organization from the Forty-sixth to the Forty-seventh Session of the General Assembly,* pp. 9–16, and Elaine Sciolino, "U.N. Secretary General Dismisses Top-Ranking Aide from the U.S.," *New York Times,* January 19, 1994, p. A9.

43. Kirkpatrick, "Boutros-Ghali's Power Grab," p. A19. For a more elaborate set of criticisms along this line, see Michael Lind, "Alboutros: The Imperial U.N. Secretary General," *The New Republic,* June 28, 1993, pp. 16–20.

44. There is especially fierce resistance to such a constitutional amendment in Japan, so much, in fact, that a cabinet minister was recently forced to resign because he declared that Japan's limitations on the use of military force were out of date and should be replaced with an amendment that permitted full Japanese participation in U.N. peacekeeping operations. See David E. Sanger, "Japan Aide Ousted; He'd Criticized Arms Role," *New York Times,* December 3, 1993, p. A6.

45. Paul Lewis, "U.S. Panel Divided in Its Study of Ways to Improve the U.N.," *New York Times,* September 13, 1993, p. A13.

46. Paul Lewis, "United Nations Is Finding Its Plate Increasingly Full but Its Cupboard Is Bare," *New York Times,* September 27, 1993, p. A8.

47. Independent Advisory Group on U.N. Financing, *Financing an Effective United Nations* (New York: Ford Foundation, 1993), pp. 7–8.

48. Ibid.

49. Ibid., p. 32.

50. Ibid., p. 2.

51. Quoted in John M. Goshko, "U.N. Chief: Political Will, Money Needed," *Washington Post,* November 22, 1992, p. A33.

52. Roger Cohen, "Dispute Grows over U.N.'s Troops in Bosnia," *New York Times,* January 20, 1994, p. A20.

53. "France to Recall Commander," *New York Times,* January 19, 1994, p. A3.

Chapter 7

1. For a discussion of this distinction, see Charles Perrow, *Complex Organizations,* 3rd ed. (New York: McGraw Hill, 1986), p. 259.

2. The phrase is borrowed from Charles Tilly, *Big Structures, Large Processes, Huge Comparisons* (New York: Russell Sage Foundation, 1984).

3. See, for example, Graham T. Allison, *Essence of Decision: Explaining the Cuban Missile Crisis* (Boston: Little, Brown, 1971); Coral Bell, *The Conventions of Crisis: A Study in Diplomatic Management* (Oxford: Oxford University Press, 1971); Michael Brecher, ed., *Studies in Crisis Behavior* (New Brunswick, N.J.: Transaction Books, 1978); and Charles F. Hermann, ed., *International Crises: Insights from Behavioral Research* (New York: Free Press, 1972). For a recent exception that gives due attention to systemic variables, see James L. Richardson, *Crisis Diplomacy: The Great Powers Since the Mid-Nineteenth Century* (Cambridge: Cambridge University Press, 1994), especially Chap. 10.

4. Most notable perhaps are Robert F. Kennedy, *Thirteen Days: A Memoir of the Cuban Missile Crisis* (New York: W. W. Norton & Co., 1968); and Nikita Khrushchev, *Khrushchev Remembers* (Boston: Little, Brown, 1970).

5. See, for example, Richard Ned Lebow and Janice Gross Stein, *We All Lost the Cold War* (Princeton: Princeton University Press, 1994), pp. 19–145; Jonathan Bendor and Thomas H. Hammond, "Rethinking Allison's Models," *American Political Science Review,* Vol. 86 (June 1992), pp. 301–322; Abram Chayes, *The Cuban Missile Crisis: International Crises and the Role of Law* (New York: Oxford University Press, 1974); and Henry M. Pacher, *Collision Course: The Cuban Missile Crisis and Coexistence* (New York: Praeger, 1963).

6. James G. Blight and David A. Welch, *On the Brink: Americans and Soviets Reexamine the Cuban Missile Crisis* (New York: Hill and Wang, 1989); and Bruce J. Allyn, James G. Blight, and David A. Welch, "Essence of Revision: Moscow, Havana, and the Cuban Missile Crisis," *International Security,* Vol. 14 (Winter 1988/1989), pp. 136–172.

7. Allyn, Blight, and Welch, "Essence of Revision," pp. 144–147.

8. Ibid., pp. 138–143.

9. Ibid., pp. 151–152.

10. Ibid., p. 144.

11. Kennedy, *Thirteen Days,* p. 11.

12. Allyn, Blight, and Welch, *Essence of Revision,* p. 155.

13. Allison, *Essence of Decision,* pp. 58–162.

14. Allyn, Blight, and Welch, *Essence of Revision,* p. 157.

15. Irving L. Janis, *Victims of Groupthink: A Psychological Study of Foreign-Policy Decisions and Fiascoes* (Boston: Houghton Mifflin, 1972), p. 164.

16. Allyn, Blight, and Welch, *Essence of Revision,* pp. 159–163.

17. Theodore Sorensen, *Kennedy* (New York: Harper & Row, 1965), p. 714.

18. Allyn, Blight, and Welch, *Essence of Revision,* pp. 166–168.

19. Orville Schell, *Mandate of Heaven: A New Generation of Entrepreneurs, Dissidents, Bohemians, and Technocrats Lays Claim to China's Future* (New York: Simon & Schuster, 1994), p. 41. We have relied on pages 33–182 of this compelling book as a basis for most of our summary of the Tiananmen story.

20. Ibid., p .88.

21. Ibid., p. 102.

22. Fred C. Shapiro, "Letter from Beijing," *The New Yorker,* June 5, 1989, p. 73.

23. *Europe: Magazine of the European Community* (April 1990), pp. 40–41.

24. Paul Lewis, "U.N. Issues New Appeal for Rwandan Cease-Fire," *New York Times,* July 15, 1994, p. A10.

25. Raymond Bonner, "Rwandan Refugees Caught 'Between Two Deaths,'" *New York Times,* July 27, 1994, p. 1.

26. Jerry Gray, "Rwandans Face Daunting Task: Reviving Trust," *New York Times,* August 12, 1994, p. A10.

27. Raymond Bonner, "Rwanda's Leaders Vow to Build a Multiparty State for Both Hutu and Tutsi," *New York Times,* September 7, 1994, p. A10.

28. Elaine Sciolino, "Top U.S. Officials Divided in Debate on Invading Haiti," *New York Times,* August 4, 1994, p. 1.

29. In early July 1994 the polls showed that more than two-thirds of the American people opposed an invasion, with more than half opposing one in which the United States would be part of a multilateral invasion force. See Garry Pierre-Pierre, "Haiti Orders U.N. to Remove Staff Monitoring Rights," *New York Times,* July 12, 1994, p. 1.

30. Quoted in Eric Schmitt, "U.S. Puts Off Any Decision on Haiti Issue," *New York Times,* August 29, 1994, p. A7.

31. Elaine Sciolino, "On the Brink of War, a Tense Battle of Wills," *New York Times,* September 20, 1994, p. 1.

32. "Haiti: Relief, not Victory," *New York Times,* September 20, 1994, p. A22.

33. Quoted in Steven Greenhouse, "U.S. Rejects Castro's Proposals for Talks," *New York Times,* August 26, 1994, p. A12.

34. Quoted in Joseph B. Treaster, "Guantanamo: Refugee Camps Fill with Fury," *New York Times,* August 30, 1994, p. A10.

35. Richard Ned Lebow, *Between Peace and War* (Baltimore: Johns Hopkins University Press, 1983), pp. 10–11.

Chapter 8

1. Marion J. Levy, "Does It Matter if He's Naked?' Bawled the Child," in Klaus Knorr and James N. Rosenau, eds., *Contending Approaches to International Relations* (Princeton: Princeton University Press, 1969), p. 93.

About the Book and Authors

Think that theory is thoroughly removed from explaining international crises such as Bosnia, Rwanda, and Korea? Think again! James Rosenau and Mary Durfee have teamed up to show that the same events take on different coloration depending on the theory used to explain them. In order to better understand world politics, the authors maintain, theory *does* make a difference.

Thinking Theory Thoroughly is a primer for all kinds of readers who want to begin theorizing about international relations (IR). Using realism—the dominant theoretical perspective in IR—and postinternationalism (Rosenau's famed turbulence paradigm) as oppositional models, the authors take us up the ladder of theory-building step by step and ask key questions along the way: Of what is this an instance? What underlying dynamic of world politics does it reflect? What different explanations might realists and postinternationalists offer?

Case studies on the U.N. and Antarctica are developed with an eye to their theoretical dimensions. Then a chapter on international crises—encompassing the Cuban missile crisis; protests in Tiananmen Square; and refugee flights from Haiti, Cuba, and Rwanda—shows how theories, and theorists, are tested in situations characterized by surprise, short timelines, and disrupted decision-making.

James N. Rosenau is university professor of international affairs at the George Washington University and the author or editor of numerous publications, including *Turbulence in World Politics: A Theory of Change and Continuity.* **Mary Durfee** is assistant professor of social sciences at Michigan Technological University and writes on the environment.

Subject Index

Author Index